ENOCH
THE
PROPHET

The Collected Works of Hugh Nibley

The Collected Works of Hugh Nibley will
include volumes on the following subjects:

The Old Testament and Related Studies
Ancient History
The Pearl of Great Price
Early Christianity
The Book of Mormon
The Doctrine and Covenants and Mormonism
Education, Politics, and Society

Other volumes in this series:

Old Testament and Related Studies

The Collected Works of Hugh Nibley: Volume 2

ENOCH
THE
PROPHET

Hugh Nibley

Edited by
Stephen D. Ricks

Deseret Book Company
Salt Lake City, Utah
and
Foundation for Ancient Research and Mormon Studies
Provo, Utah

First printing September 1986
Second printing October 1987
Third printing January 1989

Library of Congress Cataloging-in-Publication Data

Nibley, Hugh, 1910–
    Enoch the Prophet.

    (The Collected works of Hugh Nibley : v. 2)
    Includes bibliographies and index.
    1. Enoch.   2. Ethiopic book of Enoch—Criticism,
interpretation, etc.   3. Slavonic book of Enoch—Criti-
cism, interpretation, etc.   4. Hebrew book of Enoch—
Criticism, interpretation, etc.   I. Ricks, Stephen
David. II. Title. III. Series: Nibley, Hugh, 1910–
Works.   1986 ; v. 2.
BX8643.E54N53   1986   229'.913   86-11437
ISBN 0-87579-047-X

Contents

Foreword

It may seem surprising that Enoch is the only antediluvian patriarch accorded a separate volume in the *Collected Works of Hugh Nibley*, an honor that even Adam and Noah do not receive. After all, Enoch is granted scarcely seven verses in the canonical text of the Bible (Genesis 5:18-24), which give hardly more than his genealogy and inform us that he walked with God, and that, at age 365—relative youth for the superannuated preflood patriarchs—he was taken by God. And yet Enoch holds preeminent positions in the intertestamental literature and in the book of Moses in the Pearl of Great Price (Moses 6-7) that are all out of proportion to his virtual neglect in the Genesis account. From these extrabiblical writings we gain a deeper insight into the greatness of Enoch as a man and as a prophet.

As Professor Nibley notes in his paper "The Enoch Figure," Enoch is "the colossus that bestrides the Apocrypha as no other." Significantly, Enoch's importance in the Old Testament pseudepigrapha is equaled by his central role in the book of Moses. In "A Strange Thing in the Land: The Return of the Book of Enoch" (which appeared serially in the *Ensign* in 1976-77), Professor Nibley demonstrates at great length the richness of the Old Testament pseudepigraphic Enoch literature and the astonishing similarities between these writings—a body of literature that is still coming to light, very little of which was known or accessible in Joseph Smith's day—and the Enoch section in the book of Moses, even down to names of individuals.

If this volume contained nothing but a portrait of Enoch and a description of the vast Enoch literature and had placed the Enoch section in the book of Moses within that framework, it would already have merited our reading. But it is Enoch's peculiar relevance to our own day that gives the Enoch literature—and this volume—its timeliness. This literature throws into sharp relief the relevance for our own day of Enoch, a prophet in a wicked world that was on a collision course with disaster—as our world also appears to be. In "The Book of Enoch as a Theodicy," Dr. Nibley describes Enoch's world as not unlike our own, devoted to dark pleasures and resolute and sophisticated in its waywardness. Enoch cannot save a whole generation from destruction, but he does gather a group of righteous refugees from the wicked world and builds with them the City of Zion, a haven that is impregnable to the attacks of the ungodly and is ultimately taken up to heaven. In the light of Enoch's life and mission, it is fitting that one of Joseph Smith's code names in the older editions of the Doctrine and Covenants (for example, section 78 verse 1) is Enoch.

Hugh Nibley is rarely better than when placing latter-day scriptures—the Book of Mormon and the Pearl of Great Price—in their ancient setting. He assumes a near mantic role as he searches out the discontents of Enoch's time—and our own—and lays bare the significance of Enoch as a tract for our times. In this volume we have another instance of Professor Nibley at his best.

Stephen D. Ricks

PART 1

ENOCH
THE PROPHET
AND
HIS WORLD

1

Enoch the Prophet

It's been assumed, because the Pearl of Great Price is a little, thin book, that anybody can handle it and write a commentary about it. Acutally it is the most difficult and portentous of our scriptures, and we can't begin to approach the ancient aspects of this most difficult of books unless we know a lot more than we do now. The Prophet Joseph says, "The things of God are of deep import; and time, and experience, and careful and ponderous and solemn thoughts can only find them out." It's no small thing to approach a writing like the Pearl of Great Price.

In commenting on the book of Enoch, I'll refer mostly to sources outside the Pearl of Great Price. Because all the versions from which the book are taken were unknown in the time of Joseph Smith, these give remarkable confirmation of the Pearl of Great Price. Remember, Joseph Smith did give us a book of Enoch in chapters 6 and 7 of the book of Moses. I've written over a thousand pages on it, and I haven't even scratched the surface. The noncanonical stories of the Garden of Eden and the Flood have been very damaging to the Christian message, because they are the easiest to visualize, and you can popularize them more easily than any other of the Bible accounts.

Everybody has seen a garden, and everybody has been in a heavy rainstorm, so it requires no effort of the imagination for a six-year-old to convert concise, straightforward Sunday-school recitals into the vivid images that will stay

A version of "Enoch the Prophet" first appeared in Pearl of Great Price Symposium: Brigham Young University November 22, 1975 *(Provo, Utah: Brigham Young University Publications, 1976), pp. 76-85.*

with him for the rest of his life. These stories have been discredited as nursery tales because in a sense they are nursery tales, retaining forever the forms they take in the imaginations of small children, defended by grownups, who refuse to distinguish between childlike faith and thinking as a child when it is, as Paul says, time to "put away childish things." (1 Corinthians 13:11.)

It's equally easy and deceptive to fall into adolescent disillusionment, especially when "emancipated" teachers smile tolerantly at the simple gullibility of bygone days while passing stern moral judgment on the savage old "tribal god" who, overreacting with impetuous violence, wiped out Noah's neighbor simply for making fun of his boat-building on a fine summer day. The sophisticated say that these so-called myths were tolerable in bygone days, but now it's time to grow up.

Apocalyptic in general, and the writings attributed to Enoch in particular, are correctives for this myopia. They give us what purports to be a much fuller account of what happened. In the Bible we have only two or three verses about Enoch. But these parts that have been thrown out of the Bible (anciently they were part of it) give us a much fuller picture. This allows us to curb the critics' impetuosity and limit their license. The apocalyptic writings tell us in detail what happened—in much greater detail than the Bible. They also tend to make it clear to us just why it happened, and they have come to be regarded as invented "theodicies" to justify the ways of God to man.

In giving us a much fuller account than the Bible of how the Flood came about, the book of Enoch settles the moral issue with several telling parts:

1. God's reluctance to send the Flood and his great sorrow at the event.

2. The peculiar brand of wickedness that made the Flood mandatory.

3. The frank challenge of the wicked to have God do his worst.

4. The happy and beneficial side of the event—it did have a happy outcome.

Now to the first item, about God's not wanting to send the flood: In the Hebrew book of Enoch (discovered by Dr. Jellinek in 1873, long after Joseph Smith's time), Enoch introduces himself to Rabbi Ishmael, who meets him in the seventh heaven in the heavenly temple and says to him, "I am Enoch the son of Jared. When the generation of the flood committed sin, and said to God, turn away from us, for the knowledge of thy ways gives us no pleasure, then the Holy One delivered me from them that I might be a witness against them in the high heavens for all ages to come that no one might say the merciful one is cruel." In the Syriac Apocalypse of Paul, the apostle also is introduced to Enoch, being told when he is asked, "Who is this weeping angel?": "It is Enoch, the teacher of righteousness."

"So I entered into that place," Paul reports, "and saw the great Elijah, who came to meet us." He too was weeping, saying, "Oh Paul, how great are the promises of God and his benefits and how few are worthy of them!"

There is, to say the least, no gloating in heaven over the fate of the wicked world. It is Enoch who leads the weeping, as it is in the Joseph Smith account. Enoch puts forth his arm and weeps, and says, "I will refuse to be comforted." (Moses 7:44.) Enoch is the great weeper in the Joseph Smith version. Of course, he doesn't want the destruction of the human race. But in the Joseph Smith version, the amazing thing is that when God himself weeps and Enoch says, "How is it that thou canst weep?" (Moses 7:29), Enoch bears testimony that the God of heaven actually wept. It is a shocking thing to say, but here again, if we go to another Enoch text, there it is! When God wept over the destruction of the temple, we're told in one of the midrashim that it was Enoch who fell on his face and said, "I will weep, but weep not thou!" God answered Enoch and said, "If thou [Enoch] wilt not suffer me to weep, I God will go whither thou canst not come and there I will lament"—

in other words, it's none of your business if I want to weep. The significant thing is that the strange conversation in both stories is between God and a particular individual— Enoch. How would Joseph Smith know that?

In another text we are told, "When God sets about to destroy the wicked, then the Messiah lifts up his voice and weeps, and all the righteous and the saints break out in crying and lamenting with him." Here again we recall from the Joseph Smith Enoch how all the righteous and "all the workmanship of my hands" shall weep (Moses 7:40) at the destruction of the human race. The Lord says, "Wherefore should not the heavens weep, seeing these shall suffer?" (Moses 7:37.) But the same thing happens in the apocryphal writings; not only God but all the other creatures weep for the wickedness of man.

The stock reply to the charge against God of cruelty has ever been that man with his limited knowledge is in no position to judge the wisdom or charity of what God does or does not do. The extreme example of the argument is set forth in the Khadir stories. But, significantly, this argument is not emphasized in the apocalyptic writings. There God does not say to the holy man who is afflicted by the fate of the wicked, "Who are you to question what I do?" He does not blast Enoch or Abraham or Ezra or the brother of Jared on the spot for daring to question his mercy. On the contrary, he commends each one for his concern for his fellowmen and explains, in effect, "I know just how you feel, but what you fail to understand is that I had good reason for doing what had to be done, and I feel much worse about it than you could. You come far short of being able to love my creatures more than I." He commends the prophet Ezra for taking their part: "But even on this account, thou shalt be honorable before the most high because thou hast humbled thyself even as Abraham in pleading for Sodom and Gomorrah," wicked though you know they were. In the same spirit he replies to Baruch, "Do you think that there is no anguish to the angels in the presence of the mighty one?

Do you think that in these things the Most High rejoices or that his name is glorified?" He doesn't want to see men miserable. The Joseph Smith text says that "Enoch looked upon their wickedness and their misery and wept"; he saw that they weren't happy at all. Then God tells them, I am not happy about that either"; no one in heaven is, for that matter. When Enoch is distressed beyond measure at the cosmic violence he must behold, Michael comforts him: "Why art thou disquieted with such a vision? Until this day lasted the day of his mercy, and he has been merciful and long suffering toward those who dwell on the earth."

Mercy is the keynote, not vengeance. God has not hastened to unleash the forces of nature but holds them back like a dam as long as possible. When the angels, in another Hebrew Enoch fragment, beg God to get on with the work and wipe out the unworthy human race, he replies, "I have made and I remove; I am long-suffering and I rescue." After Enoch saw the angels of punishment who are prepared to come and let loose all the powers of the waters (this would be the Flood, to bring judgment and destruction on all who dwell on the earth), "the Lord of spirits gave commandment to the angels who were to go forth that they should not cause the waters to rise, but should hold them in check, for those angels were over the powers of the waters." On the contrary, the Flood was caused specifically by the cruelty of men, as we are told in Moses 7:34. God held back as long as he could while the angels were urging him to unleash the destruction. (The same thing is happening today. The angels protest, "Why do you let this go on so long?")

Thus this violence of the deluge, the completest of world catastrophes, is shown in the book of Enoch to be the only solution to problems raised by the uniquely horrendous types of wickedness that were infesting the whole world with an order that was becoming fixed and immovable. There's no other cure for it. The Enoch literature elaborates particularly on the theme of Genesis: "The earth also was corrupt before God, and the earth was filled with violence. And God looked upon the earth, and, behold, it was corrupt; for all flesh had corrupted his way upon the earth." (Genesis 6:11-12.)

"They are without affection, and they hate their own blood" is the Moses version. (7:33.) The texts say there were great disorders on the earth because of man who hates his neighbor and people who envy people: "A man does not withhold his hand from his son nor from his beloved to slay him nor from his brother."

Incidentally, the book of Enoch is quoted at least 128 times in the New Testament and very often in other places. Since the apocryphal manuscripts were discovered, we've recognized that Enoch is quoted all over the Bible and also frequently in the Book of Mormon. That is very interesting, since the Enoch literature has been discovered long since 1830.

A quotation from an Enoch text occurs in the thirteenth chapter of Helaman. "Ye have trusted in your riches," Enoch tells the people. "Ye have not remembered the Lord in the day he gave you your riches." (Cf. Helaman 13:33.) This is also Samuel the Lamanite speaking, an expert in the scriptures; he knew all about these things. He had access to the plates of brass and other records. And here Enoch speaks in a writing not discovered until 1888: "Ye have not remembered the Lord in the days he gave you your riches; ye have gone astray that your riches shall not remain, because you have done evil in everything. Cursed are you and cursed are your riches."

"Men dressing like women; women like men." The peculiar evil of the times consisted not so much in the catalog of human viciousness as in the devilish and systematic efficiency with which corruption was being riveted permanently to the social order. It was evil with a supernatural twist. The angels or "Watchers" themselves yielded to earthly temptation, mingled with the daughters of men, and used the great knowledge entrusted to them to

establish an order of things on earth in direct contradiction
to what was intended by God. Some Enoch texts tell of false
priesthoods in the days of Seth; Adam had prophesied
them, and God is angry in their attempts to surpass his
power. Angels and all the races of men use his name falsely
for deception. They're not worshipping devils. The Apocryphon of John tells us that the original attempt to corrupt
men and angels, through the lust of sex, was a failure until
the false ones set up a more powerful machinery of perversion. At first they failed, it says, so they came together and
created the *antimimon pneuma*, a clever imitation of the true
order of things, "and they brought gold and silver and metals, copper, and iron and all the treasures of the earth, so
they married the women and begat the children of darkness; their hearts were closed up, and they became hard by
this imitation false spirit." It was the deliberate exploitation
of the heavenly order as a franchise for sordid earthly ambitions.

Another text says the ordinances have degenerated
into a false baptism of filthy water. According to the
Slavonic Secrets of Enoch, it was administered by false
angels: "Woe unto you who pervert the eternal covenant
and reckon yourselves sinless." It was no open revolt
against God but a clever misuse of his name; no renunciation of religion but a perversion of piety. "The time is approaching when all life is to be destroyed on earth, for in
those days there shall be great disorder on the earth."

Another theme is quoted in our Moses 7:26. The Adversary will glorify himself and rejoice with his followers in
their works. The devil "laughed, and his angels rejoiced."
As a result, the order of the entire earth will change and
every fruit and plant will change its season, awaiting the
time of destruction. The earth itself will be shaken and lose
all solidarity. It is the reversal of all values as men worship:
"Not the righteous law; they deny the judgment and take
my name in vain." This vicious order was riveted down by
solemn oaths and covenants of which we read a great deal

in the Enoch literature. When the Sons of Heaven marry the Daughters of the Sons of Men, their leader Semiazus says, in a very recently discovered Greek fragment, "I fear you will not be willing to do this thing." So they say, "Let us swear an oath and bind ourselves all to each other. Then they all swore oaths and bound each other by them." The Lord says in the writings of Enoch in the book of Moses, "By their oaths, they have foresworn themselves, and, by their oaths, they have brought upon themselves death." The false oaths and the foreswearing is also an important theme. The systematic false teaching of the fallen angels soon "fills all the earth with blood and wickedness as the cries of the slain ascend to the gates of heaven, their groaning comes up and cannot depart because of the crimes being committed upon all the face of the earth." The passage in the book of Moses says the same thing.

The great heavenly angels, viewing these horrors from above and seeing only one solution, asked God how long he was going to permit Satan to get away with it. This is another aspect of theodicy: Must not God put an end to men when their evil deeds threaten far greater destruction than their own demise would be? The Pistis Sophia (transcribed, as it tells us in the introduction, from an earlier book of Enoch) asks, "Why did God throw the universe out of gear?" and answers, "For a wise purpose, for those who are destroyed would have destroyed everything." As it is, God had to hold back the destroyers until the last moment. The great danger to all existence was that the perverters knew too much. "Their ruin is accomplished because they have learned all the secrets of the angels and all the violence of Satan"; the threat is from them who have received the ordinances but have removed themselves from the law of the gospel. One must be willing to accept the law of God and the law of the gospel before he is qualified to receive the rest of the ordinances. They had received the ordinances, but they were not keeping the basic laws on which the ordinances were given. Still, employing the forms and knowledge they had, they set up a counter-religion and way of life. It was a time, says the Zohar, when the name of the Lord was called upon profanely. "In the days of Jared my father," says Enoch to Methuselah, "they transgressed the covenant of heaven; they sinned and betrayed the law of the gospel. They mingled with women and sinned with them. They also married and bore children, but not according to the spirit, but by the carnal order only." They changed the ordinances, they married under a different order.

Another text, first published in 1870, addresses the same issue: "Woe to you who write false teachings and things that lead astray and many lies, who twist the true accounts and wrest the eternal covenant and rationalize that you are without sin." This then was no mere naughtiness, but a clever inversion of values with forms and professions of loyalty to God that in its total piety and self-justification could never be set aright—it could only get worse. The Zohar states the general principle: whenever the Holy One has allowed the deep mysteries of wisdom to be brought down into the world of mankind, they have become corrupted, and men have attempted to declare war on God. The only redeeming feature of the thing was that the fallen angels who had perverted the human race had not learned *all* the mysteries in their heavenly condition (we're told in a Gizeh fragment), and so were not able to give away everything. As it was, their power for evil was almost unlimited.

According to the Psalm of Solomon, an early Syriac document discovered in 1906, "The secret places of the earth were doing evil, the son lay with the mother and the father with the daughter, all of them committed adultery with their neighbor's wives, they made solemn covenants among themselves concerning these things, and God was justified in his judgments upon the nations of the earth." (We're treating this as a theodicy.)

What else could he do? Part of the apocalyptic picture is the infection of the earth itself by the depravity of man, with the wicked sinning against nature and so placing themselves in a position of rebellion against the cosmos itself. It is as if one were to drive full speed the wrong way on the freeway during the rush hour. Only trouble can come from it. "While all nature obeys," Enoch tells the people, "you do not obey, you are puffed up and are vain; therefore, your destruction is consummated, and there is no mercy or peace for you." If you break all the laws, of course you will think that nature is fighting you. "They began to sin against the birds and the beasts and against each other, eating flesh and drinking blood while the earth fell under the rule of the lawless, until finally the earth itself laid an accusation against the lawless ones." All of this from an apocryphal source. That's interesting, because Enoch in the Pearl of Great Price hears a voice from the bowels of the earth, saying, "Wo, wo is me, the mother of men. . . . When shall I rest?" (Moses 7:48.)

Instead of the flood sent over a surprised community one fine day, we have in Enoch the picture of a long period of preparation during which the mounting restlessness of the elements clearly admonishes the human race to mend its ways. In the Enoch story, the darkening heavens, the torrential rains, and all manner of meteoric disturbances alternate with periods of terrible drought, and of course that is very clear in the book of Moses version: Remember how the land was blackened and utterly deserted in other parts, but remember also how "the heavens weep, and shed forth their tears as the rain upon the mountains." (Moses 7:28.) It's a dark sky, and always the water is flowing, the rivers turn from their courses, and so on. The same picture is in the apocryphal writings as in the Joseph Smith account of Enoch—the darkening heavens and the torrential rains. "Every cloud and mist and dew shall be withheld because of your sins," says one of the Enoch texts. "If God closes the windows of heavens and hinders the dew and rain from falling because of you, what will you do?" Enoch asks.

As during the twenty-five years of recurrent earthquakes that warned Abraham's Cities of the Plain to repent, the earth itself in Enoch's day became increasingly
restless. The sea was first drawn back and the fishes were
flopping around; and in the Joseph Smith version, sure
enough, "There also came up a land out of the depth of the
sea." (Moses 7:14.) Then the wicked invaded the new land,
as Enoch had foretold, and all the people were in fear and
trembling: "And fear shall seize them to the extremities of
the earth, and the high mountains shall be shaken and fall
down and be dissolved, flow down and be turned into side
channels and shall melt like wax before a flame, and the
earth will be rent with a splitting and cracking, and everything on earth shall be destroyed." This passage from the
Slavonic version describes the same scene as in Moses 7:13-
14, where the mountains flow down, the rivers are
changed, and the earth shakes, when Enoch spoke the
word of the Lord. The mountains shook, and all people
were afraid; the rivers were turned from their courses, and
the land rose up from the sea—the same picture. This does
not sound as fantastic as it once did. Any catastrophe of the
magnitude of the flood must have been accompanied by
large-scale preliminary disturbances, plus side effects,
exactly like those described. The terrible insecurity of the
times heightened the social disaster, and the people began
to fight among themselves. "A man shall not know his
brother, nor a son his father or mother. For God permitted
certain angels to go to the sons of adultery and destroy the
sons of the watchers who were among mankind and set
them to fighting against each other."

The preliminary vision is the key Enoch saw (in the
Joseph Smith version) of a great people, who dwelt in tents
in the plain in the valley known as Shum; and another great
people of Canaan, who completely exterminated the
people of Shum. They thus occupied the land and divided
themselves; the land was cursed, and they had a terrible
time. Emphasis is laid on the pollution of the earth, both

physical and moral, for the two go together, and only a great purging of water, wind, or fire can cleanse it. Without such a periodic purging, says the Zohar, the world would not be able to endure the sins of mankind. In another Gizeh fragment we read, "And thou wilt cleanse the earth from all uncleanliness and from all filthiness, and all the earth shall be cleansed from the pollution—and from all impurity, and he shall cleanse the earth from the defilement that is in it." That is what happens. In the book of Moses the earth says, "Wo, wo is me, the mother of men. . . . When shall I rest, and be cleansed from the filthiness which is gone forth out of me?" (7:48.)

Characteristic of the sweep and scope of the Enoch apocalyptic are the disturbances of the whole cosmos, for Enoch wept not just for the earth but for the heavens' sake. And he "wept and stretched forth his arms, and . . . his bowels yearned; and all eternity shook." (Moses 7:41.) Why shouldn't these and all the creations weep? And all the heavens mourn? This is a common theme in the Enoch literature. The whole cosmos shares the fate of a violated planet. The whole earth shakes and trembles and is thrown into confusion, and the heavens and their lights shake and tremble. "And I saw how a mighty quaking made the heavens to quake and the angels were disquieted with a great disquiet." Inhabitants in the other worlds weep too.

In contemplating these terrifying events, Enoch never allows us to forget that the real tragedy is not what becomes of people, but what they become. That's the sad thing. The people of Enoch's day and Noah's day were quite satisfied with themselves as they were, and they hotly resented any offers of help or advice from God's messenger; and all men were offended by Enoch's preaching. "They do not sow the seed which I give them," the Lord says to Enoch in a very important Enoch text, "but have taken another yoke and sow seeds of destruction and reject my kingship, and all the earth will be overwhelmed with iniquities and abominations." When Enoch asks the Lord why there were destructions, the first thing the Lord says is, "Behold, they are without affection"; "I gave them commandment they should have me to be their father, but they won't do it." Then he goes on, "I commanded them that they should love one another and serve me their father."

Here he says, "They don't sow the seed that I gave them; they've rejected my kingship, and all the earth will be overwhelmed." "The kings of the earth say, 'We have not believed before him; our hope was in the scepter of our kingship and in our glory.'" So when disaster strikes, they must confess that his judgments have no respect of persons. "We pass away from before his face on account of our own works." The theme often repeated in the book of Moses is that because of their own iniquities, they have brought destruction upon themselves. This is a very common theme. The refrain is ever "Wo unto you foolish ones, for you shall perish through your own folly." "They denied the Lord and would not hear the voice of the Lord but followed their own counsel. They go astray in the foolishness of their own hearts." They know not what they are doing when they say to God, "Turn away from us, for the knowledge of thy ways gives us no pleasure"—though God gave them promise of all that he would give them and all that he wanted them to do.

In the Joseph Smith version, Enoch asks, "Why are you going to destroy them? Why are we weeping?" The Lord answers, "In the day I created them I gave them three things, all they could want; I gave men knowledge, I gave them their agency, and I told them what to do—gave them a commandment that they should love one another and have me as their father. But behold they are without affection; they hate their own blood." A new fragment from the Apocalypse of Paul has the Lord explaining to Enoch what he promised men and told them he wanted them to do. "But they have defrauded themselves in refusing to keep the precepts which our Lord gave unto them. Therefore, ask no more concerning the multitude of them that perish," said the Lord, "for having received liberty [he used the word *agency* in the Joseph Smith version], they despised the Most High, scorned his laws, and forsook his way. Slavery was not given from above but came by transgression, and the barrenness of your women does not come by nature but by your willful perversions."

Peculiar to the world of Enoch is not only the arrogant quality of the sinning that went on, but the high degree of enlightenment enjoyed by the sinners, making them singularly culpable before God. Enoch explains that the Lord said, "I established Adam and gave him dominion." This verse from an old Slavonic version is practically the same verse we see in the book of Moses: "I established Adam and gave him dominion, and I gave him knowledge, I gave him his agency, and I gave him commandments, and said to him, 'This you should do, and this is bad.' What more do you want?" (See Moses 7:32-33.) God has given the human race the power of understanding and the word of wisdom. God created men last of all in his own form—put into man eyes to see, ears to hear, and a heart with which to deliberate, with eyes wide open, their choices. God says, "I hoped they would come to me, but they had no love to offer me. Rather they praised the alien one and cleaved to him ['for he loved Satan rather than God'], and for that, they deserted their mighty Lord." Their mocking kings can say, with those of Enoch's day, "We pass away on the account of our own works, descending into Sheol." The fallen angels by their own sweet choice have rebelled and are gone into captivity—"a prison have I prepared for them" (Moses 7:38); therefore they shall go into hell. "Wo unto you mindless ones, for ye shall perish through your own folly; ye have not given ear nor received what is good for you." Following their own foolish ambitions and dreams, and setting their hope not on the foundation of the inheritance of their fathers, in a spirit of apostasy they have no peace of mind and no joy, but stubbornly continue their ruinous course, ignoring God's commandments and blam-

ing others for their misfortunes "with great and hard accusations with an unclean mouth and lies—you are hard-
hearted and have no peace." They are not beyond getting
the point, for when Enoch speaks to them directly, "They
could not speak nor could they raise their eyes to heaven
for shame because of their sins and were condemned." He
showed them a book, as in the Joseph Smith version.
(Moses 6:5, 8, 46.) You cannot deny, he says "for a book of
remembrance [you] have written among [you]"; and when
he showed them the book, they "could not stand in his presence." (6:47.) This version says, "They could not speak
nor raise their eyes to heaven for shame because of their
sins when he showed them from the book."

A significant aspect of the apocalyptic picture is
the technological advancement of the doomed and wicked
world in which men defy God, confident in their tec:..no-
logical and scientific knowledge (there's a great deal about
this). To the various fallen angels designated by name, the
Enoch text assigns the introduction among men of the
study of chemistry, the manufacture of weapons and jew-
elry and cosmetics, the trade secrets of angels— formulas,
incantations, drugs, astrologies," and so forth. "They
thought to emancipate themselves from dependence on
God through their technological know-how." This is not as
foolish as it sounds, says the Zohar, for "they knew all the
arts and all the ruling principles that governed the cosmos,
and on this knowledge they relied until at length God corrected them by restoring the earth to its primitive state and
covered it with water." In the days of Enoch even the children were acquainted with the mysterious arts—what we
would call advanced sciences. Rabbi Yasah says, "With all
that knowledge could they not foresee destruction?" to
which Rabbi Isaac replies, "They knew, all right, but they
thought they were just smart enough to prevent it, but
what they did not know was that God rules the world. He
gave them respite as long as the righteous men Jared,
Methusaleh, and Enoch were alive, but when they de-

parted from the world, God let the punishment descend and they were blotted from the earth." "Alas," cries Rabbi Simeon, "for the blindness of the sons of men, all unaware as they are, how full the earth is of strange and invisible beings and hidden dangers, which could they but see them, they would marvel how they themselves can survive ten minutes on the earth." In Enoch's time, they had all sorts of engineering projects for controlling and taming nature, as did Nimrod, but the Lord altered the order of creation so that their mastery of nature became their own undoing. The same scientific prowess that led them to reject God led them to insult nature, and the upheavals that engulfed them demonstrate the very real ecological connection between the sins of men and the revolt of the elements. This was formally viewed as fatal extravagance and irrational apocalyptic.

There is more. You can find out sure enough that Joseph Smith knew what he was talking about when he wrote this book of Moses, continuing the prophecies of Enoch. Theodicy—the vindication of God's justice—is merely one aspect of the Enoch literature that is touched upon in the Enoch section of the book of Moses.

2

The Enoch Figure

It is strange that the man to whom the Bible gives only a few brief sentences should be the colossus who bestrides the Apocrypha as no other.[1] Everywhere we catch glimpses of him. He is identified with more other great characters than any other figure of the past. He is the most mysterious, individual, and unique of characters, yet he is the most universal type of them all. How can we account for "the extraordinary strength and pervasiveness of the Enoch legend"?[2]

The theologians of another day saw in his name an index of both his uniqueness and his universality. Enoch (Henoch) is "the one-and-only," Greek *hen*, "one," Latin *unicus*, "only, sole"; but at the same time he is Everyman, the universal "I," from the Semitic *anokh*. He is often identified with Enosh, "the Man" or human being *par excellence*.[3] The name *Enoch* is usually derived from the root *ḥanakh*, meaning basically to taste,[4] hence to test, "to give attention to"; from this is derived, in turn, the idea of teaching or training,[5] designating Enoch as the "first vehicle of . . . the genuine *gnosis*."[6] A related meaning is "to consecrate," making Enoch the "consecrated one, from whom authentic solutions [are] to be expected touching the secrets of this world and the one beyond."[7] This puts the figure of Enoch, A. Caquot avers, "in the center of a study of matters dealing with initiation in the literature of Israel."[8] Enoch is the great initiate who becomes the great initiator.[9]

"The Enoch Figure" was originally prepared for inclusion in "A Strange Thing in the Land: The Return of the Book of Enoch," which appeared in the Ensign from October 1975 to August 1977.

A recent study that declares the Hebrew meaning of the root to be "unknown" suggests instead the Canaanite *khanaku*, meaning "follower" (*Gefolgsmann*), that is, in the way of the initiate.[10] The idea is strengthened by "the great role which Enoch plays in Qumran," with its impressive "prophetic initiation."[11] The Hebrew book of Enoch bore the title of Hekhalot, referring to the various chambers or stages of initiation in the temple. "I will not say but what Enoch had temples and officiated therein," said Brigham Young, "but we have no account of it."[12] Today we do have such accounts.

These interpretations of Enoch's name and office are supported by his best-known epithet, that of Metatron. While some would derive it from the Latin *metator*, "guide"[13] or "leader,"[14] others prefer the Greek *meta-thronos*, the one "with the throne"[15] or "he whose throne is [the most glorious] next to [*meta*] the Throne [that is, the 'Throne of Glory'; or 'the throne greatest next to *the* Throne']."[16] Others insist that the derivation still remains unsolved and that "the Metatron combines various traits derived from different systems of thought."[17] K. Kohler went so far as to trace it to Mithra, noting especially the prominence of the fiery chariot (Hebrew *merkābāh*) in various Oriental cults.[18] "I have seventy names," says Metatron Sar ha-Pānīm, "matching the 70 tongues of the world, and all of them are the name of the King of Kings of Kings, but my King calls me Na'ar [the Lad]. I asked him: 'Why is such a one called the Lad?' He answered me:'I am Enoch the son of Jared!'"[19]

Matthew Black would see in Enoch's mystical epithet of Metatron a means of transmitting "the Enoch figure" to later times under the philosophical epithet of "Man as the measure (*metron*) of all things," designating at once "the elect Community, and the Head of the elect . . . the immortalized patriarch, the elect One, the Son of man."[20] The tendency today is to define Enoch as the eponymous pe-

rennial head of any of the many groups of sectaries that
broke off from the rest of Judaism or Christianity from time
to time, the society of the elect, some little aspiring Zion
that withdrew from the wicked world and fancied itself as
the elect community of Israel hiding in the wilderness. The
Enoch-figure is both a teacher-leader and a hider.[21]

The combination of certain traits—independence, intelligence, compassion, and power—is Enoch's signature,
setting him apart from all others by the superlative degree
to which he possesses them.

His is the independent intelligence always seeking
further light and knowledge. He is the great observer and
recorder of all things in heaven and earth, of which God
grants him perfect knowledge. The great learner, he is also
the great teacher: Enoch the Initiator into the higher mysteries of the faith and secrets of the universe; Enoch the
Scribe, keeper of the records, instructor in the ordinances,
aware of all times and places, studying and transmitting
the record of the race with intimate concern for all generations to come. He offers the faithful their greatest treasure
of knowledge. He is the seer who conveys to men the mind
and will of the Lord.[22]

Enoch is the great advocate, the champion of the
human race, pleading with God to spare the wicked and
"refusing to be comforted"[23] until he is shown just how that
is to be done. He feels for all and is concerned for all. He is
the passionate and compassionate, the magnanimous one
who cannot rest knowing that others are miserable. He is
the wise and obedient servant, the friend and helper of all,
hence the perfect leader and ruler.[24]

For his work Enoch is endowed with power—the
power of the priesthood.[25] He had but to speak the word of
the Lord and mountains shook and rivers turned from their
courses.[26] He is the king who is given power from on high
to organize and lead the people of God in their migration
and in the building of their city and in the great missionary

program that went out from it. He is their leader as both priest and king, the founder and director of their sacred society on earth.[27]

But since the "Enoch-figure" meets us everywhere, we are constantly confronted with questions of identity. How can Enoch be "identified" (as he has been) with Adam, Seth, Methusaleh, Melchizedek, Noah, Abraham, Isaac, Levi, Moses, Elijah, Job, Isaiah, Daniel, Ezra, Baruch, Zerubabel, Zadok, Lehi, Zosimus, John the Baptist, Peter, John, Rabbi Ishmael, and Joseph Smith? For that matter, how can each member of that list (a sampling only) be identified with one or more others in the roster? Religious literature abounds in facile metaphor and allegory, but that is something else; a reading of John 14-17 or 3 Nephi 10 will make it clear that when these people are declared to be "one," it really means something, amounting to an actual fusion of persons. In the above list each one has his own peculiar intimate relationship with Enoch—we have seen in passing how Joseph Smith as the president in Zion took the name on certain occasions—and since all their stories cannot be told here, certain of the more important ones must serve.

At the head of the list comes Noah, with whom Enoch shared the common mission of warning mankind against the coming Flood; the Enoch story overlaps with the Noah story in a way that scholars have found disturbing and have attributed to bungling and confusion. Here the Joseph Smith version in the book of Moses proves most enlightening, for while the same overlapping is very apparent, it is also explained with perfect clarity. The trouble is that God addresses Enoch *as if* he were Noah and Noah *as if* he were Enoch. "At a very early date," writes Van Andel, "the Noah Tradition and the Enoch Tradition are interwoven. The connection lies in the figures themselves. Their righteousness shows much similarity and their works make them interesting both for an Enoch-circle and a Noah-circle."[28] The points of resemblance between the two figures—their preaching mission, their speaking with God face to face, their importance as key figures in "a turning point in history," and so on, suggest "how easily the Noah Tradition can be woven through that of Enoch and vice versa."[29] "Which of the two traditions is older," Van Andel leaves for further investigation,[30] but the mixing of the figures accounts for the mingling of the texts, suggesting to R. H. Charles that the book of Enoch is "built up on the debris of" an older Noah saga.[31] Sir F. G. Kenyon, on the other hand, gives priority to Enoch at least in the Michigan Codex "in its original state . . . containing a fragment of a Book of Noah, of which other portions are interspersed elsewhere in Enoch."[32] Though scholars following the standard German procedure formerly insisted that the Noah elements were a corruption, an intrusion, or "Christian interpolations" in the Enoch text,[33] they now recognize, as Jellinek did from the first, that "the Enoch- and the Noah-books belonged together";[34] after all, they were contemporaries and had the same mission. The Joseph Smith text shows how easily Noah and Enoch can trade places, a phenomenon so marked that some scholars now go so far as to maintain that "Enoch is really Noah."[35] Parallel passages show how the two are consciously related:

Moses 7:41. . . .wherefore *Enoch* knew, and looked upon their wickedness, and their misery, and *wept* and stretched forth his arms . . . and his bowels yearned . . . and all eternity shook.
44. And as Enoch saw this he had *bitterness* of soul, and *wept* . . . and said unto the heavens: I will refuse to be comforted; but the Lord said . . . look.

1 Enoch 65:1. [When] *Noah* saw the earth . . . that its destruction was nigh,
2. . . . He arose . . . and went to the ends of the earth, and cried aloud to his grandfather *Enoch*; and Noah said three times in an *embittered voice*: "Hear me, hear me, hear me!" . . . And thereupon there was a commotion on the earth. . . . And Enoch my grandfather came and stood by me, and said to me: Why hast thou cried unto me with a *bitter cry* and *weeping*?

When Enoch "refused to be comforted" in view of the
impending flood, God showed him Noah and he was comforted (Moses 7:44-45), a reminder of the closing line of the
Chester Beatty Papyrus (107:3): "And his name was called
Noah, comforting the earth after destruction." He also
showed him the ark and "that the Lord smiled upon it and
held it in his own hand" (Moses 7:43), even as in 1 Enoch
67:2 he sees the mysterious structure built by the angels,
which on later evidence turns out to be the ark, with the
promise, "I will place my hand upon it [the ark] and preserve it." In the Joseph Smith text the Earth says to Enoch,
"When shall I rest, and be cleansed from all the filthiness
which is gone forth out of me? . . . that I may rest and righteousness for a season abide upon my face?" (Moses 7:48.)
In the Greek Enoch, on the other hand, it is Enoch who
says, "Noah shall be the remnant in whom you will rest for
a season and his sons from all the impurities and the filthiness, sins and wickedness . . . of the earth"[36] It is the same
story with a shift of characters. Again, in the Joseph Smith
Enoch when Satan's rule "veiled the whole face of the earth
with darkness . . . Enoch beheld angels descending out
of heaven . . . and [many] were caught up by the powers
of heaven into Zion." (Moses 7:26-27.) In the recently discovered Apocryphon of John, on the other hand, when
"darkness was poured out over every place upon the entire
earth, He [God] took counsel with his angels, and their
angels were sent down to the children of men"; but it was
not Enoch's people but Noah and those with him who were
carried away to heaven in a cloud of light.[37]

The first five columns of the Genesis Apocryphon, an
old Aramaic text belonging with the Dead Sea Scrolls, "deal
with the birth of Noah," according to Professor Avigad, in
terms not found in "the brief Biblical account in Genesis
[5:28-29], but [which] resembles Enoch [106] in most essential points."[38] When first discovered, it was thought to be a
Book of Noah "embedded in Enoch, properly derived from
the Book of Lamech,"[39] but the story turns up elsewhere,

for example, in the Greek Enoch text in exactly the same context. It tells of a marvelous child, Noah, who had been born to Lamech, who could not believe it to be his own, but charged his wife (Bit-Enosh, "Daughter of Man") with having consorted with "one of the angels" (sons of God). Only when Lamech's father, Methusaleh, goes to a far place to inquire of his father, Enoch, does he receive assurance that the child is legitimate.[40] Even this interesting twist does not escape the Joseph Smith version.

Moses 8:2. *Methusaleh*, the son of Enoch was not taken . . . for he [God] *truly* covenanted with *Enoch* that *Noah* should be the fruit of *his* loins. Moses 8:3. And . . . Methusaleh prophesied that from his loins should spring all the kingdoms of the earth [through Noah], and he took glory unto himself. 4. And there came forth a great famine into the land . . .	C. Beatty, 107:2. *Enoch:* Now run child [*Methusaleh* was already a grandfather] and signify to Lamech *thy* son that the child [*Noah*] born to *him* is *truly* his and not in falsehood. Beatty, 106:16. It is to *Methusaleh* that *Enoch* foretells that the issue of Noah will populate the whole earth through his three sons. Slavonic Enoch 22. But I will preserve *Noah*, the firstborn of Lamech, and I will cause to rise from his seed another world, and his seed will endure through the ages. And Methusaleh awoke from his sleep and was sorely distressed because of the dream.

Here we are told not only that Noah was legitimate after all and that Methusaleh was promised that his grandson Noah would be the parent of the race, but also, surprisingly, that the news caused Methusaleh distress.[41] Of this there is nothing in the Bible.

But what leads to a natural confusion of Enoch with Noah is that both receive the same promise. Again, the Joseph Smith version is right on target:

Moses 7:45. . . . from *Noah*, he beheld all the families of the earth; and he cried unto the Lord, saying: When shall the day of the Lord come . . .

7:49. And . . . *Enoch* . . . ? cried unto the Lord, saying: O Lord, wilt thou not have compassion upon the earth? Wilt thou not bless the children of *Noah*?

50. . . . I ask thee . . . that thou wilt have mercy upon *Noah* and his *seed*. . . .

51. And the Lord . . . covenanted with *Enoch* . . . that he would call upon the children of *Noah*. . . .

52. . . . That a remnant of *his seed* should always be found among all nations, while the earth should stand;

53. And the Lord said: Blessed is he through whose seed Messiah shall come; for he saith—I am Messiah, the King of Zion, the Rock of heaven. . . .

Moses 7:42. And *Enoch* also saw *Noah* . . . that the posterity of all the sons of *Noah* should be saved with a temporal salvation.

43. Wherefore *Enoch* saw that *Noah* built an Ark. . . .

45. And . . . *Enoch* looked; and from *Noah* he beheld all the families of the earth. . . .

1 Enoch 65:6. To *Enoch:* A command hath gone forth from the presence of the Lord. . . .

12. And He hath destined *thy name* to be among the holy . . . And has destined *thy righteous seed* both for kingship and great honors, and from thy seed shall proceed a fountain of the righteous and holy without number forever.

67:2. . . . And there shall come forth from it [the *Ark*] the *seed* of life. . . . And I will make fast thy [*Enoch's*] seed before me forever and ever, and I will spread abroad those who dwell with thee. . . . It shall be blessed and multiplied on the earth in the name of the Lord.

1 Enoch 84:5. *Enoch:* And now, O Lord and Great King, I implore thee and beseech thee to fulfill my prayer, and to leave me [*Enoch*] a *posterity* on earth, and not destroy all the flesh of man.

Secrets of Enoch 23:82. And *I* know that this race will be destroyed entirely, and *Noah* my brother will be saved for the procreation of offspring, and that a numerous race will arise from his seed, and Melchizedek will become the head of the priests.

Thus the covenant of Noah is made also with Enoch: "And the Lord said unto *Enoch:* As I live, even so will I come in the last days . . . to fulfill the oath which I have made unto you concerning the children of *Noah*." (Moses 7:60.)

The general principle on which one great patriarch can be identified with another is set forth in the Zohar:

> Noah [cf. Enoch] walked with God, meaning that he never separated himself from Him, and acted so as to be a *true copy* of the supernal ideal, a "Zaddik [righteous one], the foundation of the world", and embodiment of the world's covenant of peace. 59b. Righteousness and Justice are the foundation of thy throne [cf. Moses 7:32]. . . . It is the Zaddik who produces offspring in the world, . . . the souls of the righteous, these being the fruit of the handiwork of the Holy One. (Zohar, Bereshit 59b-60a.)

As the one who conveys the promise concerning Noah from Enoch to Lamech, Methusaleh also shares in the knowledge and the promise. Indeed in 1 Enoch 83:8ff., it is Methusaleh rather than Enoch who is told to "make petition . . . that a remnant may remain on the earth, and that he may not destroy the whole earth. . . . And . . . I . . . wrote down my prayer for the generations of the world." Now according to Moses 8:2, Methusaleh was spared specifically to ensure the carrying out of the covenant God made with Enoch "that Noah should be the fruit of his loins," which agrees perfectly with the other sources. The same adding of links to the chain is repeated in the story of Nir, the son of Methusaleh who, when his wife Sophonim brought forth another "Wunderkind" like Noah, accused her as Lamech did his wife, of unfaithfulness,[42] while he and Noah (his nephew) looked upon the newborn child in wonder and fear.[43] Nir doubles also for Enoch in a passage that reveals the borrowing:

> From the day that Nir, the son of Methusaleh, became High Priest, there was peace and order on all the earth for 202 years but after that the people apostatized . . . envying each other, and people rose against people and nation against nation, and there was a great

trouble, and Nir the priest . . . was greatly afflicted and
said in his heart: The time is approaching of which the
Lord spoke to Methusaleh, the father of my father . . .
and he stretched forth his arms to the heavens and as he
prayed his spirit departed.[44]

In the same account Methusaleh, like his father Enoch,
doubts his worthiness: "And Methusaleh stretched forth
his arms to the heavens and called upon the Lord saying:
'Alas O Lord, who am I to be at the head of thine altar and
thy people?'"[45] And then, exactly like his son Nir, "While
Methusaleh was speaking to the people his spirit was troubled, and bending his knees he stretched forth his arms toward the heaven, praying to the Lord; and as he prayed his
spirit departed."[46] One begins to wonder what difference it
makes who is in the stellar role. "Methusaleh became king
under his fathers," as the Hebrew source puts it, "and did
according to all that his father Enoch showed him . . . and
he did not turn from the Good Way to the right or to the
left."[47] Guided by "another book [that] Enoch wrote for his
son Methusaleh,"[48] keeping strictly in the same path, one
great leader resembles another, which is not surprising
where each repeats the words and actions of his father by
the father's specific instructions:

Moses 7:50. Enoch: I ask
thee, O Lord . . . that the
earth might never more be
covered by the floods.

51. And the Lord could not
withhold; and he covenanted
with Enoch . . . that he would
call upon the children of
Noah;

52. And he sent forth an
unalterable decree, that a
remnant of his seed should
always be found.

1 Enoch 83:8. And now my
son [Methusaleh] arise and
make petition [as Enoch
himself had] . . . that a
remnant may remain on the
earth, and that He may not
destroy the whole earth;

10. And I [Methusaleh]
wrote down my prayer for the
generations of the world.

After doubling for Enoch, Methusaleh, and Noah, Nir proceeds to have a son, who, following the pattern, is another wonder-child, Melchizedek:

> Noah and Nir feared greatly, for the child was completely grown and spoke with his mouth and blessed the Lord. And Noah and Nir examined the child and declared: This is from the Lord, my brother! Behold the seal of the priesthood on his breast! Noah said to Nir: Brother, behold the Lord has restored the dwelling of his sanctification among us. And they washed the child and clothed him in the robes of the high Priest and he ate the bread of benediction, and they called him Melchizedek. And Noah said to Nir: Guard the child, for the people have become wicked on all the earth and will try to kill him. Nir, praying to God, was told in a vision of the night: "A great destruction is coming. . . . As to the child [Melchizedek], I will send my archangel Michael and he will take the child and place him in the Paradise of Eden . . . and he will be my priest of Priests forever, Melchizedek. And Nir . . . said I know that this race will be destroyed entirely, and Noah my brother will be saved for the procreations, and that a numerous race will arise from his seed and Melchizedek will become the head of Priests."[49]

Thus the apparent confusion of Enoch and Noah is progressively confounded down the line of succession. But there is the same line from beginning to end: "Now this same Priesthood, which was in the beginning, shall be in the end of the world also." (Moses 6:7.) It centers in the Messiah of the seed of Enoch and Noah as "the King of Zion, the Rock of Heaven, which is as broad as eternity." (Moses 7:53.) In the Secrets of Enoch we are told that Melchizedek will be priest and king in a place at the center of the earth when the Lord will bring him forth as "another Melchizedek of the lineage of the first Melchizedek."[50] Here is identity indeed—Melchizedek succeeding himself! In the Pistis Sophia, Jesus says that "the higher mysteries" tell how all "are to be saved in the time and in the number of Melchizedek the Great Mediator of the Light, the agent of all who is at the center of the world."[51]

"All the prophets," said Joseph Smith, "had the Melchizedek Priesthood and were ordained by God himself."[52] And in an Enoch text a voice comes from Adam's coffin and blesses Melchizedek as "the only Priest among the people consecrated by God's own hand. Then the Lord told Melchizedek to take twelve stones and make an altar and put the bread and wine of Shem on it . . . in similitude of the sacrifice of the Lord."[53] When in a like demonstration Methusaleh prayed at the altar and asked God to let the people know by a sign "that it is thou who hast ordained the Priest for thy people. . . . While he was praying the altar was shaken, and the knife of its own accord turned away from the altar and flew out of the hand of Melchizedek in the presence of all the people. And all the people were seized with trembling and glorified the Lord."[54] To assure us that this is not an unconscious plagiarism, we are told that Melchizedek was with Abraham at the time, having met him on Mount Nabus near Jerusalem, where he embraced and blessed him, Abraham and Melchizedek receiving from the people exactly the same acclamation that was once given Methusaleh and Enoch.[55]

Abraham is our model (D&C 132:29ff.) and is as notable as Enoch for a peculiar combination of intelligence, independence, and humanity:

Abraham 1:2. Desiring also to be one who possessed great knowledge, and to be a greater follower of righteousness, and to possess a greater knowledge, and to be a father of many nations. . .

BHM 4:129. The soul of Enoch clung to the discipline of God and to knowledge and intelligence; and he knew the ways of God, and he was set apart in himself from the children of men.

Christ turns the liberated Adam over to Michael, and they all enter the gate of heaven, where Enoch and Elijah receive them.[67] In the Metatron, as Käsemann observes, "both Michael and Metatron-Enoch belong in the series of Moses and Elijah as heavenly high priests."[68] And so, by an easy transition, to Elijah, more often paired with Enoch than any other figure: "The angel containing the name Yahweh referred to in Exodus 23:20-21 is . . . 'Metatron Prince of the Face,' and is identified with the prophet Elijah."[69] As the Lord approaches the gates of hell in the drama just referred to, Beliar asks Hades, "Look carefully who is coming, it looks like Elijah or Enoch or one of the prophets to me!" Yet it is Jesus—so much are the three alike.[70] In a related source, after Christ leads the procession up out of hell and the righteous dead are redeemed with the help of Enoch and Elijah, those who live on "until the end of the world, at which time they will be sent down to earth by God during the rule of the Antichrist to be put to death by him and rise after three days to be caught up into the clouds and meet the Lord."[71] Other sources report the same tradition but include the Lord in the holy trio who are slain and ascend to heaven in their respective times.[72] John the Baptist, too, was identified with Elijah—"this was Elijah to come if ye can receive it."[73] Just as the sectaries of the desert believed John the Baptist, "the Wild Man," to be the returned Enoch,[74] so the Manichaeans in the third century identified their own founder, Mani, with Enoch.[75]

So we have a society of intimates, all sharing and doing the same things: "Abraham received the priesthood from Melchizedek, who received it through the lineage of his fathers, even till Noah. And from Noah till Enoch . . . and from Enoch to Abel." (D&C 84:14-15.) "Enoch was 25 years old when he was ordained under the hand of Adam, [who also] blessed him. And he saw the Lord, and he walked with him, and was before his face continually." (D&C 107:48-49.) That intimate, personal, face-to-face contact is emphasized throughout—it is all one family living by the

same rules and looking forward to one single great event—
the coming of the heavenly Zion to join with the earthly
ones. That intimate touch is important—it puts all the
leaders of the dispensations, including our own, on the
same footing: "Let my servant Ahashdah and my servant Gazelem or Enoch [Joseph Smith, Jr.], and my servant
Pelagoram, sit in council with the Saints which are in
Zion." (D&C 78:9.)

Joseph Smith has been charged with gross ignorance in
depicting Elijah and Elias as two different persons, yet they
very well could have been. The Gospel of Philip says that
the Lord had one name, Jesus, which was the same for all
people and all languages, while his Greek name of Christ
was not used by the Syrians, who said "Messiah" instead;
the name of Nazarene was a secret one whose real meaning
was known only to his immediate followers.[76] Conversely,
one name could designate different prophets while taking
a slightly different form to avoid confusing them.[77] Thus
Caesar was a man, but scores of men have borne the same
name; to make distinction among them the name may be
rendered, for example, Czar, Kaiser, Kezar. Elijah is identified repeatedly in ancient sources with both Enoch and
John the Baptist. Who is to say at this distance in time
whether or not Elias is a doublet of this illusive figure? Sir
Frederick Kenyon has explained how the Son of Man is
"the Lord, whose life was in many respects prefigured by
many of the patriarchs and prophets. . . . This is he who in
Abel was slain, in Isaac was bound, who in Jacob dwelt in a
strange land, in Joseph was sold, in Moses was cast out, in
the Lamb was sacrificed, in David was hunted, in the
prophets was dishonored."[78]

The repeated emergence of "Enoch figures" in the
course of sacred history should cause no perplexity to
Latter-day Saints, who have already seen three "Joseph
Smiths" as prophet, seer, and revelator.[79] What arguments
that could stir up among scholars three thousand years
from now! As the mantle of Elijah fell on Elisha (note the

suspicious resemblance of names), and that of Moses on
Joshua in a more than figurative sense, so many of the
Saints testified as eyewitnesses that for a moment in the
bowery at Nauvoo Brigham Young *was* Joseph Smith.

There is one parallel that has exercised the experts more
than all the others put together, and that is the puzzling relationship between Enoch and the Son of Man. No question has been more diligently discussed in the journals than
the identity of the son of Man; few scholars can resist the
temptation of pointing out with magisterial ease just who
he is, but with little or no agreement among themselves.
Aside from Jesus, it is Enoch who of all the candidates lays
by far the most convincing and challenging claim to the Son
of Man title "as teacher, wise one, advocate, prophet, ideal
man, bringer of salvation, revealer of hidden mysteries,
etc."[80] The key to the identification as R. Otto sees it is that
Christ "lived and preached in the role and in the name of
the Son of Man, just as Enoch also in his preaching was a
functionary of the Son of Man and his Righteousness."[81] In
1 Enoch 37:71, "Enoch has become the eschatological
Saviour himself, the ideal of the pious community," officially designated as the "Son of Man."[82] Though earlier
scholars were disturbed by the outright identity of the two
(R. H. Charles deliberately alters the ancient text to avoid
it),[83] their identity was fully recognized by ancient theologians; indeed, the Christian "tendency to identify Adam in
all his characteristics with Jesus, who similarly is represented as 'The Perfect Man,'"[84] matches the practice of
identifying Enoch also with Adam. Eusebius states the case
thus: "The Son of Man and the Son of Adam are the same
thing, so that Adam and Enosh are the same; carnal (*sarki-
kon*) through Adam, rational (*logikon*) through Enosh."[85] He
also makes it perfectly clear that by Enosh he means *Enoch*:
"The Hebrews say that Enosh not Adam was the first true
man. . . . He 'was not found' [said only of Enoch] means
that truly wise men are hard to find. He withdrew from the
world of affairs and thereby became the Friend of God [cf.

Abraham]. The Hebrews call him 'The Friend,' signifying thereby the favor (*charin*) of God."[86] For the Mandaeans, the Son of Man is necessarily the Son of God, "for he is Enosh, the first man created," in the direct image of God.[87]

In the intertestamental period, "the Son of Man tradition [was] in a fluid state and could be adapted to any Messianic Figure."[88] The individual is unique, but the type can be shared. Thus in the Dead Sea Scrolls Michael is the Son of Man, but for that matter so is Melchizedek.[89] "The fact that the prophets spoke in the person of God or Christ was a common observation," as Rendell Harris pointed out. "It [was] inevitable that this impersonation should cause difficulties of interpretation."[90] Impersonation? Was it not enough to be the agent without actual impersonation? Time and again when we think we have discovered an overlooked "Enoch figure," it turns out that the ancient author was quite aware of the parallel. Thus Zerubbabel or Paul or Rabbi Ishmael or Isaiah in their heavenly journeys all meet with Enoch before the story is over.[91] Are these men guilty of impersonation? The question concerns C. P. Van Andel, who acquits them all: A man who performs the function of Enoch has, he concludes, a perfect right to assume the name of Enoch.[92]

Today emphasis is being placed on the society of the faithful itself as the actual embodiment of the Son of Man: "Enoch has become the eschatological Saviour himself, the ideal of the 'pious community'"[93] officially designated as the "Son of Man." Such "Enoch circles" naturally identified whoever was their leader with Enoch.[94] Matthew Black, seeing the Metatron title "Man as the Measure," equates "the elect community" with the "Head of the Community, the immortalized patriarch, the elect one, the Son of Man."[95] The communities that followed John the Baptist regarded him as both Enoch and Elijah. "How could John [the Baptist also] be Elijah?" L. E. Keck asks. This was one of the great mysteries to which various sects claimed to have the key, secretly passed down from the Lord to the

Apostles.[96] The passing down thus took place during the forty-day ministry of the Lord, at which time he appears exactly in the manner of Enoch as one whose comings and goings are as thrilling and mysterious as are the great secrets of knowledge he imparts.[97]

In the Old Testament, the expression "Son of Man" is found only in four poetic passages, in which it is hardly more than an expression for an ordinary human.[98] In the New Testament, it is not, as anyone would naturally expect, the unassuming title of one who would depict himself humbly as a common mortal "delicately and modestly,"[99] or even in "self-depreciation."[100] For in all the occurrences of the title in the New Testament, it refers to the Lord in his capacity as the exalted one from on high whose real nature and glory are hidden from men.[101] Aside from these occurrences, the title "Son of Man" "is never used as a title in the intertestamental literature *except* in the Similitudes of Enoch."[102] Here is a very neat test for Joseph Smith: the "Son of Man" title does not occur once in the Book of Mormon, either, and in the Pearl of Great Price it is confined to one brief section of the Book of Enoch where it is used no fewer than seven times—again the prophet is right on target. Several verses are cited below to explain how the titles *Sons of God* and *Sons of Man* in the plural related to the singular *Son of God* and *Son of Man* (all emphasis supplied):

Moses 6:68. Behold thou [Enoch] art one in me . . . and thus may *all* become *my sons*.	Ethiop. Bk. of Mysts., in *Patriologiae Orientaliae* VI, 430. Next after *Adam* comes *Enoch*, the 7th, the Righteous One, who saw all that was to come and saw a vision of the cosmos. In such a way *all the prophets are symbols of the Son*.
7:18. And the Lord called his people *Zion*, because they were of *one* heart and *one* mind. . . . 7:69. And Enoch *and* all his people walked with God, and he dwelt in the midst of Zion; and . . . God received it up into *his own bosom*.	The Lord the Father wrote with his own fingers the 10 words indicating the various dispensations—all centering in "the subject of the *Son*."

7:24. Enoch was . . . even in the *bosom* of the Father and the *Son of Man*.

7:63. And the Lord said unto Enoch: . . . thou and all thy city. . . . *We* will receive them into *our bosom* . . . and we will fall upon their necks and they shall fall upon our necks.

431. In the 2nd Week [Disp.] Enoch saw "that the Man was saved," "the *Man*" being *Noah*, who was also a type of the Savior since he saved the race. . . . Even so in the 3rd Week, the Lord chose *Abraham*.

432. In the 4th Week he chose *Moses*; in the 5th Week he chose the *Prophets*, in the 6th the *Apostles*, in the 7th [a dispensation coming after the Apostles] he chose the *Saints* those who believe on the coming of the Lord.

434. Thus "*Noah*" was the symbol of the Son, as the Flood was of Baptism;

436. *Abraham* was the symbol of Jesus in 10 things, including baptism and *Enoch* was the exemplar of all 10 [signs and dispensations; cf. Clementine Recognitions I].

Van Andel, *Structuur*, p. 23 on the 10 dispensations. 1 Enoch 1:1. Enoch directs his writings to "the Elect and righteous who will be living in that day of tribulation . . . 2. . . . but *not* for this generation, but for a remote one which is to come."

Recalling that Enoch is the initiate, it is suggested that it was by initiation that Enoch became "in a way identified with the Son of Man."[103] Here Van Andel notes that we are skating on thin ice, that "the concept is a dangerous one in our ignorance," since the whole thing was treated by the ancients themselves as a carefully guarded secret.[104] Through anointing, a Catholic writer suggests, Enoch is "next to God, but not God,"[105] recalling those wonderful words of Enoch, "thou art God, and I know thee . . . that I should ask in the name of thine Only Begotten; thou hast made me and given me a right to thy throne." (Moses 7:59.) Also a right to become his son: "Behold I am a Son of God in the *similitude* of his Only Begotten; and where is thy [Satan's] glory that I should worship thee?" (Moses 1:12-13; emphasis supplied) for God said, "I have a work for thee, Moses, *my son*; and thou art in the *similitude* of Mine Only Begotten [who] . . . is and shall be the Savior." (Moses 1:6; emphasis supplied.) That "*is* and *shall* be" is important, showing the Son of Man's recurrent missions; even more important is "similitude" as the key to identity between one of God's sons and another. "The Man Adam" is "many," and yet there is but one great archetype; there are saviors on Mount Zion, but there is only one Savior; lords many, but only one Lord; there are prophets and *the* Prophet; there is a Daniel and *the* Daniel; an Elijah and *the* Elijah, anointed ones and *the* Anointed One, devils and *the* devil. We need not be disturbed when the Odes of Solomon report that Enoch is "raised up to become the Son of God,"[106] or when an Ethiopian text teaches that only the prophets by ascending a high mountain to a high place "can hear the fearful name of God," pending which God is known only by epithets, the first of the list being Enoch.[107] Enoch here is only an epithet, not the true and essential name.

The fullest explanation of the divinity of Enoch is given by the Prophet Joseph:

> They are they who are priests and kings, who have received of *his* fulness, and of *his* glory. And are priests of the Most High, after the *order* of Melchizedek, which was after the *order* of Enoch, which was after the *order* of the Only Begotten Son. Wherefore, as it is written, they are gods, even *the sons of God*. (D&C 76:56-58; emphasis supplied.)

Our Father Adam, Michael, he will call his children together and hold a council with them to prepare them for the coming of the Son of Man. . . . The Son of Man stands before him, and there is given him glory and dominion. Adam delivers up his stewardship to Christ . . . as holding the keys of the universe, but *retains* his standing as head of the human family; I saw Adam in the valley of Adam-Ondi-Ahman. . . . The Lord appeared in their midst and he [Adam] blessed them all. (*Teachings,* pp. 157-58.)

Those who share the same exalted order have a claim to the same honorific titles. Such were not limited to the ancient prophets, "for pious theists claim for themselves the attribute of Enoch," and the words of Psalms 73:49 "seem not unworthy of the poet who identified himself with Enoch."[108] The initiate has become a scribe, a sage, and an interpreter himself, an initiator—a veritable Enoch. This is confirmed by the Prophet Joseph: "I say in the name of the Lord that the kingdom of God was set up on the earth from the days of Adam to the present time, *whenever there has been a righteous man* . . . unto whom God revealed his word."[109]

The Enoch Tradition in the Ancient Near East

The Dead Sea Scrolls have expanded the sphere of Enoch studies, which until now have been confined to the world of the intertestamental writers taking their cue from apocalyptic Daniel (about 165 B.C.), with occasional brief looks at the classical and Indo-Iranian elements vaguely designated as belonging to the Gnostics or the Mysteries. But the Enoch tradition takes an immense leap backward as soon as we begin to examine the oldest records of the race, in which the most eminent authorities have detected not only the figure but even the name of Enoch repeatedly, and which also contain full and vivid descriptions of the world of Enoch as described in our later sources.

At least as early as the second century B.C., learned

men were making a "fusion of the Bible with Berossus and Hesiod," the former being a highly trustworthy historian who was "entirely dependent on Babylonian traditions,"[110] while the latter rivals Homer as the earliest and most venerated of Greek writers. The common meeting ground of the hoariest legends and histories of many peoples was the Flood story, and down through the centuries the figure of Enoch "was widely equated with the Oannes of Berossus," he being the seventh mythical king of Babylon (as Enoch was the seventh patriarch), the bringer of heavenly wisdom to men, builder of the holy city, and God of the Flood, whose name also suggests that of Enoch.[111] W. Hallo notes that Oannes may be the Greek form of the Sumerian name Ur-an, equated "in late texts . . . playfully . . . with Akkad, *ummanu*, sage, teacher, while *Hnwk* [Enoch] is derived from a root meaning to train, educate."[112] Another seventh king, the Sumerian En-men-dur-an-ki(na), Caquot equates with Enoch, he being the founder of the Mesopotamian priesthood, "the king of Sippar in whose hands the Gods place the secret of Anu, Bel, and Ea, the tablet of the Gods, the seal of the oracle of the heaven and earth."[113] His Sumerian name means "Lord of the Decree, of Totality of heaven and earth."[114] The name *Enoch* also suggests that of Enki-Ea, "the King of Wisdom who created intelligence. He knows everything that has a name," like the Egyptian Thoth, and like Thoth he is also the great guide to the rites of initiation into the mysteries.[115]

As "recent studies emphasize the significance of the Flood story for the understanding of pre-patriarchal history,"[116] Enoch assumes a central position. It will be recalled that in the Genesis Apocryphon and other Lamech texts, Methusaleh goes to Enoch at the ends of the earth to inquire about the birth of Noah. Now in the long familiar Babylonian epic of Gilgamesh, that hero in dire perplexity goes to consult Utnapishtim, also at the ends of the earth, and Utnapishtim is none other than Noah, who tells the hero the Flood story even as Enoch predicts the Flood to

Methusaleh.[117] It is held today that "Enoch is a kind of demi-god corresponding to (and inspired by) the Redeemer-god or Wisdom-God of the Babylonian Flood-legend . . . Ea-Oannes; Enoch is the Jewish Redeemer from the Flood," the real hero of the Flood story, "a highly privileged mediator between God and man, enjoying the distinction of being human yet immortal."[118]

Indeed J. G. Davies goes so far as to maintain that the Utnapishtim story "is the immediate source of the Enoch legend."[119] In the Sumerian version of the epic, Utnapishtim also goes by the name of Atrahasis, "the exceedingly Wise One," "the Super-clever One."[120] As Kraeling describes it, the Atrahasis story is even closer to Enoch's than is the Old Babylonian version.[121] In the latter not only Utnapishtim but Gilgamish himself is an Enoch figure: "He saw the secret things and revealed hidden things; he brought intelligence of the days before the Flood; he went on a long journey. . . . He engraved on a tablet of stone all the travail; he builded the wall of Uruk, the Holy City" (cf. Enoch's City).[122]

Moving west into Canaan, the Ugaritic writings of the fourteenth century B.C. contain lines and situations that seem to come right out of Enoch. There is a great assembly of fallen Gods on Mount Hmry—the Mount Hermon on which the heavenly Watchers held their convention in the Enoch story.[123] There is the upheaval of nature in "violent rains and storms," the colossal roaring of the elements that marks the end of an old age and the beginning of a new.[124] We find a ritual drama in which "we may visualize such a scene as the classic encounter between Elijah and the Prophets of Baal,"[125] thus bringing Enoch's double onto the scene. There is a haunting familiarity in some lines: "Who is Kret that he should weep? Or shed tears, the Good one, the Lad of El?"[126] These texts share common elements and names with the Minoan-Mycenaean, Babylonian, and Egyptian holy books, showing their common archaic ritual background.

A very early Egyptian ritual text, Papyrus Salt 825, has recently been reexamined. It gives a vivid picture of world upheaval amidst universal weeping:

> O make lamentation, Gods and Goddesses. . . . The earth is desolate, the Sun does not come forth, the moon is reversed in her course; Nun [the watery firmament] trembles, the earth is overturned, all mortals shall weep and mourn, the gods and goddesses also, all mankind, the Akhw, the dead, the beast of the field, the herds . . . with a sore weeping.[127] [cf. Moses 7:28, 37]. Hor has wept, the water descending from his eye to the earth. . . . Then Shw and Tefnut set to weeping with a great weeping [this pair represent the heavens above and the earth beneath; cf. "The whole heavens shall weep over them. . . . Wherefore should not the heavens weep? (Moses 7:37; see also verses 28-34, 40)]. Then Re wept anew, and the water that came down to earth from his eye became a bee ('fy).[128]

E. Hornung points out that the common Egyptian root *rem*, meaning both "tears" and "mankind," shows the "deep association," the mood (*Stimmigkeit*) of the world as reflected in language. "It hits us like lightning when the Creator says: 'I must weep because of the raging against me! Men are blind.'"[129] How well our Joseph Smith Book of Enoch captures the spirit of the thing!

> And it came to pass that the God of heaven looked . . . and he wept; and Enoch bore record saying: how is it that the heavens weep, and shed forth their tears as rain upon the mountains? (Moses 7:28.)

Here the weeping sky is equated with the weeping Creator and the rain to its tears and to his tears. Or again:

Moses 7:34. The *fire* of mine indignation is *kindled* against them; and in my *hot* displeasure will I send Floods upon them, for my *fierce* anger is *kindled*.	Salt 825. III, I. Re spat or vomited in this indisposition [*bdsh*] bitumin [*mrhw*] . . . 2. he was indisposed again and the liquid that came from his mouth grew up and became Papyrus [*twfn*, a cleansing substance].

If rain can be divine, cleansing tears, lava can be divine, purifying wrath!

An important class of writings contained in the "oldest book in the world," the Pyramid Texts of Egypt, is what Faulkner labels "Ascension Texts."[130] They describe the ascension to heaven of the hero snatched up in the whirlwind amidst vast thunderings and lightnings and upheavals of nature. The imagery is impressive, but where does it come from? "The king is Osiris in a [whirlwind] . . . bound for the sky on the wind, on the wind!" (PT 258.) "The king travels the air and traverses the earth. . . . There is brought to him a way of ascent to the sky, and it is he who performs the errand of the storm. The Sun Folk have testified concerning me; the hail storm of the sky has taken me and they raised me up to Re." (PT 261-62.) "The sky is overcast, the stars are darkened, the celestial expanses quiver, the bones of the earth-gods tremble. . . . Commend me to the four blustering winds which are about you . . . who contend . . . with those whom they would destroy. May they not oppose me when I . . . come to tell you the report of the great Flood which is coming forth from the great one." (PT 273-74, 311.) So Enoch might have spoken. It is interesting to read that in the king's entourage are the "Great Ones" and the "Watchers" (so rendered by Faulkner), suggesting personnel of very ancient traditions: "The Great Ones care for you, the Watchers wait upon you." (PT 373.) We read of the opposing hand of the Great Fetterer or Chainer in PT 384, and think of Satan clutching his great chain in Moses 7:26. The departure to heaven is a triumphant one though it leaves mortals stunned: "Geb laughs, Nut shouts for joy before me when I ascend to the sky. The sky thunders for me, the earth quakes for me, the hail storm has burst apart for me, and I roar as does Seth. Those who are in charge of the parts of the sky open the celestial doors for me, and I stand on air, the stars are darkened for me with the aid of the gods' water jars [the virga of falling rain]. . . . I will leave a record of myself among men and the love of me among the Gods." (PT 511.) This reads like some "primitive" version of the scores of "testaments" left behind by prophets, patriarchs, and apostles who at a later time tell of their journeys to heaven, following the archetypal Enoch; what can be the connection?[131] After the Pyramid Texts, the Coffin Texts continue the story in which "the voyages to heaven assume an infinity of astronomical allusions, the greater part of which are incomprehensible," according to L. Speleers, who concludes that "the original texts and contexts have plainly been lost."[132] The 178th chapter of the Book of the Dead contains a Flood story text that the ancient scribes profess themselves at a loss to explain, lost as it is in the mists of the remote past. "What is this?" writes one of them; and the answer: "This storm was the raging of Re. Thoth removed the thundercloud—and restored the eye. Others say, however, that the thunder cloud is caused by sickness in the eye of Re which weeps."[133] The title of this chapter is "The Rite for Not Dying a Second Time," reminding us that Gilgamesh visited the Babylonian Noah expressly to learn the secret of not dying again.

> What has become of the human race? They make war, stir up all manner of iniquity and violence, and commit every kind of crime. They contrive rebellion, conspiracy and terror; killing has become a way of life; they plot and carry out murders, for the strong takes advantage of the weak in all their doings [Budge]. Thou [Thoth speaking for God] canst not look upon evil, thou wilt not be patient. Make short their years! Cut short the times of their months; because they do crime in secret in everything they have done unto thee. I have [am] thy writing-tablet O Thoth, thy inkpot has been brought to me. I am not among those who return to their secret deeds of iniquity. (2-9.)

Here the scribe specifies: "Words to be spoken by Ani [the Candidate or Initiate]":

O Atum, what land is this toward which I wander?
For it has no water, it has air; it is very *md* [deep, like a
valley, cf. Moses 7:5-8]. It is black as night [Moses 7:26,
etc.] and ever vainly seeking is he who lives in it; none of
the sweet things of life are in it. . . . So said Atum,
speaking with me face to face, saying, I cannot look upon
thy iniquities [or afflictions, difficult times, lit. "straits"].
Spoken by Atum . . . I have ordained that my likeness
shall be seen in him; my face shall look upon the face of
the Lord Atum. . . . I have permitted him to send the
Great Ones [cf. angels] and now all my works shall be for
destruction. This earth is destined to return to the water
of Nun, into primeval chaos [*hwhw*] as in the beginning.
(10-18.)

The god next promises Ani the continuation of his line,
his son being, as he is, the heir upon the throne (line 20, cf.
Moses 7:45, 49.) In the lines that follow, the hero survives
in the great "ship of millions" [cf. facsimile no. 2, fig. 41],
which supports the life of the race. Then (lines 23-26)
comes a renewing of the covenant: "Thou doest for me
what thy father did for thee, Re has placed me upon the
earth that I might prepare my throne that my heir . . . and
my garden might thrive . . . to place mine enemies . . . in
bonds in the embraces of Sekhet. I am thy son, O my father
Re, thou hast made me for this. . . . Thou causest me to
come, to rise up, to advance to a glorified state."

To escape from the Flood every god takes his place in
the "ship of millions"—what better name for the Ark?[134]
The same story is told in other texts: Heliopolis joins in
weeping, as the earth returns to its watery chaos, and
Osiris departs in the Great Ship to go to the great God in
the midst of the sky.[135] The funerary nature of the event in
no way conflicts with historical contexts, since the final
leave-taking of the hero, his *Petirah*, is necessarily his last
farewell—to all intents his funeral—to those left behind on
earth. A hieratic papyrus in the British Museum has the
righteous escaping from the diluvial punishment of the

wicked in two ways—one in a great boat, the other by taking off into the sky; and, as we have seen, the Slavonic texts supply both escape routes for Enoch's people.[136]

The recorder of all these events is the Egyptian Thoth, Hermes, who bore God's message to a depraved humanity in the time of the Watchers and, as he warned them, recorded all that happened in "the Book of Remembrance of All Things."[137] "He saw all things as a whole, and having beheld he comprehended . . . he had the power to reveal unto others, and . . . the things which he learned he engraved and having engraved them he hid them," so that succeeding generations would have to seek diligently for such knowledge in order to find it (cf. Moses 1:41).[138] The Egyptian equivalent of Watchers were those who conspired under Typhon and took terrible oaths in which Aso, the queen of Ethiopia, took the lead, reminding us of Lamech's wife. The evil aspirations of this woman were checked by the mysterious prophet Si-Osiris whose wondrous birth matches that of Noah and others.[139] Guided by his father, this Wunderkind journeyed to the celestial court and, like Enoch and others, "entered the seventh hall and saw Osiris upon a golden throne."[140] Fifteen hundred years later, this prophet returns again, appearing as a superboy and superscribe in the royal court, where he overcomes the evil woman and her son and sends them packing to Nubia in an airship of his own invention. Like the Messiah, Si-Osiris returns in every "time of wickedness and vengeance."[141] A Thoth figure, he is personified as Sia, "who bears the gods' book, he who is in charge of wisdom being great even Sia who is at the right hand of Re." "Sia," Faulkner notes, "is the personification of intelligence and understanding."[142] He is also the Arabic Idris, who is Enoch.[143] Thoth, like Enoch, is in charge of the rites of initiation, as "Lord of the Divine Words, Keeper of the Secret Knowledge that is in heaven and earth, the great God of the beginning . . . who established speech and writing, causing the temples to flourish."[144] "This way was taught by

Hermes (Thoth) and was interpreted by the prophet Bitus to Ammon the king when he found it written in Hieroglyphs. . . . He transmitted the name of God and it spread throughout the entire earth."[145]

The stock Egyptian picture of the king mounting up to heaven in the vast updrafts of a cumulo-nimbus thunderhead is recognized today as referring to real natural phenomena that must have made an enormous impression.[146] The mysterious cords or ropes often referred to by which one is carried up into the sky are interpreted by Wainright as meteoric trails, and he compares the ascensions of Moses and Elijah "in a thunderstorm," the latter with a "chariot of fire and horses of fire" to "the entry into heaven made by some of the early Pharaohs."[147]

Indo-Aryan tradition fairly swarms with Enoch-figures, and the early Christians resented the competition with their own. "Stupid men regarded Zoroaster as a martyr," said Clement of Rome, "worshipped at his tomb, and said he had been carried up to heaven as the Friend of God in a heavenly chariot, they dared to worship him and cherish him as the Living Star."[148] To go into Book of Mormon (1 Nephi 1:8-11) and other analogies would take us too far afield (though G. de Santillana finds very significant ties between Enoch and Quetzalcoatl),[149] as would the frequent parallels with Enoch of various heroes of Classical literature, noted by scholars of the Renaissance and Reformation.[150]

Pindar, in his ninth Olympian Ode, tells of the rebellion of men against God and the horrid convulsions of nature that followed, of Deucalion and the ark and of his son Japetus (Japheth), the ancestor of the Greeks. If ever there was a perfect description of a half-heavenly, half-earthly society, it is Pindar's picture of the Hyperboreans dwelling in a state of bliss atop "the inaccessible unattainable mountain."[151] B. Z. Wacholder saw in Atlas, standing amidst the thunder between heaven and earth, "but a Greek adaption of Enoch" through Phoenician ties.[152]

Greek mythology is an endless procession of familiarly recurring themes—the abominations of the ancients, the deeds of inspired holy men, upheavals of nature, fearful punishments and glorious ascensions, and so on, as Greek imagination and speculation suggest ever more combinations and embellishments of the motifs. Take, for example, the case of Aeacus. At a time when gods were mating with the daughters of men, Zeus, blasting the earth with fires from heaven, took the maiden Aegina to an uninhabited island and there begot Aeacus, causing the island to be peopled by turning its ants into humans and surrounding it with reefs so that no one could approach it.[153] Others say that Aeacus himself led the people up onto the land where the prehistoric rites of all the Greeks were held atop a high mountain.[154] He was the most pious man who ever lived, and was "held in such honor that men longed to keep their eyes on him . . . and join his holy company on the island of Aegina." When mankind became treacherous and murderous the earth was smitten with a great drought, and the oracle said that only the prayers of Aeacus, who, incidentally, was married to a water-nymph, the daughter of Nereus [cf. Nir, brother of Noah in the Enoch-legends], could save the race. So he ascended the highest mountain, where "his prayers were answered by a loud thunderclap, clouds obscured the mountain summit that has ever since been an unfailing portent of rain."[155] To this day the Athenians call it the cloud of St. Elijah, sure sign of a downpour. Aeacus, greatest of kings and leaders, also built the holy city of Dia (some say Troy), and many sources describe him (as others do Enoch) as one of the three judges of the dead (the other two being Michael and Elijah). His name, according to Worner, means "divine," and he is to be identified originally with Zeus.[156] Thus we may see that Greeks have all the original building blocks, but they have admittedly lost the blueprints and never tire of trying to put the parts back together again in the proper order. I. E. S. Edwards says much the same thing about the Egyptians.[157]

Hesiod's Theogony, the Greek Genesis, begins with rain upon the mountains with the chorus of Muses singing in the darkness "veiled in thick clouds" (lines 1-11). We are told of the revolt in heaven; of horrible conspiracies on earth with a race of giants rebelling against Kronos, who had earlier revolted against his own father, Uranus; of a land that emerged from the sea and how people went up on the new land and there celebrated the lascivious rites that produced the race of Titans by those who had been the children of heaven. (207ff.) Then comes a long genealogy of horrors and troubles that still afflict the earth (211-336), interrupted only by the righteous Nereus (the Nir of the Slavonic Enoch), from whom sprang a host of daughters who are most fair to look upon, and a generation of proud and cruel descendants. (240-69.) The next rebel is Zeus, who takes over the earth with his faithful companions, force and violence. Zeus has an ambivalent character. He is responsible for the afflictions of mankind on earth and yet he is still the god of heaven. The Greeks have more than a sneaking suspicion that their ancestors at an early time got off on the wrong track in their worship. All is not sweetness and light: "We can lie like truth," the holy Muses tell Hesiod, "but we can tell the truth when we want to." (27-28.) The idea that something went seriously wrong early in the human story is not out of place in religious people; one is reminded that the initiates of Qumran began their discipline with a solemn recitation of how *their* fathers had taken the wrong way, as indeed does the story of Abraham. (Abraham 1:5-7.)

Zeus calls a great council on Olympus (cf. the Watchers on Mount Hermon) to plan his war against the Titans. (389-403.) The first to join him was Styx, the lady of the oath, who gave him his power (397-403); but it is Hecate, the dark lady of the oaths, whom men and gods honor above all others, for it is she whose methods promise success to all— power and gain, authority and riches (411-52). Zeus and Hades were born together, and the birth pangs of their mother Rhea are the major upheavals of earth and heaven respectively. (453-506.) Kronos ate his children to prevent any of them seizing his power, but Zeus was saved by Earth's wise tricks and got the upper hand. The whole epic is a tale of horrendous crimes, conspiracies, oaths, and betrayals. Next we hear of a new race, the line of Japetus (Japheth), who, with the daughter of Oceanus, begot Atlas, Meoetius, Prometheus, and Epimetheus. Meoetius was blasted for his pride and ambition; Epimetheus was the first immortal to marry among the daughters of men and got what he deserved, his wife being Pandora (cf. Lamech). Atlas and Prometheus suffered the same afflictions between heaven and earth for showing too much affection toward the human race. Hesiod tells of the Flood (775ff.) as well as the great burning at the end of the world (845ff.), and of the city of perfect peace and harmony that exists somewhere suspended between heaven and earth where Charis and Himeros (all that is lovely and desirable respectively) have their dwelling (63-64).

The leader and hero-ancestor of the Greeks, according to Hesiod, is Prometheus, the son of Japheth. (526.) Some Jewish doctors associate him with Adam and indirectly with Enoch,[158] and the recently discovered Apocryphon of John, No. 3, says that the fall of the first Archon was revealed to Noah by Pronoia and Epinoia, "Foreknowledge" and "Reflection," whose names perfectly match those of Prometheus (Fore-thought) and his brother Epi-metheus (Hind-sight), who taught the people at a time when "darkness was poured out over all that was on earth."[159] Note that the time of wickedness was not the first such period, even as we read in Moses 5:13-16 of the great time of evil even before the days of Cain.

The *Prometheus* of Aeschylus takes place at the ends of the earth (line 1): no wholly human character appears in the play. Prometheus is being crucified[160] for the crime of showing too much affection (*philanthropia*) for the human race and betraying the secrets of heaven to mortals. (Lines

28-38, 104ff.) The once heavenly Zeus has in his ambition
become cruel and tyrannical; only Prometheus has the
courage to resist him and champion suffering mankind.
The chorus enters in a spaceship—an aerial chariot—weeping and shedding their tears upon the mountains. (190ff.)
We learn from them that Zeus, for all his ferocity, is still the
president of the Blessed Ones, and Prometheus prophesies
that he and Zeus will one day become loving friends again.
(277-283.)

Prometheus tells of the war in heaven and how he
changed sides and brought men a hope of salvation that
frees them from fear, compared with which gift the accom-
panying gift of fire was merely a bonus. (291ff.) He himself
appears as one who must suffer and be raised up on high in
order to redeem the race. (269.) The leader of the chorus,
Oceanus, arrives on a winged horse, which he calls a
"swift-winged bird." (279ff.) Why the ocean here in the
tops of the mountains? It is because his presence presages
the Flood. His opening speech is quoted by Paul: "Do not
kick against the pricks!" (325.) Oceanus says he is bringing
the solution to the whole problem, as indeed the Flood
was. (390ff.) Hearing him, the chorus sheds rain-tears
while all Asia weeps (399ff.), the seas are in turmoil, the
waters are troubled (431ff.), and the sky and the earth's
volcanoes throw fiery bolts at each other. (360ff.)

Prometheus is depicted as the great teacher, the bringer
of knowledge and intelligence to the human race, and
again he supplies a line to the scriptures when he says of
mankind, "Having eyes they saw not, having ears, they
heard not." (447-48.) He tells how he has taught them astronomy, mathematics, medicines, technology, divination
(456ff.), and like Enoch announces that he has been promised the right to God's throne (510). But the human race lies
in darkness as the maiden Io enters describing the drought
and desolation of the seas. (561.) The girl wheedles the
Great Secret out of Prometheus (just as Pandora did of his
brother Epimetheus). Prometheus reports to Io his univer-

sal vision of all the earth (707ff.); he knows what happens
from beginning to end and prophesies the overthrow of
Zeus by his own folly for seeking to marry a mortal woman
(760ff.). He tells Io that her wanderings will end in Egypt,
where she will beget a king from whom fifty maidens, five
generations removed, will flee from their fifty Egyptian
cousins and murder all but one, who will beget Heracles
the Deliverer. The chorus prays not to be wedded "to any
bridegroom who descends from heaven!" and declares
mixed marriages to be the great source of misery and disaster. (890ff.)

Prometheus remarks that just such a marriage will
overthrow Zeus, and then he describes the great upheavals
of nature with the waters of the Flood out of control.
(907-35.) Hermes the oath-maker comes to persuade Prometheus to listen to reason and come back to the court of
Zeus, but Prometheus refuses, saying he has already seen
two tyrants fall and knows that Zeus is the next in line.
Hermes tells Prometheus that he can hope for no relief unless some God of his own free will offers to suffer for him
and descend below all things. (1026ff.) Prometheus declares himself willing to abide his deliverance rather than
yield to the enticing offer held forth by Hermes as the personal representative of Zeus. Hermes, warning against the
coming destruction, says that Prometheus and the Chorus
can blame only themselves for what is about to happen to
them; and as he departs, the whole universe is thrown into
confusion as "the sky mingles with the sea," and all that remain are the basic elements of earth, sky, water, and fire.

There are other versions of these sad events in the
myths and legends of many people, but by now it should
hardly be necessary to multiply examples or to point out
parallels to the reader. Of comparative studies there is no
end, but where do they lead us? What can we say for sure
about Enoch? For one thing, that the Enoch story is not just
another myth. More than two thousand years ago, able
scholars were trying to account for the common Flood story

and the Enoch figure found throughout the ancient world; with the progress of modern research, Enoch, instead of dissolving as so many figures have done in the light of science, has become progressively more real, and the old familiar claims to his hoary antiquity do not vanish at the touch of modern research but do just the opposite. "Curiously," writes B. Z. Wacholder, "it is now generally agreed that the link between the Babylonian traditions and Genesis was much *more* profound than conceived either by Pseudo-Eumolpus or Alexander Polyhistor," two sound and competent scholars of the second or third century B.C.[161]

As Enoch's base is spread ever broader on the map and deeper into the past, its importance for Jews, Christians, and Moslems becomes more evident and more baffling: "The relationship between Luke and the Enoch tractate becomes more and more of a puzzle to me the more I think of it," writes one eminent scholar. "Was the relationship in question more than a literary one? Was Luke personally acquainted with the man who translated 1 Enoch? Or was he perhaps himself this man?"[162] Luke himself as one of the transmitters of the old Enoch text! Bold speculation indeed, but for such surprises the student must now be prepared.

In 1835, the Latter-day Saints were told that all things contained in the Book of Enoch were "to be testified of in due time." (D&C 107:57.) Meantime, they had been given a preview in chapters 6 and 7 of the book of Moses. The Pearl of Great Price might well be called the Book of Six Testaments, namely: (1) the Book of Moses, including the Visions of Moses and the Writings of Moses, designated in the ancient manner as "the words of God which he spake unto Moses" (Moses 1:1); (2) A Revelation of the Gospel unto Our Father Adam, excerpted from his Book of Remembrance and quoted in (3) the Prophecies of Enoch;[163] (4) the Book of Abraham Written by His Own Hand upon Papyrus [this is the *title* of the book after the ancient fashion, not merely the colophon of one particular manuscript only];[164] (5) an Extract from the New Testament, "being the 24th Chapter of Matthew," also called "the Little Apocalypse" and with equal propriety "the Little Enoch"; (6) Extracts from the History of Joseph Smith, the Prophet.

Without exception these are all parts of larger writings—extracts and fragments. The same holds true for the Book of Mormon, containing "an abridgment of the record of the people of Nephi, and also of the Lamanites" with "an abridgment taken from the Book of Ether also." (Title page, Book of Mormon.) The abbreviated and fragmentary nature of all these writings should be emphasized; every one of them is only a sampling, but in each case a large enough sampling to permit extensive comparison with ancient writings claiming the same authorship and thus establishing their right to serious attention. The repetition of the same themes in all of them is a mark of authenticity, for not only does all authentic apocalyptic writing tell the same story,[165] but even secular history follows patterns to such a degree that throughout the ages the ever-recurring events of sowing and harvest, coronation and conquest, marriage and burial, war and peace, and so on, have been endlessly rehearsed in set ritual cycles all over the world. The many parallel passages we have cited from sources far removed from each other in time and place may once have raised eyebrows; yet any thought of plagiarism by Joseph Smith is out of the question, and if there is one thing that recent manuscript discoveries have made clear for the first time, it is that ancient texts of the greatest importance have been preserved throughout thousands of years of copying with almost uncanny accuracy. Even more impressive is the dawning realization of the immense age and historical plausibility of those legends found throughout the world to which Enoch holds the key.[166]

NOTES

1. Aside from brief genealogical notes, all that the Bible tells us about Enoch is that "he walked with God, and was not" (Genesis 5:25), and that he prophesied the coming of the Lord to execute judgment (Jude 1:14).

2. Quoted from G. W. Anderson, in *Encyclopedia Britannica* (Chicago: Encyclopedia Britannica, Inc., 1973) 8:605.

3. R. Eisler, *Iesous Basileus ou Basileusas*, 2 volumes (Heidelberg: Carl Winter, 1930) 2:32, 46-52, 102-3; M. J. bin Gorion, *Die Sagen der Juden*, 5 volumes (Frankfurt am Main: Rutten u. Loening, 1926) 2:285.

4. A. Caquot, "Pour une étude de l'initiation dans l'ancien Israel," in C. Bleeker, ed., *Initiation* (Leiden: Brill, 1965), p. 121.

5. B. Davies, *A Compendious and Complete Hebrew & Chaldee Lexicon to the Old Testament* (Andover: W. F. Draper, 1882), p. 220.

6. C. von Orelli, "Enoch," in S. M. Jackson, ed., *The New Schaff-Herzog Encyclopedia of Religious Knowledge*, 15 volumes (Grand Rapids, Mich.: Baker Book House, 1977) 4:148.

7. Caquot, "Pour une étude," p. 121.

8. Ibid., p. 121; von Orelli, "Enoch," p. 148.

9. Caquot, "Pour une étude," p. 121.

10. A. van der Born, "Henoch," in H. Haag, ed., *Bibel-Lexikon* (Zurich: Benziger Verlag, 1968), p. 711.

11. Ibid.

12. *Journal of Discourses* 18:303.

13. Ludwid Blau, "Metatron," in *Jewish Encyclopedia*, 12 volumes (N.Y.: Funk and Wagnalls Co., 1904) 8:519.

14. G. H. Box, "The Hebrew Book of Enoch," in *Jewish Quarterly Review* (hereinafter *JQR*) 7 (1895): 592.

15. Ibid.

16. Ibid., p. 583.

17. L. Blau, "Metatron," p. 519.

18. K. Kohler, "The Pre-Talmudic Aggada. II. C. The Apocalypse of Abraham and his Kindred," *JQR* 7 (1895): 592.

19. A Jellinek, *Bet ha-Midrash* (hereinafter *BHM*), 6 volumes, (Jerusalem: Wahrmann Books, 1967) 5:171.

20. M. Black, "Eschatology of the Similitudes of Enoch," *Journal of Theological Studies*, NS 3 (1952): 6-8.

21. Cf. Lehi. Such elect societies are typified as "Rekhabite." Eisler, *Iesous Basileus* 2:68, 171, 242ff., etc.; U. Mauser, *Christ in the Wilderness* (London: SCM Press, 1963), ch. 2.

22. Moses 6:21ff., 36; Van Andel, *De Structuur van de Henoch-traditie en het Nieuwe Testament* (Utrecht: V. H. Kemink, 1955), p. 61.

23. Moses 7:44.

24. Moses 7:41, 44, 49-50.

25. D&C 107:48.

26. Moses 6:34.

27. Moses 7:13, 19.

28. Van Andel, *Structuur*, p. 119. As Noah preaches the first end, so Enoch *Redivivus* preaches the second end of the world (25); both take a special position between heaven and earth (29); Noah as Preacher of Righteousness was identified by the early Christians with Enoch (83), etc.

29. Ibid., p. 117.

30. Ibid., pp. 41-42.

31. R. H. Charles, *The Book of Enoch* (Oxford: Clarendon Press, 1912), xlvii.

32. F. G. Kenyon, *The Chester Beatty Papyri* (London: Emery Walker Ltd., 1941), fasc. VIII, Enoch and Melito 8.

33. So A. Dillmann, cited in G. B., "Enoch," in J.-P. Migne, *Dictionnaire des Apocryphes*, 2 vols. (Paris: J.-P. Migne, 1856) 1:395; thus Lagrange, cited by J. B. Frey, "Apocryphes de l'Ancien Testament," in L. Pirot, *Dictionnaire de la Bible* (Paris: Letouzey et Ane, 1928) 1:368.

34. A. Jellinek, *BHM* 3:32-33; frg. XIV, 155-60; 2:83-108, 114ff.

35. R. Graves and R. Patai, *Hebrew Myths: The Book of Genesis* (New York: McGraw Hill, 1964), p. 119.

36. M. Black, ed., *Apocalypsis Henochi Graecae* (Oxford: Clarendon Press, 1976), x:20; 106:18.

37. Apocryphon of John, No. 1, 73:7.

38. N. Avigad, *Genesis Apocryphon* (Jerusalem: Magnes Press), 1956), p. 19.

39. J. C. Trevor, "Identification of the Aramaic Fourth Scroll from 'Ain Feshkha,'" *Bulletin of the American Schools of Oriental Research* 115 (October 1949): 9-10, n. 4.

40. The story is told in the Greek Enoch (Black, *Apocalypsis*, pp. 10, 12-13, 18, and Kenyon, *Chester Beatty* 106:1–107:2),and in the Genesis Apocryphon.

41. Secrets of Enoch, 22ff., in Andre Vaillant, ed., *Le livre des secrets d'Hènoch* (Paris: Institut d'études Slaves, 1952), pp. 72, 77. The story is repeated a generation later in the Apocalypse of Adam, where it is Noah who doubts the legitimacy of his child, swearing with an oath, "This race was not begotten of me!" for which God rebuked him. (Apocalypse of Adam 71:116ff.)

42. Secrets of Enoch, 22ff., in Vaillant, ed., *Le livre des secrets*, p. 72.

43. Ibid.

44. Ibid.

45. Secrets of Enoch 21 in Vaillant, ed., *Le Livre des secrets*, p. 66.

46. Secrets of Enoch 22 in Vaillant, ed., *Le livre des secrets*, p. 72.

47. *BHM* 4:132. When "Methusaleh served as High Priest, he explored all the earth, and searched out all those who believed in the Lord, and those who had changed, and he corrected them and converted them," as indeed did his father Enoch and his grandson Nir. (Secrets of Enoch 22.)

48. Book of Noah 108:1, in R. H. Charles, ed., *Apocrypha and Pseudepigrapha of the Old Testament* (Oxford: Clarendon Press, 1963-64) 2:280.

49. Secrets of Enoch 23, in Vaillant, *Le livre des secrets*, pp. 80, 82.

50. Secrets of Enoch, Ms. R 23, in *ibid.*, pp. 114ff.

51. Pistis Sophia, p. 24 (34). In the Book of Adam (G. B., "Le livre du combat d'Adam," in Migne, *Dictionnaire des Apocryphes*, 1:357-59), Melchizedek remains with the body of Adam "celebrating the ordinances forever" at the place in the center of the earth, where salvation will be accomplished (1:367); that spot is the site of Enoch's New Jerusalem (1:377), to which the kings of the earth come and bow down to Melchizedek, begging him to dwell with them.

52. *Teachings of the Prophet Joseph Smith* (Salt Lake City: Deseret Book Co., 1976), p. 181.

53. G. B., "Le livre du combat," pp. 375-76.

54. Secrets of Enoch 21, in Vaillant, *Le livre des secrets*, p. 66. Now this is exactly the sign that convinced the people of divine favor over Abraham on the altar, after which all the princes and the people came and bowed down to him. Discussed at length in Hugh W. Nibley, "The Unknown Abraham," *Improvement Era*, 72 (March 1969):3, 76, 79-80, 82, 84; Midrash, Lekh Lekha.

55. G. B., "Le livre du combat," pp. 375-76.

56. K. Kohler, "The Pre-Talmudic Aggada," p. 588, where he also compares Abraham with Enoch and other patriarchs, pp. 592-94.

57. Thus, in Apocalypse of Abraham 1:1, Abraham's genealogy begins with Enoch; he, like Enoch, is shown the universal vision (9:61); spends forty days on a high mountain and is shown the fate of the human race (9:8); is caught up and taken on a cosmic journey (9:14); is overcome and has to be reassured in the presence of God (10:14); moved amidst vast meteorological and geological disturbances (11:1-6); is caught up as on wings to a high mountain and hence to heaven, where he beholds all things (12:1-9); has a bout with Satan in the manner of Moses (Moses 1); learns the story of Satan's fall and the sins of the Watchers (13:14); describes the throne of God where "naught but peace" is found (13:18), etc., ending with

the vision of the return of the temple, the priesthood, and the celestial Zion (13:26ff.).

58. Zohar, Noah 65b.

59. Joseph Smith, *Teachings*, pp. 157, 168, 169.

60. Ibid.

61. Ibid.

62. An important part of the book of Enoch is the "Book of Weeks," each "week" being a dispensation represented by an inspired central figure: Enoch, Noah, Abraham, Moses, the temple, Elijah, and the Chosen Ones of the seventh period. (Van Andel, *Structuur*, p. 25.) Since Enoch is the seventh figure of the first period, he is particularly involved in the seventh dispensation, that of the end; hence, Van Andel, *ibid.*, p. 26, suggests that down through apocalyptic history, the "Enoch Church or Society, is a constant factor, with the figure of Enoch dominating throughout."

63. "Pour une étude," p. 121.

64. Above, note 3. The Primal Man who comes down to earth at the beginning and returns at the end is both Adam and Enoch in early Christian lore. (R. Bultmann, "Die Bedeutung der neuerschlossenen mandäischen und manichälischen Quellen fur das Verstandnis des Johannesevangeliums," *Zeitschrift fur die Neutestamentliche Wissenschaft* 24 [1924-25]: 104.) Adam and Enoch have the same pattern of years, marking their functional identity. (George Syncellus, Chronolog. 13; Book of Jubilees 3:32; Jellinek, *BHM* 5:172.)

65. Van Andel, *Structuur*, p. 126.

66. The Metatron in his capacity as Great High Priest is both Enoch and Michael. (E. Käsemann, *The Wandering People of God*, tr. Roy A. Harrisville and Irving L. Sandberg [Minneapolis: Augsburg Publishing House, 1984], p. 215.) "It is not clear how he [Melchizedek] is to be distinguished from Michael," writes J. T. Milik, in "Milki-ṣedeq et Milki-reša dans les anciens écrits juifs et chrétiens,"*Journal of Jewish Studies* 23 (1972): 95-144.

67. Gospel of Nicodemus 9:25.

68. *The Wandering People*, pp. 213-15.

69. P. Mordell, "The Origin of Letters and Numerals according to the Sefer Yeṣirah," *JQR* 2 (1912): 580-81. On the widespread identification of Enoch with Elijah, see J. S. Soggin, "Enoc ed Elia come profeti escatologici nel folklore romanesco," *Studi e Materiali*, 30(1959): 119ff. For many points of comparison, see H. P. Houghton, "The Coptic Apocalypse of Elias," *Aegyptus* 39(1959): 179-210.

70. A. Wilmart and E. Tisserand, "Fragments grecs et latins," *Révue Biblique* 22(1913): 186-87, being Evang. Barthol. 1:16-17 (Gk. frg.).

71. Gospel of Nicodemus 9:25.

72. Geo. Cedrenus, "Historiarum Compendium," in J.-P. Migne, ed., *Patrologiae Graecae* (hereinafter *PG*) (Paris: Freres Garnier, 1894) 121:476, says they will lie three days unburied on the very spot where the Lord was crucified; F. Tempestini, "Livre d'Adam," in Migne, *Dictionnaire des Apocryphes* 1:167; J. G. Davies, *He Ascended to Heaven* (New York: Association Press, 1958), p. 16.

73. Mark 9:11-13; Matthew 17:10-13. The identity of Enoch-Enosh and John the Baptist is treated at length by Eisler, *Iesous Basileus* 2:101, 439, 445, 736.

74. Ibid. 2:18ff.

75. *Coptic Manichaean Manuscripts* (Berlin, 1960), I, 47.

76. Gospel of Philip 104:3, 110:9ff.

77. Cf. "Jesus" and "Joshua."

78. F. G. Kenyon, *Chester Beatty Papyri*, fasc. VIII, 9-10.

79. Joseph Smith, Jr., Joseph F. Smith, and Joseph Fielding Smith.

80. Van Andel, *Structuur*, pp. 35-36, citing Rudolf Otto.

81. Ibid., pp. 36-37.

82. Ibid., p. 118.

83. Noted by B. Lindars, "Re-Enter the Apocalyptic Son of Man," *New Testament Studies* 22 (1976): 58. While the great Catholic scholar C. Lapide found it "daring and improper" to speculate on Christ's activities after the Crucifixion, he conceded that "probably as some believe he was with Elijah and Enoch in paradise." (*Commentaria in Sacram Scripturam*, 21 volumes [Paris: Ludovicus Nives, 1858], 17:490.)

84. Leo Jung, "Fallen Angels," *JQR* 16 (1925-26): 312-13.

85. Eusebius, Praeparatio XI, 6, in *PG* 21:856-58.

86. Ibid., VII, 8, in *PG* 21:521.

87. G. Widengren, *The Gnostic Attitude* (Santa Barbara: Institute of Religious Studies, University of California at Santa Barbara, 1973), pp. 29-30.

88. L. Jansen, cited by Van Andel, *Structuur*, p. 75. What we have in the Old Testament, according to Van Andel, is a line of prophets who are also teachers and leaders of the people out of dire straits: Saviors of the people. The line runs from Adam to the Messiah through Abraham, Noah, Moses, and Elijah, each bringing through a "remnant" and each planting the seed for a later dispensation, all in fulfillment of the promise to Enoch, who remains the figure around whom the whole process crystalizes. (Van Andel, *Structuur*, pp. 25-27.)

89. B. Lindars, "Re-Enter," pp. 56, 57, 60.

90. R. Harris, *The Odes and Psalms of Solomon* (Cambridge: Cambridge University Press, 1909), p. 103.

91. Book of Zerubbabel, in *BHM* 2:54; Apocalypse of Paul (Syriac) in G. Ricciotti, "Apocalypsis Pauli syriace," in *Orientalia* 2 (1933):2ff.; Ishmael in *BHM* 5:xliii.

92. Van Andel, *Structuur*, pp. 17, 115: "He does not conceal himself behind the name, but he bears the name and the name bears him."

93. Ibid., p. 118.

94. Ibid.

95. M. Black, "Eschatology," p. 7, cites Manson: "May it not be that we are here [En. 71] by the 'oscillation' between the individual and the corporate?" in which "Enoch . . . is regarded as the first human individual to embody the Son of Man idea, the nucleus of the group of the elect and righteous ones." Cf. ibid., p. 6: "Enoch is not only translated and transfigured; he is declared to be the Son of Man, *the Man par excellence*, 'born unto righteousness,' in union with whom the righteous 'shall have peace and an upright way.'"

96. L. E. Keck, "John the Baptist in Christianized Gnosticism," in C. Bleeker, ed., *Initiation* (Leiden: Brill, 1965), pp. 185-87.

97. See H. Nibley, "The Forty-day Mission of Christ—the Forgotten Heritage," *Vigiliae Christianae* 20(1966): 1-24, reprinted in *When the Lights Went Out* (Salt Lake City: Deseret Book Co., 1974), pp. 33-54.

98. Job 16:21; Ps. 12:8, 89:45; Eccles. 3:21, though all are subject to a wide variety of interpretation, of course.

99. So Vermes and Lievestad, both cited by Lindars, "Re-Enter," p. 53.

100. Ibid.

101. Ibid., pp. 65-67. W. Bauer, *Das Johannesevangelium* (Tubingen: Mohr, 1933), p. 40.

102. Ibid., p. 53, with italics added.

103. Van Andel, *Structuur*, p. 37. Upon reaching heaven, Enoch is exalted to the level of the Son of Man (1 Enoch 70-71); while as a reward, all the righteous may receive "the secrets of the Son of Man, who is still a mystery now" (1 Enoch 118). The standard mounting up to the seventh heaven, for example, of R. Ishmael, is an initiation, reflected in the Hechalot concept.

104. Ibid., p. 15.

105. E. de San Marco, "Henoch," in *Enciclopedia Cattolica*, 12 volumes (Citta del Vaticano: Ente per l'Enciclopedia Cattolica e per il Libro cattolico, 1951) 6:1407-8.

106. Odes of Solomon 36.

107. In S. Euringer, "Die Binde der Rechtfertigung (Lefafa Ṣedek)," *Orientalia* 9 (1940): 248, the name is Honake.

108. T. K. Cheyne, *Jewish Religious Life After the Exile* (New York: G. P. Putnam's Sons, 1908), pp. 238-39.

109. Joseph Smith, *Teachings,* pp. 59-60: "For our own part, we cannot believe that the Ancients in all ages were so ignorant of the system of heaven as many suppose. Because the Ancients offered sacrifice it did not hinder their hearing the Gospel."

110. B. Wacholder, "Pseudo-Eupolemus: Two Greek Fragments on Abraham," *Hebrew Union College Annual* 34 (1963): 92.

111. Ibid., p. 97, n. 86; K. Koch, "Die Hebräer," *Vetus Testamentum* 19 (1969): 58; Van Andel, *Structuur,* p. 117.

112. W. W. Hallo, "Antediluvian Cities," *Journal of Cuneiform Studies* 23 (1971): 64.

113. A. Caquot, "Pour une étude," p. 121. C. von Orelli, "Enoch," p. 148, notes that Enmeduranki has Enoch's solar affinities—calendar, holy city, and so forth.

114. S. Mayassis, *Mystères et Initiations* (Athens: B.A.O.A., 1961), p. 154.

115. Ibid., p. 181; cf. p. 175 on Hammurabi as such an Enki-figure.

116. W. M. Clark, "The Righteousness of Noah," *Vetus Testamentum* 21 (1971): 261, giving references.

117. C. von Orelli, "Enoch," p. 148, notes that there has been the usual confusion of Noah and Enoch in the Babylonian version, in which the Babylonian Noah is translated to heaven like Enoch while "by analogy [with Noah] it was assumed that Enoch instead of Noah was meant."

118. M. Black, "Eschatology," p. 5, citing L. Jansen and R. Otto.

119. J. G. Davies, *He Ascended to Heaven* (New York: Association Press, 1958), p. 17.

120. L. Matous, "Die Urgeschichte der Menschheit im Atraḫasīs-Epos in der Genesis," *Archiv Orientální* 37 (1969): 5. Kraeling finds the two versions reflected in the P and J texts of Genesis: "In P's Enoch we seemingly have the whole biography of the Babylonian Flood here *in nuce,*" whereas the hero of the other version is Terah, whose "name could be an abridgement of Atraḫasīs or Atarḫasīs." (E. G. Kraeling, "The Earliest Hebrew Flood Story," *Journal of Biblical Literature* 66 (1947): 292.)

121. Kraeling, "The Significance and Origin of Genesis 6:1-4," *Journal of Near Eastern Studies* 6 (1947): 193-94, discussing Phoenician and Greek ties especially with regard to the Giants.

122. Gilgamesh Epic, I.i, 5-9.

123. "The Story of Baal and Anat," 67:11:10ff., in C. Gordon, *Ugaritic Literature* (Rome: Pontificium Institutum Biblicum, 1949), p. 36.

124. J. Gray, *The Legacy of Canaan* (Leiden: Brill, 1957), pp. 47-52ff., with "perpetual tension between fertility and drought," p. 56.

125. Gray, *The Legacy*, p. 148.

126. C. H. Gordon, *Before the Bible* (N.Y.: Harper & Row, 1962), p. 135. As in the Adam-Enoch literature, we see the hero lying helpless on the ground at the mercy of Satan-Mot, while his wife tries to revive him (Gray, *The Legacy*, pp. 61ff.); again he is smitten when the adversary comes to "challenge him to a final combat" (pp. 73-74) and must suffer in expiation for his brother's blood—making him also a Cain-figure (pp. 75-76).

127. Pyr. Text No. 309; 250: "I have come to my throne, which is for the spirit, I unite hearts, O you who are in charge of wisdom, being great, I become Sia, who bears the God's book, who is on the right hand of Re . . ."—a typical Enoch passage. (R. Faulkner, *Ancient Egyptian Pyramid Texts* [Oxford: Clarendon Press, 1969], pp. 61, 96.)

128. Ph. Derchain, *Le Papyrus Salt 825* (Brussels: Academic, 1965) 1:137; 2:1, with much more to the same effect.

129. E. Hornung, *Der Eine und die Vielen* (Darmstadt: Wissenschaftliche Buchsgesellschaft, 1973) p. 142; Adriaan de Buck, *The Egyptian Coffin Texts*, 7 vols. (Chicago: University of Chicago Press, 1956) 6:344.

130. Faulkner, 58ff., from which our quotations are taken.

131. Some are discussed by K. Kohler, "The Pre-Talmudic Aggada," p. 592ff.

132. L. Speleers, *Les Textes des Cerceuils du Moyen Empire Egyptien* (Brussels: n.p., 1946), p. xxvi.

133. E. A. W. Budge, *Book of the Dead: Papyrus of Ani* (New York: G. W. Putnam's, 1912), p. 3, plate 29; 2:562ff.

134. Texts are full of navigational terms suggestive of the Flood, for example, 1366: "The sky weeps for you, the earth quakes at you . . . and you ascend to the sky as a star."

135. J. Zandee, "Sargtexte, Spruch 75," *Zeitschrift für Aegyptische Sprache* 99 (1975): 52-54; cf. de Buck, *Coffin Texts* 4:180d; 6:32k; 7:187b.

136. A. H. Gardiner, *Hieratic Papyri in the British Museum* (London: Trustees of the British Museum, 1910), col. V (pt. ii): 11, 5-22. So also PT 521.

137. T. Hopfner, *Fontes Historiae Religions Aegypticae* (Bonn: A. Marci u. E. Weberi, 1922-25) p. 391:38.

138. Ibid.

139. F. L. Griffith, *Stories of the High Priest of Memphis* (Oxford: Clarendon, 1900), pp. 145-47; Plutarch, de Iside 13.

140. Ibid., p. 153, with Thoth (Enoch) standing at the right side of the throne keeping the record while Anubis on the other side brings up the dead for judgment.

141. Ibid., pp. 205-6, 201.

142. Pt 309; 250: "I have come to my throne, which is for the spirit, I unite hearts, O you who are in charge of wisdom, being great, I become Sia, who bears the God's book, who is on the right hand of Re."—a typical Enoch passage. (R. Faulkner, *Pyr. Texts*, pp. 61, 96.)

143. In G. Vajda, "Idris," in *Encyclopedia of Islam* (Leiden: Brill, 1971) 3:1030, Idris is identified "most frequently with Hanokh, more rarely with Elijah (Ilyas)," and by the Shi'i with Elisha as well; also he is Hermes. The Enoch quotation known to the Middle Ages was attributed to Enochus philosophus qui lingua Arabica cognominatur Edris, cit. in "Enoch," in Migne, *Dictionnaire des Apocryphes* 1:397.

144. Prayer of Kheriuf, in G. Roder, *Urkunden zur religion des Alten Aegypten* (Jena: E. Diedrichs, 1915), p. xxv.

145. Iamblichus, de Mysteriis 8:5. Like Setme's Book of All Knowledge and Power (Griffith, *Stories*, p. 20), hidden in the depths of the sea, even so Adam's Book of Razael (the Divine Secret) was thrown into the sea by envious angels and recovered by Rahab "the Celestial Prince of Egypt" in a later dispensation. (L. Ginzberg, *Legends of the Jews*, 7 volumes [Philadelphia: The Jewish Publication Society of America, 1909] 1:156.) Neferhotep, a pharaoh of the XIII dynasty (1785 B.C.), reports in an inscription how he said to his courtiers, "My heart yearns to see the records of the primal time of Atum (Adam), unfold them for me for a thorough investigation; help me to know what God is in his true form." M. Pieper, *Die Grosse Inschrift des Konigs Neferhotep* (Leipzig: Hinrichs, 1929), p. 73, Text Roman I lines 3-5.

146. J. Spiegel, "Das Auferstehungsritual der Unaspyramide," *Annales du Service des Antiquités de L'Egypte* 53 (1956): 379; G. de Santillana, *Hamlet's Mill* (Boston: Gambit, 1969), pp. 77-78.

147. E. A. Wainwright, "Letopolis," *Journal of Egyptian Archaeology* 18 (1932): 168-69; cf. 2 Kings 2:11.

148. Clementine Recognitions, P.G. 1:1327. R. Otto has investigated the Indo-Aryan ties with Enoch. (Van Andel, *Structuur*, p. 71.)

149. De Santillana, *Hamlet's Mill*, pp. 77-78, 360.

150. For example, the key expression "and he was not" may be detected in Livy, I, 16: "nec deinde in terris Romulus fuit"; in

Diodorus, History 2:20: "Semiramis sese subduxerit tanquam migratura ad deos"; Lysias, Orations 31:494: "Herakles ex anthropōn ephaisthē"; Homer, Odyssey *Odyssey*, 4:561: "For God took him." Other references are given in E. Rosemüller, *Scholia in Vetus Testamentum* (Leipzig: J. A. Barth, 1810), 1:147-50. Josephus del., *Antiquities* 1:3:4, is disturbed, in fact at not finding the report of Enoch's passing in the official records.

151. O. Schroeder, "Hyperborer," *Archiv fur Religionswissenschaft* 8 (1905): 76, 80-84; quotation from p. 83.

152. B. Wacholder, "Pseudo," pp. 96-97.

153. E. Wörner, "Aiakos," in W. H. Roscher, *Ausführliches Lexikon der Griechischen und Römischen Mythologie*, 7 volumes (Hildesheim: Georg Olms Verlagsbuchhandlung, 1965) 1:109-10.

154. Ibid.

155. R. Graves, *The Greek Myths*, 2 volumes (Harmondsworth, N.Y.: Penguin Books, 1960) 1:214.

156. Wörner, "Aeacus," pp. 113-14.

157. I. E. S. Edwards, *The Pyramids of Egypt* (Baltimore: Pelican Books, 1961), pp. 27-28.

158. *BHM* 5:xlviiif.

159. Apocryphon of John, no. 3, 37.

160. His punishment differs from typical Roman crucifixion only in being on stone instead of wood. He is "raised up on high" (1.277), "nailed" (21, 56) sleepless in a standing position (32), and pierced with a spear-head. (64)

161. Wacholder, "Pseudo," p. 93.

162. Aalen, "St. Luke's Gospel and the Last Chapters of I Enoch," *NTS* 13 (1967), 13.

163. These titles are found in the English Pearl of Great Price, published by F. D. Richards, Liverpool, 1851, p. 1.

164. "Written by his own hand" is typical of colophons to Egyptian books, as is the mention of the writing material, as in the Memphite "Shabaka" text, which we are told was written upon leather. This does not mean that the copies of Egyptian texts and drawings in the possession of the Church today are the actual first-hand manuscripts coming directly from Abraham to us. See H. Nibley, "As Things Stand at the Moment," *BYU Studies* 9:1 (Autumn 1968): 74-79.

165. K. Koch, *Ratlos vor der Apokalyptik* (Gerd Mohn: Gutersloher Verlag., 1970), pp. 20-24.

166. De Santillana, *Hamlet's Mill*, pp. 77-78, and G. de Santillana, *The Origins of Scientific Thought* (New York: Mentor Books, 1961), p. 20.

3

The Book of Enoch as a Theodicy

The stories of the Garden of Eden and the Flood have more than any others damaged the credibility of the biblical message, being the easiest to visualize, popularize, and satirize of any Bible accounts. Everyone has seen a garden and been caught in a pouring rain, and it requires no effort of the imagination for a six-year-old to convert concise, straightforward Sunday-school recitals into the vivid images that will stay with him for the rest of his life. These stories are discredited as nursery tales because they are nursery tales, retaining forever the forms they take in the imaginations of small children, defended by grownups who refuse to distinguish between childlike faith and thinking as a child when it is time to "put away childish things." (1 Corinthians 13:11.) It is equally easy and deceptive to fall into adolescent disillusionment, and with emancipated teachers to smile tolerantly at the simple gullibility of bygone days while passing stern moral judgment on the savage old tribal God who, overreacting with impetuous and sadistic violence, wiped out Noah's neighbors simply for making fun of his boat-building on a fine summer's day. The most resounding denunciation of the Christian God

---

The strongest argument of the atheist has ever been the indiscriminate cruelty of great natural catastrophes and wars. The most effective refutation of the argument is provided by the Book of Enoch, once accepted by Jews and Christians alike, but renounced by the schools and no longer found in the Bible. The following paper was read at a gathering of ministers and priests (a regional meeting of the Society for Biblical Literature in 1974), to whom both the thesis and the sources were unfamiliar, and who received the message most gratefully. To keep things simple, references were confined to non-LDS sources. These have been added here in parentheses, which, though annoying to the reader, supply interesting confirmation for both the ancient and apocryphal accounts and the inspiration of the Prophet Joseph Smith.

since the days of Celsus has been his indiscriminate cruelty in sending the flood.

Aeschylus's Prometheus reflects that long, traditional background of shock and dismay and resentment: Zeus is held responsible for the world upheaval, which makes him appear cruel, capricious, and arbitrary, overreacting violently to any opposition to his will. Prometheus is the pleading Enoch-figure, the champion of the downtrodden race.

But now it is time to grow up. Apocalyptic in general and the writings attributed to Enoch in particular are correctives to the old myopia. By giving what purport to be much fuller accounts of what happened than those contained in the Bible, these texts curb the critics' impetuosity and limit their license. But are these writings to be trusted? Well, what is the purpose of this long line of documents that report repeated calamities and upheavals in dispensation after dispensation and in the process also tell us why such things befell the race? Why should these writers invent horrors which they then have to explain? Why should they depict events that put God in a bad light? How does it happen that they all describe the same types of calamities (though they are charged with letting their Oriental imaginations run wild in what Bousset calls "a brain-sick daydream"), and that what they describe is completely devoid of those miraculous elements of supernatural intervention that became the stock-in-trade of the later Apocrypha? How is it that those same calamities match so closely the events attendant upon the upheavals now put forward as the normal result of a geology of plate tectonics? These apocalyptic writings were so detested by the Christian and Jewish doctors alike that they were completely expunged from the canon of scripture—without a vestige of right or authority. Never written to be popular, they show all the marks of good faith and historical reliability in their authors. K. Koch notes that whereas the Bible stories were once taken seriously by the ministry and derided by science, the powerful substantiation of those stories, which is now being provided by the emergence of a large and growing corpus of newly discovered apocalyptic writings, is today being taken seriously by the scientists while being decried and resisted by the ministry.

The apocalyptic writings, in the process of telling us in detail what happened in the times of great natural upheavals, necessarily make it clear just why it happened, and they may justly be regarded as intended theodicies. In giving us a much fuller account than the Bible's of how the Flood came about, the book of Enoch settles the moral issue without argument. The telling points we shall note here are (1) God's reluctance to send the Flood and his great sorrow at the event; (2) the peculiar brand of wickedness that made the Flood mandatory; (3) the frank challenge of the wicked to God to do his worst; and (4) the happy side and beneficial outcome of the event.

1. The Hebrew Sefer Hekalot or Book of Enoch (discussed by Jellinek in 1873) has the hero introduce himself to Rabbi Ishmael, who meets him in the seventh heavenly temple, where he is the angel Metatron Sar ha-Panim: "I am Enoch the son of Jared. When the generation of the Flood committed sin and said to God, 'Turn away from us, for the knowledge of thy ways give us no pleasure!' then the Holy One delivered me from them that I might be a witness against them in the high heavens for all ages to come, that no one might say, 'The Merciful One is cruel!'"[1] (Cf. Moses 5:13.) In the Syriac Apocalypse of Paul, that apostle is also introduced to Enoch, being told when he asks "Who is this weeping angel?" that "This is Enoch, the Teacher of Righteousness. So I entered into that place," Paul reports, "and saw great Elias who came to meet me; he too was weeping, saying, O Paul, how great are the promises of God and his benefits, and how few are worthy of them!"[2] There is, to say the least, no gloating in heaven over the fate of the wicked world of Noah; it is Enoch who leads in the weeping (cf. Moses 7:44), but the surprising thing is that

God himself weeps! "When God wept over the destruction of the Temple, Metatron fell on his face and said: 'I will weep; but weep not thou!' God answered and said: 'If thou wilt not suffer me to weep, I will go wither thou canst not come and there I will lament.'"[3] (Cf. Moses 7:28, 29, 31.) The picture of God weeping is one of the surprising contributions of the Enoch literature and in itself exonerates God of cruelty. The "two measures of chastisement" that come upon the race are not to be distinguished from "two tears of the Holy One,"[4] and, when God sets about to destroy the wicked, "then the Messiah lifts up his voice and weeps . . . and all the righteous and Saints break out in crying and lamenting with him."[5] The angels do not envy God his painful task: "Who can endure the severe judgment which has been executed, and before which they melt away?" says Michael. (Cf. Moses 7:37.) "Who is he whose heart is not softened concerning it, and whose reins are not troubled . . . because of those!" (Cf. Moses 7:41.) Yet as they "stood before the Lord," Michael did not dare intercede lest he seem to challenge the justice of God—it was Enoch alone who dared do that.[6]

The stock reply to the charge of cruelty against God has ever been that man with his limited knowledge is in no position to judge the wisdom or charity of what God does or does not do, the extreme example of the argument being set forth in the Moslem Chadir stories. But this argument significantly is not emphasized in the apocalyptic writings. There God does not say to the holy man who is afflicted by the fate of the wicked, "Who are you to question what I do?" He does not blast Enoch or Abraham or Baruch or Ezra or the Brother of Jared or Job on the spot for daring to question his mercy, but on the contrary commends each for his concern for his fellowman (cf. Moses 7:45), and he explains in effect, "I know just how you feel; what you fail to understand is not that I had good reason for doing what had to be done, but that I feel much worse about it than you ever could!" "For thou comest far short of being able to love

my creation more than I!" he tells Ezra,[7] and commends the
prophet for taking his part (cf. Moses 7:44): "But even on
this account thou shalt be honourable before the Most
High; because thou has humbled thyself,"[8] even as did
Abraham in pleading for Sodom and Gomorrah. In the
same spirit he replies to Baruch: "Dost thou think that there
is no anguish to the angels in the presence of the Mighty
One? . . . Dost thou think that in these things the Most
High rejoices, or that his name is glorified?"[9] When Enoch
is distressed beyond measure at the cosmic violence he
must behold (cf. Moses 7:44), Michael comforts him: "Why
art thou disquieted with such a vision? Until this day lasted
the day of His mercy; and He hath been merciful and long-
suffering towards those who dwell on earth."[10] Mercy is
the keynote, not vengeance; God has not hastened to unleash the forces of nature but holds them back as long as
possible. When the angels beg God to get on with the work
and wipe out the unworthy human race, he replies in a
Hebrew Enoch fragment, "I have made and I remove, and I
am long-suffering, and I rescue!"[11] Further, "[Enoch]
showed me the angels of punishment who are prepared to
come and let loose all the powers of the waters . . . to bring
judgment and destruction on all who dwell on the earth.
And the Lord of Spirits gave commandment to the angels
who were going forth, that they should not cause the
waters to rise, but should hold them in check; for those
angels were over the power of the waters."[12] On the contrary, the Flood was sent specifically because of the cruelty
of *men*. (Genesis 6:11-12; cf. Moses 7:33.)

2. The violence of the Deluge, the completest of world
catastrophes, is shown in the book of Enoch to be the only
solution to problems raised by a uniquely horrendous type
of wickedness that was infesting the whole world in an
order that was by nature fixed and immovable. The Enoch
literature elaborates and goes into particulars on the theme
of Genesis 6:11-12: "The earth also was corrupt before God;
and the earth was filled with violence. And God looked

upon the earth, and behold, it was corrupt; for all flesh had corrupted his way upon the earth." Enoch sees "great disorder on the earth, because a man hates his neighbor, and people do evil to people, and nation rises in war against nation, and all the earth will be filled with blood and disorder"[13] and "a man does not withhold his hand from his son, nor from his beloved, to slay him . . . nor from his brother,"[14] at a time when "covetousness held in her hand the head of every kind of lawlessness."[15] "Ye have trusted in riches," Enoch tells them, ". . . ye have not remembered the Most High in the days of your riches."[16] Elsewhere, Enoch tells the people, "Ye have gone astray that your riches shall not remain . . . because you have done evil in everything,"[17] with all manner of perversions, including "men dressing like women and women like men."[18]

The peculiar evil of the times consisted not so much in the catalog of human viciousness, long as it was, as in the devilish and systematic efficiency with which corruption was being riveted permanently on the social order. (Cf. Moses 5:58.) It was evil with a supernatural twist: Those angels or "Watchers" who had been sent down to correct the vices of the race and impart heavenly instructions to men themselves yielded to earthly temptation, mingled with the daughters of men, and used the great knowledge entrusted to them to establish an order of things on earth in direct contradiction to what was intended by God.[19] "There will be false priesthoods in the days of Seth," Adam had prophesied, "and God will be angry with their attempts to surpass His power. . . . The angels and all the race of men will use His name falsely for deception."[20] The Apocryphon of John tells us that the original attempt to corrupt men and angels through the lusts of sex was a failure, until they set up a more powerful machinery of perversion: "At first they failed, so they came together and created the *antimimon pneuma*," a clever imitation of the true order of things, "and they brought gold and silver and gifts of all metals and copper and iron, all the treasures of the earth. So they got the women and begot children of the darkness. Their hearts were closed up and became hard by this imitation false spirit."[21] This was a deliberate exploitation of the heavenly order as a franchise for sordid earthly ambitions. "The ordinances had degenerated" to a false baptism of "filthy water,"[22] administered by false angels. "Woe unto you who pervert the eternal covenant, and reckon yourselves sinless."[23] This was no open revolt against God but a clever misuse of his name; no renunciation of religion but a perverse piety: "The time is approaching when all life is to be destroyed on the earth. For in those days there shall be great disorder on the earth . . . and the Adversary will glorify himself and rejoice in [his followers'] works, to my Lord's affliction." As a result, "the order of the entire earth will change, and every fruit and plant will change its season, awaiting the time of destruction . . . the earth itself will be shaken and lose all solidity." It is the reversal of all values as they "worship not the righteous law, . . . deny the righteous judgment, and . . . take His name in vain."[24]

This vicious order was secured down by solemn oaths and covenants: When the sons of heaven married the daughters of the sons of men, their leader Semiazas said, "I fear you will not be willing to do this thing. . . . So they said: Let us swear an oath, and bind ourselves to each other by them."[25] (Cf. Moses 5:29.) The systematic false teachings of the fallen angels soon "fill all the earth with blood and wickedness," as "the cries of the slain ascend to the Gates of Heaven, and their groaning comes up and cannot depart because of the crimes being committed upon the face of all the earth."[26] The great heavenly angels viewing these horrors from above could see only one solution, and they asked God how long he was going to permit Azazel to get away with it.[27] This is another aspect of theodicy: Must not God put an end to men whose evil deeds threaten far greater destruction than their own demise would be? The Pistis Sophia [transcribed, as it tells us, from an earlier book of Enoch] asks: "Why did God throw the universe out of gear?" It answers: "For a wise purpose; for those who were destroyed would have destroyed everything." As it is, God had to hold back the spirits until the last moment. And when the power of the wicked aspirants had to be broken, it was done in a twinkling, that is, as painlessly as possible.[28]

The great danger to all existence was that the perverters knew too much: "Their ruin is accomplished because they have learnt all the secrets of the angels, and all the violence of the Satans, and all their powers—the most secret ones."[29] The threat is from those "who have received the ordinances, but have removed themselves from the Way of Life."[30] They have claimed the ordinances without keeping the law of God—that they would observe them his way; while still employing the forms and knowledge brought from on high, they have to set up a counter-religion and way of life.[31] It was a time, says the Zohar, when "the name of the Lord [was] called upon profanely."[32] "In the days of Jared my father," says Enoch to Methusaleh, "they transgressed . . . from the Covenant of Heaven . . . sinned, and betrayed the *ethos* [law of the gospel], mingled with women and sinned with them; they also married and bore children, but not according to the Spiritual but by a carnal order only."[33] "Woe to you who write false teachings (*logous*) and things that lead astray with many lies; who . . . twist the true accounts and wrest the eternal Covenant, and rationalize that you are without sin!"[34] This, then was no mere naughtiness, but a clever inversion of values, with forms and professions of loyalty to God, which, in its total piety and self-justification, could never be set right and could only get worse. The Zohar states the general principle that "whenever the Holy One allowed the deep mysteries of wisdom to be brought down into the world, mankind were corrupted by them and attempted to declare war on God."[35] The only redeeming feature of the thing was that the fallen angels who perverted the human race "had not learned all the mysteries" in their heavenly condition.[36]

As it was, their power for evil was almost unlimited, "for in secret places of the earth were they doing evil; the son had connexion with the mother and the father with the daughter: and all of them with their neighbors' wives: and they made solemn covenants among themselves concerning these things . . . [therefore] God was justified in His judgments upon the nations of the earth."[37]

Part of the apocalyptic picture is the infection of the earth itself by the depravity of man, with the wicked sinning against nature and so placing themselves in a position of rebellion against the cosmos itself; as if one were to drive full speed the wrong way on the freeway during rush-hour. "While all Nature obeys," Enoch tells them, "you do not obey; you are puffed up and vain . . . therefore your destruction is consummated and there is no mercy or peace for you."[38] More aggressively, "they began to sin against the birds and the beasts . . . and against each other, eating flesh and drinking blood, while the earth fell under the rule of the lawless"[39] until finally "the earth laid accusation against the lawless ones."[40] Instead of the Flood sent over a surprised community one fine day, we have in Enoch the picture of a long period of preparation during which the mounting restlessness of the elements clearly admonishes the human race to mend its ways. In the Enoch story, darkening heavens, torrential rains, and all manner of meteoric disturbances alternate with periods of terrible drought, when "every cloud and mist and dew shall be withheld because of your sins. . . . If God closes the windows of heaven and hinders the dew and rain from falling because of you, what will you do?" Enoch asks them.[41] And, as during the twenty-five recurrent earthquakes that warned Abraham's cities of the Plain to repent, the earth itself became increasingly restless. The sea was first drawn back and then invaded the land,[42] and as Enoch foretold, "all the people shall fear . . . and trembling and great fear shall seize them to the extremities of the earth (cf. Moses 7:14), and the high mountains shall be shaken and fall down and be dissolved (cf. Moses 7:13) . . . flow down and be turned into side-channels, and shall melt like wax before a flame; and the earth will be destroyed."[43] In the light of the new plate tectonics, this does not sound as fantastic as it once did; any catastrophe of the magnitude of the Flood must have been accompanied by large-scale disturbances exactly like those described.

The terrible insecurity of the times heightened the social disaster as the people began to fight among themselves. "A man shall not know his brother, nor a son his father, or his mother."[44] For God permitted certain angels to go to "the sons of adultery, to destroy the sons of the Watchers from among mankind: Set them fighting against each other in war and in destruction."[45] (Moses 7:7.) Emphasis is laid on the *pollution* of the earth, both physical and moral, for the two go together, and only a great purging of water, wind, or fire, could cleanse it (cf. Moses 7:48), for without such periodic purging, says the Zohar, "the world would not be able to endure the sins of mankind."[46] "And thou wilt cleanse the earth from all uncleanness . . . and all the filthiness [*akatharsias*] . . . and all earth shall be cleansed from all the pollution [*miasma*] and from all impurity [*akatharsias*]."[47] "And he shall cleanse [*praunei*] the earth from the defilement [*phthoras*] that is in it."[48]

Characteristic of the sweep and scope of the Enoch apocalypse is the disturbance of the whole cosmos sharing the fate of the violated planet and its destruction: "The whole earth shall be shaken, and tremble, and be thrown into confusion . . . and the heavens and its lights be shaken and trembling."[49] (Cf. Moses 7:41, 13.) "I saw how mighty quaking made the heaven to quake, . . . and the angels . . . were disquieted with great disquiet."[50] (Cf. Moses 7:56.) The "quaking" of the heavens, often referred to, suggests to present-day knowledge of the shifting or unsteadiness of the earth's axis.

3. In contemplating these terrifying events, Enoch never allows us to forget that the real tragedy is not what

becomes of people but what they become. The people in the days of Enoch and Noah were quite satisfied with themselves as they were, and they hotly resented any offers of help or advice from God's messengers. "They will not carry the yoke which I have placed upon them," the Lord told Enoch, "but they will cast off my yoke, and they will accept a different yoke. And they will sow worthless seeds . . . and they renounced my uniqueness. And all the world will be reduced to confusion by iniquities and wickedness."[51] (Cf. Moses 6:28.) "The Kings of the earth say, We have not believed before Him . . . but our hope was in the sceptre of our kingship, and in our glory," so that when disaster strikes they must confess that "his judgments have no respect of persons, and we pass away from before his face on account of our own works."[52] The refrain is ever "Wo unto you foolish ones, for you shall perish through your own folly!"[53] "They denied the Lord and would not hear the voice of the Lord, but followed their own counsel."[54] (Cf. Moses 6:43.) "They go astray in the foolishness of their own heart."[55] (Cf. Moses 8:21-22.) They know what they are doing when they say to God, "Turn away from us, for the knowledge of thy ways gives us no pleasure!"[56] "God gave them promise of all that he would give them and what he wanted them to do; but they have defrauded themselves in refusing to keep the precepts which our Lord gave unto them."[57] "Therefore ask no more concerning the multitude of them that perish," said the Lord to Ezra, "for having received liberty they despised the Most High, scorned his Law, and forsook his ways."[58] (Cf. Moses 7:32.) "Sin has not been sent upon the earth, but man of himself has created it."[59] "Slavery was not given from above but came by transgression, and the barrenness of your women does not come by nature but by your own willful perversions."[60]

Peculiar to the world of Enoch is not only the monstrously arrogant quality of the sinning that went on, but the high degree of enlightenment enjoyed by the sinners, making them singularly culpable. To Enoch God explains, "I established Adam, and gave him dominion; and I gave unto him his free agency, and showed him the Two Ways . . . and I said unto him: This is good for you, and this is bad."[61] (Cf. Moses 7:32.) What more could anyone ask? God had given the race the power of understanding and the word of wisdom. "God created man last of all, in His own form, and put into him eyes to see, ears to hear, and a heart to reflect, and intelligence to deliberate."[62] With eyes wide open they made their choice: "For I waited so they might come to me, but they did not deign to. (Cf. Moses 7:33, 37.) And they glorified an alien [god]. And they joined [to him] . . . and they abandoned the Lord who gave them strength."[63]

The theme of willfully proud and stubborn men whose rejection of God's word is their undoing rings through Greek literature, beginning with the spoiled young men of Odysseus' crew destroyed in spite of all his heroic exertions to save them—by their own intractable lack of self-control (atasthaloi).[64] This is followed immediately by Zeus's complaint about how men are constantly blaming the gods for the results of their own folly.[65] The resounding roll of dios eteleueto boule ("the decision of Zeus has been made") seems to make the buck stop there, deafening the reader to the important fact that Zeus had to lower the boom because his messenger, a prophet of sweet reasonableness, had been cynically thrown out of the camp and had appealed to the god to do something about it. In a way, Odysseus, Chryses, and Tereisias are all Enoch figures, portending dire results but not without offering a way of escape. The mocking kings can say with those of Enoch's day, "We pass away . . . on account of our [own] works . . . descending . . . into . . . Sheol."[66] "The Fallen Angels of their own sweet will plotted, conspired, and apostatized along with their prince."[67] (Cf. Moses 5:51.) "Wo to you mindless ones [aphrones], for ye shall perish through your own folly, and ye shall not give ear, and not receive what is good for you."[68] Following their own foolish ambitions and dreams, engaging in lying works to realize them, "setting at naught the foundation of the inheritance of their fathers in a spirit of apostasy, they have no peace of mind and no joy."[69] Stubbornly and morosely they continue their ruinous course, ignoring God's commandments and blaming others for their misfortunes with "great and hard accusations with an unclean mouth and lies—you are hard-hearted and have no peace."[70] They are not beyond getting the point, for when Enoch speaks to them straight, "they could not speak, nor could they raise their eyes to heaven for shame because of their sins, and they were condemned."[71] (Cf. Moses 6:47.)

A significant aspect of the Apocalyptic picture is the technological advancement of the doomed and wicked world, in which men defy God confident in their technical and scientific knowledge. To the various fallen angels, designated by name, the Greek Enoch texts assign the introduction among men of the studies of chemistry, "the manufacture of weapons and jewellery, cosmetics, the trade-secrets of the angels," formulas and incantations, drugs, astrology, *semeiotika*, asteroscopy, *selenagogias*, and so on.[72] They thought to emancipate themselves from dependence on God through technological know-how,[73] in the manner of the doomed super-race of Peleus and Thetis.[74] "This is not as foolish as it sounds," says the Zohar, "for they knew all the arts . . . and all the ruling chieftains in charge of the world, and on this knowledge they relied, until at length God disabused them by restoring the earth to its primitive state and covering it with water."[75] In the days of Enoch, even the children were acquainted with the mysterious arts (what we would have called advanced science); R. Yesa asks: "With all that knowledge could they not foresee destruction?" To this R. Isaac replies: "They did know, but they thought they were safe because they had means of preventing [the angel in charge of fire and the angel in charge of water] from executing the judgment upon them. What they did not know was that God rules the world. [Cf. Moses 4:6.] . . . God gave them a respite all the time that the righteous men Jared, Methusaleh, and Enoch were alive, but when they departed from the world, God let the punishment descend . . . and they were blotted out from the earth."[76] "Alas," cries R. Simeon, "for the blindness of the sons of men, all unaware as they are how full the earth is of strange and invisible beings and hidden dangers, which could they but see they would marvel how they themselves can survive on the earth."[77] In Enoch's time they had all sorts of engineering projects for controlling and taming nature (as did Abraham's Nimrod), but the Lord altered the order of creation so that their very mastery of nature as they understood it became their undoing.[78] The same scientific hubris that led them to reject God led them to insult nature, and the upheavals that ensued demonstrate the very real ecological connection between the sins of men and the revolt of the elements that was formerly viewed as the fatal extravagance and irrationality of Apocalyptic.

4. What is consistently overlooked in summing up the grim pages of Enoch is that the terrible fate that overtakes the wicked is more than counterbalanced by the benign and constructive forces that reduce the damage to a minimum and follow it up with quick and complete repair. For one thing, in the Enoch account nobody suffers who does not deserve to: The Flood is by no means an indiscriminate slaughter. True, when the destroying angel is abroad, he makes no distinction among his victims, but by that time the wicked as well as the righteous have received ample warning and time to take cover (cf. Moses 7:21), so that no one can complain of cruel or unfair treatment.

From the first, God provided a way out. When "the Great Angels, seeing the bloodshed and violence and all the unrighteousness and lawlessness upon the earth went and reported to God, asking him, What are we to do?" the Lord sent the angels "to teach the righteous what to do

to preserve his soul and to flee."[79] (Cf. Moses 5:58.) In the
Secrets of Enoch, the Lord appears to Nir "in a vision of
the night, saying a great destruction is coming upon
the earth. . . . As to the child [Melchizedek] I will send
my archangel Michael and he will take the child and place
him in the paradise of Eden."[80] Enoch himself was carried
away in such manner physically: "While Enoch was speaking,
. . .darkness covered the people who were standing with
Enoch. And the Angels hastened and took Enoch and carried him to the upper heaven. . . . And the darkness withdrew from the earth and it was light again, and the people
saw, and understood how Enoch had been taken, and they
glorified God and returned to their houses [temples]."[81]
(Cf. Moses 7:26-28.) Again, "in those days a whirlwind
carried me off from the earth, and set me down at the end
of the heavens. And there I saw another vision."[82] Another time, "an angel of the Lord called out to Enoch from
heaven . . . and said that he should take him up to heaven,
to make him King over the Bene ha-Elohim, even as he
ruled over the Children of God on earth."[83] So Enoch was
the one who mysteriously vanished, "and he was not; for
God took him." (Genesis 5:24.)

But he is not alone in his heavenly junkets: the other
biblical statement about Enoch is that he led his city of Zion
to safety, transported beyond the earth, to return at a later
time and join hands with the earthly Jerusalem, the two
meeting, in the common concept, in mid-air. It was
foretold that when "the rainshowers of God the Almighty
[shall] destroy all flesh . . . great angels will come down on
high clouds to bring those men to the place where the spirit
of life is to be found."[84] (Cf. Moses 7:27.) This passage from
the Apocalypse of Adam is given more fully in the Chester
Beatty Enoch text: "And angels shall come down, descending into secret places in that day; all who aided unrighteousness shall be gathered together in one place . . . and
over all the righteous and holy he will set a guard of holy
angels . . . and they shall be preserved as the apple of his

eye until the tribulations and sin shall give over."[85] The
image is that of the righteous spirits in the *anapausis* or
refrigerium, but the type is the heavenly city of Enoch.
According to R. H. Charles, "the most complete and self-
consistent of all the sections" of First Enoch is that dealing
with Zion and the New Jerusalem.[86] (Cf. Moses 7:62.) The
peculiar allure of the tradition is the possible element of
tangible reality in it, the haunting science-fiction plausibility of it.[87] When God comforts the righteous with the
assurance, "I have mounted up to the heights, and this that
I might lift up from among them the Elect . . . as a reward," we are reminded of verses like John 12:32, but the
Jewish text insists on a mechanism for the thing with "my
ranks and hosts and Cherubs and wheels and Seraphim" all
taking part.[88] There is a separation of the righteous and the
wicked, the former being removed physically from the
earth: "I will bring upon all earthly creation ten plagues.
. . . And then from your seed will be left the righteous
men . . . who strive in the glory of my name toward the
place prepared beforehand for them,"[89] that is, when "my
judgments will come upon the heathen who have acted
wickedly through the people of your seed who have been
set apart for me."[90] The separation is a prerequisite:"Therefore have I now taken away Zion, that I may the more
speedily visit the world in its season."[91] "Afterward great
angels will come on high clouds to bring those people to
the place where the spirit of life dwells . . . [then they will
come] from heaven to earth [and back again], but the whole
multitude of flesh will be left behind in the waters."[92] At
that time "fear and trembling shall seize all men . . . and
everything which is upon the earth shall be destroyed," the
Lord tells Enoch. "I shall give peace to the righteous, and
for the elect I will provide security [*synteresis*, physical pro-
tection] and peace . . . and a light will appear and bestow
peace upon them."[93]

At that same time Enoch takes charge of the operation
from the earth side, being from time to time "raised aloft on

the chariots of the spirit" while "the angels took the cords to measure for me the place for the elect and righteous, and there I saw the first fathers and the righteous who from the beginning dwell in that place."[94] There is a sort of shuttle service operating over a period of time, for it has ever been the practice that "the angels of the ministry are rising and descending from heaven to circulate (*l^{e}tawel*) over all the earth."[95] In Enoch's day, they gathered all who would be saved into a special *topos*, a sort of marshaling area or refugee camp, which according to the Apocryphon of John later became confused with the Ark: it was a sort of island of light in a vast surrounding darkness, barricaded (*skepazein*) against the forces of destruction; "they entered and wrapped themselves in a cloud of light, and the Lord was among them, for darkness was poured out over all the earth."[96] (Cf. Moses 7:26.) "When all the earth was shaking . . . and in confusion, the angels came down and carried out their assignments," which included both "destroying all bastard spirits and sons of the Watchers because of the unrighteousness of men" and seeing to it that "all the righteous shall escape, and continue to go on living for a thousand generations!"[97] How? "But ye are come unto Mount Sion [Enoch's community!], and unto the city of the living God, the heavenly Jerusalem, and to an innumerable company of angels." (Hebrews 12:22.)

The City of Enoch is the symbol of escape; the Berlin Manichaean Manuscript sees in the removal of the Church from the wicked world the equivalent of the removal of Enoch's Zion from the same,[98] and the Psalms of Solomon 17 depicts the pious sectaries of the desert as fleeing to the place of safety in the same manner.[99] We are warned, "Forget not Zion!" against the days "when everything that is shall become the prey of corruption."[100] Enoch leads the parade: "When my Apostle shall raise himself up he shall be lifted up along with his Church, and they shall be lifted up from the earth. And it shall take the form of my *ekklesia* and be free above [in the height]."[101] There is a real motion implied as in the return: "In those days [the] elect and holy children will descend from the high heaven, and their seed will become one with the children of men."[102]

In the book of Enoch all this traffic between heaven and earth is definitely something more than a spiritual or intellectual beatitude—it is precisely the persistent harping on the physical reality of the thing that turned the Church Fathers against Apocalyptic in general and Enoch in particular. Enoch in his primary role of heavenly scribe is able to visit various levels of heaven and earth and to view things from strange and unfamiliar angles and vantage points. This aspect of Apocalyptic, which has been singled out as its greatest weakness (ancient and modern doctors have only contempt for his harping on a very unspiritual cosmology), may well be its greatest strength. It is the ultimate foundation of all theodicy: we are in no position to judge what is going on because we see things from literally only one angle, and we therefore have no conception of reality. In Enoch, it is not only God who sees things from different levels, but holy men as well are given that privilege—and that makes everything different.[103]

Though science has conceded an infinite number of possible viewpoints for describing any object, in practice it has always insisted that there is really only one valid viewpoint: the down-to-earth, no-nonsense reality of everyday experience. We see everything, as it were, through a long, thin tube set up at an immovable point and welded in position to face in one direction only. What do we know of reality? For two thousand years the doctors have allowed God in theory unlimited perception while taking it upon themselves to decide how things look from God's point of view. All the astronauts knew quite well what to expect when viewing the earth from outer space; yet several reported that when they actually saw it, they were stunned and overwhelmed with the reality of the thing, and they knew with absolute certainty that there was more going on than science could ever know. The words of Whitehead on his

deathbed that the Bible teaches us of infinite possibilities
and that "these possibilities are REAL!" admonish us not to
be too hasty in condemning Enoch: we really don't see
things as they are.

The ultimate vindication of God's goodness in Enoch is
the final disposal of the issue. The fallen angels and their
followers were to be cast into a special prison (cf. Moses
7:38) and kept in chains of darkness, but only for a certain
set period of time, after which they were to be given
another chance to repent (cf. Moses 7:39) and then stand a
fair trial. Repentance would receive forgiveness through
the power of the atonement. To make sure that they receive
every opportunity of salvation, they receive the *kerygma*
from the Lord himself (cf. Moses 7:47), among others, who
goes down to teach and deliver the very spirits who rejected Enoch's teachings: "For Christ also hath once suffered for sins, the just for the unjust . . . quickened by the
Spirit: By which also he went and preached unto the spirits
in prison; which sometime were disobedient, when once
the longsuffering of God waited in the days of Noah." (1
Peter 3:18-20.) "Why art thou disquieted?" Michael asks
Enoch. "That day is prepared . . . for sinners an inquisition . . . that the punishment of the Lord of Spirits may not
be in vain. . . . Afterward the judgment shall take place according to his *mercy* and his *patience.*"[104]

A longsuffering God is not a cruel one. Enoch's mission—warning against the Flood—is from first to last a
humane one. As to the slaying of innocent animals (a
charge brought by the Sophists against Zeus as well), R.
Ishmael can only conclude that if the animals suffered they
must have deserved it: "For they have sinned, all of them,
the multitudes of that time, their wives, sons, daughters,
horses [mules], their property, and all the birds that were
in the world, which God destroyed with them in the Flood.
All that sinned were swept away."[105] Note that R. Ishmael
insists on the proposition that not one innocent creature
suffered. But if death is the ultimate disaster, then God is

cruel to all creatures. At what point does justice become a serious matter? Always. God is always just. At what point does pain? There we are dealing with a very relative matter. This is not the same thing. What does it take to frighten a child? All creatures experience fear and alarm, unpleasant sensations, as a basic prerequisite to survival. And we can take God's word for it to Ezra: "You come far short of being able to love my creation more than I love it."[106]

But Ezra gives a clear rebuttal to Rabbi Ishmael's hardline reasoning when he reminds us that men and animals experience things differently, so much so that death is tragic only to humans, for animals know nothing of it at all: "We perish and we know it. Let the human race lament, but let the beasts of the field be glad! Let all the earth-born mourn, but let the cattle and the flocks rejoice! For it is far better with them than with us; for they have no judgment to look for, neither do they know of any salvation promised to them after death." As far as they are concerned, it is all just one unchanging life; the real anguish of death is the anticipation of annihilation, and of that the brute creation knows nothing.[107]

NOTES

1. A. Jellinek, *Bet ha-Midrash* (hereinafter *BHM*), 6 volumes (Jerusalem: Wahrmann Books, 1967) 5:xlii, 171.

2. "Apocalypsis Pauli Syriace," *Orientalia* 2 (1933): 2ff., 19.

3. L. Blau, "Metatron," in *The Jewish Encyclopedia* (New York: Funk & Wagnalls, 1904) 8:519.

4. Zohar, Shemoth 19b.

5. Zohar, Shemoth, 8a.

6. 1 Enoch 68:2-4.

7. 4 Ezra 8:47.

8. 4 Ezra 8:49.

9. 2 Baruch 67:2-3.

10. 1 Enoch 60:5-6.

11. Jellinek, *BHM* 5:172.

12. 1 Enoch 66:1-2.

13. Secrets of Enoch 22, in Andre Vaillant, ed., *Le livre des secrets d'Hènoch* (Paris: Institut d'études slaves, 1952), p. 72; 2 Enoch 34:1-2.

14. 3 Enoch 4 (99, 15).

15. Apoc. Abraham 24:9; cf. 1 Timothy 6:10; 1 Enoch 67:8-11; 3 Enoch 5:7-9.

16. 1 Enoch 84:8; cf. Helaman 13:22.

17. F. G. Kenyon, *The Chester Beatty Papyrus* (London: Emery Walker Ltd., 1941) 96:10. Samuel the Lamanite plainly drew on the Enoch texts that must have been included in the brass plates of Lehi. (Cf. Helaman 13:31.)

18. Ibid., 98:1.

19. Apocalypse of Adam 3:12-15 (71).

20. Apocryphon of John I, 73-74.

21. Apocalypse of Adam 84:78.

22. Greek Enoch 3; cf. 1 Enoch 99:2.

23. Secrets of Enoch 22, in Vaillant, *Secrets*, p. 72.

24. 1 Enoch 60:6.

25. Charles, R. H., *The Book of Enoch* (Oxford: Clarendon Press, 1912), appendix 1, "The Gizeh Greek Fragment of Enoch," VI, 1, 2, 5 (hereinafter "Gizeh Fragment").

26. Greek Enoch 7:4, 9:8-10.

27. Ibid., 9:1-4.

28. Pistis Sophia, G. R. S. Mead, ed. and tr. (London: John M. Watkins, 1921), pp. 31-33.

29. 1 Enoch 65:6.

30. F. Tempestini, "Le livre d'Adam," in J.-P. Migne, *Diction-naire des Apocryphes*, 2 vols. (Paris: J.-P. Migne, 1856) I:161.

31. 2 Enoch 12.

32. Zohar, Bereshith 56a.

33. Kenyon, *Beatty*, 106:13.

34. Greek Enoch 98:15.

35. Zohar, Noah 75b.

36. Gizeh Fragment, XVI, 3.

37. Psalms of Solomon 8:9-11, 27.

38. Greek Enoch 3:4-5.

39. Gizeh Fragment, VII, 4.

40. 1 Enoch 7:6.

41. Greek Enoch 100:11.

42. 1 Enoch 60:16.

43. Gizeh Fragment, I, 5.

44. 1 Enoch 56:5-7.

45. Gizeh Fragment, X, 9.

46. Zohar, Bereshith 58b.

47. Gizeh Fragment, X, 20-22.

48. Kenyon, *Beatty*, 106:176.

49. Greek Enoch 102:1.
50. 1 Enoch 60:1.
51. 2 Enoch 34:1-2.
52. 1 Enoch 63:7-8.
53. Greek Enoch 98:2.
54. Secrets of Enoch 4, in Vaillant, *Secrets*, p. 8.
55. Kenyon, *Beatty* 99:8.
56. Jellinek, *BHM* 4:171.
57. "Apocalypsis Pauli Syriace," *Orientalia* 2 (1933): 2ff.
58. 4 Ezra 8:55-56.
59. 1 Enoch 98:4.
60. Greek Enoch 98:5.
61. Secrets of Enoch 22, in Vaillant, *Secrets*, p. 100-1.
62. Secrets of Enoch 18, in Vaillant, *Secrets*, pp. 60-63.
63. Apocalypse of Abraham 31:6-8.
64. Odyssey, I, 6-9.
65. Ibid., I, 32-34.
66. 1 Enoch 63:9-10.
67. Secrets of Enoch Ms. R 3 in Vaillant, *Secrets*, P. 93ff.
68. Kenyon, *Beatty* 98:9.
69. Ibid., 99:8.
70. Gizeh Fragment, II, 3-5.
71. Gizeh Fragment, XIII, 3.
72. G. Syncellus, Chronol., 23; Greek Enoch 8:3.
73. Zohar, Noah 74b.
74. P. Oksala, "Die Göttliche Hochzeit und der Hain der Götter—Catulls Gedicht 64," *Temenos* 4:81-91.
75. Zohar, Bereshith, 56a.
76. Ibid., 56b.
77. Ibid., 55a.
78. M. J. bin Gorion, *Sagen der Juden* (Frankfurt am Main: Rütten & Löning, 1913-27) 1: 167-68.
79. Gizeh Fragment, VII-X, G^{s}3.
80. Secrets of Enoch 23, in Vaillant, *Secrets*, p. 80.
81. Secrets of Enoch 18, in Vaillant, *Secrets*, p. 64.
82. 1 Enoch 39:3-4.
83. Jellinek, *BHM* 4:130.
84. Apocalypse of Adam 96.
85. Kenyon, *Beatty* 100:4.
86. Charles, *The Book of Enoch*, pp. 1-1i.
87. The Moslems teach that the Kaaba was put into orbit around the earth during the flood, descending again after the danger was over, certainly suggesting the nature of the thing as a meteoric stone (Tha'labi). (Qiṣaṣ al-Anbiyā' [Cairo: Muṣṭafā Bāb al-Halabī, A. H. 1340], p. 214f.)

88. Jellinek, *BHM* 5:173.

89. Apocalypse of Abraham 29:15-17.

90. Apocalypse of Abraham 29:14.

91. 2 Baruch 20:1-3.

92. Apocalypse of Adam 3:4-5.

93. Gizeh Fragment, I, 8.

94. 1 Enoch 70:1-4.

95. Jellinek, *BHM* 5:127.

96. Apocryphon of John I, 73; III, 37.

97. Kenyon, *Beatty* 102:2-3.

98. *Manichäische Handschriften der Staatlichen Museen Berlin* (Stuttgart: 1940), p. 12.

99. Psalms of Solomon 17:16-20.

100. 2 Baruch 31:3-5.

101. *Manichäische Handschriften*, p. 12.

102. 1 Enoch 39:1.

103. 2 Enoch 39:5.

104. 1 Enoch 60:5.

105. Jellinek, *BHM* 5:171.

106. 4 Ezra 8:47.

107. 4 Ezra 7:64-66.

PART 2

A STRANGE THING IN THE LAND: THE RETURN OF THE BOOK OF ENOCH

4

A Strange Thing in the Land:
The Return of the Book of Enoch

Certain visions once given to Moses were also "revealed to Joseph Smith the Prophet, in June 1830."[1] In De-
cember of the same year, "The Writings of Moses" were
also revealed, comprising what are now chapters 2 to 8 of
the book of Moses. (See the chapter headings.) This purports to be the translation of a real book originally written
by Moses: "And now, Moses, my son, I will speak unto
thee concerning this earth upon which thou standest; and
thou shalt write the things which I shall speak.

"And in a day when the children of men shall esteem
my words as naught and take many of them from the book
which thou shalt write, behold, I will raise up another like
unto thee; and they shall be had again among the children
of men—among as many as shall believe." (Moses 1:40-41.)

In his writings Moses renewed the revelations and
carried on the books of earlier prophets, according to our
text, which also includes what the Prophet Joseph entitled
"Extracts from the Prophecy of Enoch." Of this, B. H.
Roberts explains: "It will be understood . . . that the
'Prophecy of Enoch' itself is found in the 'Writings of
Moses,' and that in the text above [Moses, chapter 7] we
have but a few extracts of the most prominent parts of
'Enoch's Prophecy.'"[2]

What was given to the Church in 1830 was, then, not
the whole book of Enoch, but only "a few extracts," a mere
epitome, but one composed, as we shall see, with marvel-

---

*"A Strange Thing in the Land: The Return of the Book of Enoch" first appeared in the En-
sign from October 1975 to August 1977.*

ous skill; five years later the Saints were still looking forward to a fuller text: "These things were all written in the
book of Enoch, and are to be testified of in due time." (D&C
107:57.) The Enoch sections of the book of Moses were published in England in 1851 under the heading, "Extracts
from the Prophecy of Enoch, containing also a Revelation
of the Gospel unto our Father Adam, after He was driven
out from the Garden of Eden."[3]

The revelation of Adam also went back to a *written*
source, for, speaking of his ancestors, Enoch is reported as
saying that, though they are dead, "nevertheless we know
them, and cannot deny, and even the first of all we know,
even Adam. For a book of remembrance we have written
among us, according to the pattern given by the finger of
God." (Moses 6:45-46.) Enoch, we learn, had this book of
Adam, and read it to the people, and handed it on with his
own writing in the corpus that Moses later edited and
Joseph Smith finally translated: "Soon after the words of
Enoch were given, the Lord gave the following commandment [December 1830]: 'Behold, I say unto you that it is not
expedient in me that ye should *translate* any more until ye
shall go to the Ohio.'" (D&C 37:1; italics added.)[4]

The excerpts from the works and days of Enoch found
in the Pearl of Great Price supply us with the most valuable
control yet on the bona fides of the Prophet. What has confused the issue all along in dealing with the Book of Mormon and the book of Abraham as translations is the question of the original documents. Almost all of the time and
energy of the critics has been expended in vain attempts to
show that Joseph Smith did not translate correctly from certain ancient manuscripts, or that such manuscripts did not
exist. This has been a red herring, since nobody has been
able to prove yet that Joseph Smith claimed to be translating from any specific known text. Moreover, the experts
have strangely and stubbornly overlooked hundreds of
passages from the Old and New Testaments that Joseph
Smith translated in a way that does not agree with the

translations of the scholars. Why don't they nail him on that? Because such a demonstration ends in proving nothing against the Prophet: manuscripts and translations of the Bible differ so widely, and so many baffling issues are being raised today about the nature of the original text, that there is no way of proving that any of his interpretations is completely out of the question. Always in these cases the discussion comes back to the original manuscripts.

But with the book of Enoch the question of an original manuscript never arises. Although chapters 2 through 8 of the book of Moses are entitled "The *Writings* of Moses," the Prophet nowhere indicates that he ever had the manuscript in his hands. Eighteen months earlier he recorded a revelation concerning John the Apostle, "translated from parchment, written and hid up by himself." (See D&C 7: heading.)[5] Since the discovery of the Dead Sea Scrolls, we know that writing revelations on parchment and hiding them up in caves was standard practice among the ancient Saints, thereby confirming this remarkable passage of modern revelation. But even more significant is the idea that though Joseph Smith saw and "translated" the document in question, he never had it in his hands, and, for that matter, it may have long since ceased to exist. The whole thing, document and translation, was "*given* to Joseph Smith the Prophet, and Oliver Cowdery" by revelation "when they inquired through the Urim and Thummim." (D&C 7: heading; italics added.)

So it was with the book of Enoch, transmitted to us by Joseph as it was given to him. Though his work was far more demanding and probably required far more concentration and sheer mental effort than we can even imagine, that task did not include searching for a lost manuscript or working out a translation.

So we are forced back on the one and only really valid test of the authenticity of an ancient record, which does not depend on the writing materials used, nor the language in which it was written, nor the method of translation, but simply asks the question, "How does it compare with other records known to be authentic?" This is what the critics of the Book of Mormon and the book of Abraham have never been willing to face up to; with the book of Enoch they have no other choice—and so, through the years, they have simply ignored the book of Enoch. Yet there never was a more delightfully vulnerable and testable object. It offers the nearest thing to a perfectly foolproof test—neat, clear-cut, and decisive—of Joseph Smith's claim to inspiration.

The problem is perfectly simple and straightforward: There was once indeed an ancient book of Enoch, but it became lost and was not discovered until our own time, when it can be reliably reconstructed from some hundreds of manuscripts in a dozen different languages. How does this Enoch redivivus compare with Joseph Smith's highly condensed but astonishingly specific and detailed version? That is the question to which we must address ourselves. We do not have the golden plates nor the original text of the book of Abraham, but we *do* have at last, in newly discovered documents, a book which is *the* book of Enoch if there ever was one. And so we have only to place the Joseph Smith version of the book of Enoch—Moses 6:25 through 8:3 with associated texts—side by side with the Enoch texts, which have come forth since 1830, to see what they have in common and to judge of its significance.

For those who seek divine guidance in troubled times, the book of Enoch has a special significance, not merely by virture of its pertinent and powerful message, but also because of the circumstances under which it was received. As the *History of the Church* records: "It may be well to observe here, that the Lord greatly encouraged and strengthened the faith of His little flock, which had embraced the fullness of the everlasting Gospel, as revealed to them in the Book of Mormon, by giving some more extended information upon the Scriptures, a translation of which had already commenced. Much conjecture and conversation frequently occurred among the Saints, concerning the books mentioned, and referred to, in various places in the Old and New Testaments, which were now nowhere to be found. The common remark was, 'They are *lost books;*' but it seems that the Apostolic Church has some of these writings, as Jude mentions or quotes the Prophecy of Enoch, the seventh from Adam. To the joy of the little flock, which in all . . . numbered about seventy members, did the Lord reveal the following doings of olden times, from the prophecy of Enoch."[6]

The book of Enoch was given to the Saints as a bonus for their willingness to accept the Book of Mormon and as a reward for their sustained and lively interest in all scriptures, including the lost books: they were searchers, engaging in eager speculation and discretion, ever seeking like Adam and Abraham, for "greater [light and] knowledge." (Abraham 1:2.) And we have been told that if we stop seeking we shall not only find no more, but lose the treasures we already have. That is why it is not only advisable but urgent that we begin at last to pay attention to the astonishing outpouring of ancient writings that is the peculiar blessing of our generation. Among these writings the first and most important is the book of Enoch.

The Lost Book of Enoch

Early Christian writers knew all about the book of Enoch: indeed, "nearly all the writers of the New Testament were familiar with it, and were more or less influenced by it in thought and diction," according to R. H. Charles, who notes that "it is quoted as a genuine production of Enoch by St. Jude, and as Scripture by St. Barnabas. . . . With the earlier Fathers and Apologists it had all the weight of a canonical book."[7] Its influence is apparent in no less than 128 places in the New Testament,[8] and Charles can declare that "The influence of I Enoch on the New Testament has been greater than that of all the other apocryphal and pseudepigraphical books taken together."[9] He further lists some thirty passages in early orthodox Jewish and Christian writings in which the book of Enoch is mentioned specifically,[10] plus numerous citations from the book that are found in the important Jewish apocalyptic writings of Jubilees, the Testament of the Twelve Patriarchs, the Assumption of Moses, 2 Baruch, and 4 Ezra, and quotations from Enoch found in more than thirty Christian Patristic writers.[11]

To these we might add the wealth of Enoch lore contained in the Zohar, a work whose prestige and respectability have greatly increased of recent years, and the interesting fact that the *Pistis Sophia*, that important link between the sectaries of Egyptian, Mesopotamian, and Palestinian Christianity and Judaism, claims to contain important material taken from "the two Books of Jeu which Enoch has written. [12] "They should find the mysteries which are in the Book of Jeu which I caused Enoch to write in Paradise . . . [which I spake out of the tree of knowledge and the tree of life], and I caused him to place them in the rock of Ararad."[13]

"Shortly before the Christian era, Enoch became the hero of a whole cycle of legends," which enjoyed immense popularity.[14] The Christians got their enthusiasm for the book of Enoch as well as the book itself from the Jews, that being "the most important pseudepigraph of the first two centuries B.C."[15] The Hasidic writings of the time as well as the later Cabalistic works show dependence on Enoch.[16] But it is important to note that Enoch is not popular with the gnostics and philosophers; he is quoted almost exclusively by the most respected and orthodox writers among both Jews and Christians. Thus "large parts of the lost Book of Enoch were included in the Pirke of Rabbi Eleaser and in the Hechalot," both highly respected works.[17] Recently some of the oldest and most important fragments of Enoch have turned up among the Dead Sea Scrolls, and far more important ones are still being held back by their uneasy Christian editors.[18] More than a century ago, when A. Jellinek began his zealous search for surviving traces of a

Hebrew book of Enoch, he declared that the Enoch literature was the work of the Essenes.[19] And thereon hangs the
principal clue to their disappearance.

How could a book of such long-standing influence, authority, and veneration possibly have become lost? Very
simple: it ran afoul of ideas held by the doctors of the Jews
and Christians alike after those worthies had fallen under
the influence of the University of Alexandria, whose modern descendants resumed their censure of it after it was discovered and have continued to condemn it to this day.

"But our book contained much of a questionable character," writes R. H. Charles with a sigh, "and from the
fourth century of our era onward it fell into discredit; and
under the ban of such authorities as Hilary, Jerome, and
Augustine, it gradually passed out of circulation, and became lost to the knowledge of Western Christendom."[20]
Enoch "fell early into disuse," according to C. C. Torrey,
because it had no strong appeal for the Christians and "was
too bulky" to copy and handle.[21] This explanation is as
feeble as that of St. Augustine, who, while admitting that
"we cannot deny that Enoch . . . wrote some inspired
[divine] things, since the canonical Epistle of Jude says so,"
refuses to accept it solely on the grounds that the Jewish
doctors reject it—an argument that bore no weight whatever with the earlier Christians.[22]

"Of a questionable character" to whom? For what Christians did Enoch have "no strong appeal"? The answer is
perfectly clear: it was the learned rabbis and doctors of the
fourth century who were offended by it.

In his recent study of Hellenistic Judaism, H. F. Weiss
comes to the point: It was as inspired or revealed writings
that such great apocalyptic works as Enoch, Fourth Esdras,
and Baruch "were by the 'official' rabbinic-pharisaic Judaism . . . systematically suppressed and removed, ostensi-
bly on the grounds of their apocalyptic content."[23] They did
not just fade out; they were deliberately and systematically
destroyed.

Thus, until recently, the only surviving fragments of Enoch have come from Christian copyists, and not a single Jewish text of the Twelve Patriarchs, which draws heavily on Enoch, survives; moreover, not a single picture of Enoch has ever been identified in either Jewish or old Christian art.[24] The trouble was, says Charles, that in Enoch the "apocalyptic or prophetic side of Judaism" was confronted by the rabbinical or halachic, that is, by the "Judaism that posed as the sole and orthodox Judaism . . . after 70 A.D.," which damned it forever as a product of the Essenes.[25]

It was the same story with the Christians; it was "such authorities as Hilary, Jerome and Augustine" who put the book of Enoch "under the ban." They were all learned schoolmen steeped in the rhetorical and sophistic education of the time, admitting quite freely that the Christians of an earlier time held ideas and beliefs quite different from theirs.[26] They also knew that Enoch was treasured as a canonical book by the early Christians, but they would have none of it. The transition is represented by the great Origen, another product of Alexandria, who lived a century before them; he quotes Enoch, but with reservation, finding that he cannot agree with the teachings of the book, no matter how the first Christians may have venerated it.[27]

At the present time, sensational new manuscript discoveries are forcing both the Jewish and the Christian doctors to view Enoch with a new respect. Consider two items from Catholic encyclopedias—then and now. In 1910 the *Catholic Encyclopedia* brushed aside the idea that the epistle of Jude testifies of the existence in ancient times of the book of Enoch: "Some writers have supposed that St. Jude quoted these words from the so-called apocryphal Book of Henoch; but, since they do not fit into its context [Ethiopic], it is more reasonable to suppose that they were interpolated into the apocryphal book from the text of St. Jude. The Apostle must have borrowed the words from Jewish tradition."[28] But the *New Catholic Encyclopedia* of 1967 tells a different story: not only does Jude actually quote from the book of Enoch, but the "entire passage found in Jude v. 4-15 reveals a dependence on Ethiopic Enoch."[29] When a recent article in *Scientific American*, of all places, seeks to demonstrate how all our ideas of early Jewish and Christian religions have been drastically expanded and altered in the past few years, its star witness is the newly discovered book of Enoch.[30]

The last lingering remnant of Enoch's words from the ancient world was a passage cited by the Byzantine writer George Syncellus, about A.D. 800. This, however, was a mere excerpt of less than a page in length; the writings themselves had by that time long since vanished.[31] For, "from the 4th century on, the Latin Church ceased to concern itself" with Enoch, while "only a few traces are still found, persisting for a short time longer, in the Greek Church."[32] All that the Middle Ages had to show as the sole remnant of the book of Enoch was a miserable Arabic proverb, "piety brings easy money," which is not from Enoch at all.[33]

The Rumors Fly

With the first dawn of the Reformation, rumors of the existence of a real book of Enoch began to stir. About the time that Columbus set sail, Johann Reuchlin was excited by the report that the famous Pico della Mirandola (d. 1494) "had purchased a copy of the book of Enoch for a large sum of money."[34] The report may well have been authentic, according to Nathaniel Schmidt, who notes that "it is possible . . . that Pico's collection contained a copy of the Hebrew Enoch. . . . There may also have been a copy of the Ethiopic Enoch."[35] Rumors gave rise to the usual impositions and frauds, and in 1494 Reuchlin wrote against those who produced books with exciting titles, claiming that they were the books of Enoch, proven by their age to be more holy than other books, falsely claiming some to have been Solomon's, and so easily beguiling the ears of the ignorant.

He had heard, he states, of one such book for sale, which he assumes to be a late forgery based on Josephus.[36] This did not mean that Reuchlin ceased to look for the real book of Enoch. In 1517 he wrote that "the books of Enoch and Abraham, our father, were cited by men worthy of faith," and countless examples of ancient authors whose works are now lost to our age confirm the probability of their works having been lost in the same way, still we do not doubt that a great number have survived.[37]

With the widespread "rediscovery" of the Bible in the Reformation, "the Book of Enoch excited much attention and awakened great curiosity,"[38] just as it did among those to whom the Book of Mormon came in a later age of enlightenment. But, as is well-known, the great reformers in their all-out zeal for the Bible condemned the "wretched Apocrypha" for presuming to be classed with it.[39] John Calvin considered Enoch to be no more than an ordinary mortal, whose translation to heaven was nothing more than "some extraordinary kind of death," and he held with the Jewish doctors that Enoch's "walking with God" meant no more than that he received inspiration.[40] In 1553, the humanist Guillaume Postel, acclaimed at the court of France for his firsthand knowledge of the Near East, announced, "I have heard that there is reason for believing that there are Books of Enoch at Rome, and an Ethiopian priest has told me that that book is held to be canonical and is attributed to Moses in the Church of the Queen of Sheba [the Abyssinian Church]."[41] The famous Codex Alexandrinus, which was presented to Charles I of England in 1633, was accompanied from Egypt as far as Constantinople by a Capucinian monk, Gilles de Loches, who had been living in Egypt. That monk told Peiresc, the famous scholar and manuscript collector of Pisa, about a monastery possessing eight thousand volumes, in which he had seen a book of Enoch.[42] As the German Orientalist Ludolf recounted a generation later, "Gassendi, in his Life of Peiresc, writes among other things of a certain Capuchin,

Aegidius Lochiensis, who had spent seven years in Egypt: He says he mentioned among other things a Mazhapha Einok, or Prophecy of Enoch, declaring what would happen up to the end of the world, a book hitherto not seen in Europe, but written in the character and language of the Ethiopians or Abyssinians among whom it was preserved. By this Peiresc was so excited and so on fire to buy it at any price that he spared no means to make it his own."[43] It is now known that this was the authentic Ethiopian Enoch, but Schmidt comments that the scholarly reaction at the time was to suppose that Peiresc had been duped.[44]

The last authentic excerpt to be written from the book of Enoch was the first to be discovered, 800 years later: it was that prince of scholars, Joseph Justus Scaliger, who around 1592 recognized the passage mentioned above when it was quoted by the Byzantine historian Syncellus as a genuine excerpt from the lost book of Enoch. Yet Scaliger "spoke in very disparaging terms of the book . . . although he maintains that the apostle Jude has quoted it."[45] So there the matter rested, with Enoch discredited and dismissed by the very man who had discovered him.

Toward the end of the seventeenth century, scholarship lost its former imagination and drive, thanks to the competitive skepticism of experts determined to demonstrate their solid conservatism to each other. Peiresc's manuscript of Enoch ended up in the Mazarin Library in Paris, whither in 1683 the Prussian scholar Job Ludolf repaired with considerable publicity to put it to the test. Schmidt records that Ludolf promptly concluded that it was not the book of Enoch at all: "But that it is not Enoch is at once apparent from the title alone: 'Revelations of Enoch in Ethiopian' "[46] As for the content of the book, it simply nauseated him: "To tell the truth it contains such gross and vile stinking [putidas] fables that I could hardly stand to read it. . . . Let the reader then judge how beautiful these 'revelations' of Enoch are, how worthy of their magnificent binding and sumptuous edition! We would rather keep silent regarding this most idiotic of books, were it not that so many illustrious men have made mention of it."[47] Ludolf examined it at the Mazarin Library, and declared it utterly bad; but then, Schmidt sums it up, "Ludolf, who did not believe there ever was a book of Enoch, may be pardoned."[48] May he? That was his trouble to begin with—he did not believe that there ever was such a book, just as those Egyptologists who were asked to pass judgment on the book of Abraham approached their task with the settled conviction that there never was such a book. For him, as for them, only one conclusion was possible.

But the Christian world gratefully received the final verdict of the learned (even as they did again in 1912!), and as a result the study of Enoch was dropped for ninety years, until the discovery of new manuscripts broke the intellectual logjam. Until Ludolf's pronouncement, the search for Enoch had been a "subject richly productive of criticism and theological discussion"; but once Berlin had spoken, "the idea that a book of Enoch existed in Ethiopia was completely abandoned, and no one gave it another thought."[49] As one scholar observed with relief as late as 1870, "But when Job Ludolf went afterwards to Paris to the Royal Library, he found it [the Enoch manuscript] to be a fabulous and silly production. In consequence of this disappointment, the idea of recovering it in Ethiopic was abandoned."[50] As a result of Ludolf's authoritative contribution, "all hopes of obtaining the book seem to have died away throughout Europe. . . . It was generally supposed, that it must be ranked among the books irrecoverably lost."[51] Even down to the present time, when they should know better, "modern editors and commentators," according to N. Schmidt, go on "repeating with approval the disdainful remarks of Ludolf."[52]

And so, following the well-worn path of self-certified scholarship, the experts would have gone on automatically repeating each other for generations with the book of Enoch safely laid to rest as a myth, were it not for three copies of that same Ethiopian version, which the famous explorer James Bruce brought home with him from his epoch-making journey to the sources of the White and Blue Nile in 1773.

Bruce was six years in Abyssinia and had learned the language, "and brought home with him a large collection of curious and interesting objects,"[53] including some of the most valuable Christian Coptic manuscripts ever discovered, as well as the three priceless Ethiopian Enoch texts.[54] "Of these three copies, one he retained in Kinnaird House [the family seat in Scotland], another he presented to the Bodleian Library in Oxford, the third he gave to the Royal Library in Paris."[55]

Bruce himself wrote: "Amongst the articles I consigned to the library at Paris was a very beautiful and magnificent copy [Ludolf had commented caustically on such waste of effort in the Peiresc manuscript] of the prophecies of Enoch in large quarto. Another is amongst the books of Scripture which I brought home, standing immediately before the Book of Job, which is its proper place in the Abyssinian Canon; and a third copy I have presented to the Bodleian Library at Oxford."[56]

But Dr. Ludolf had done his work well. There was a flurry of interest in Bruce's finds, but it quickly subsided, and "for more than a quarter of a century these manuscripts remained as unknown as if they had still been in Abyssinia."[57] "Whatever may have been the curiosity of the public at the time of Bruce," a Catholic scholar reports, "it seems to have been long since pacified; and as for the exemplar deposited in the library at Oxford, it slept a profound sleep."[58] The first public notice of the text was on the Continent, when in 1800 the famous Orientalist Sylvestre de Sacy translated into Latin the first three chapters of the Paris manuscript and the opening lines of some other chapters;[59] in the following year a German named Rink published a few of the same chapters at Königsberg. That was about it—and then silence for another twenty years.

It was a great and good man, Archbishop Richard Laurence of Cashel in Ireland, who restored the book of Enoch to the world. In "A Charge Delivered at Munster" in 1826 he pleaded, as the Protestant bishop of the most important Irish see, for Catholics and Protestants to learn to live together. For taking and holding this position through the years, Laurence was subjected to savage and relentless attacks from both the Protestant and the Catholic clergy. "His fears for the public peace," wrote the editor of *The British Critic, Quarterly Theological Review,* and *Ecclesiastical Record,* "appear to have strangely overpowered his anxiety for the cause of Scriptural truth. That the endeavor to break down the strong holds of Popery in Ireland may occasion some discord and provoke some retaliation, is, indeed, more than probable. But his Grace must know perfectly well that the gospel itself produced, at first, a formidable dislocation of society," etc., etc.[60]

From the other side, the Roman Catholic prelate attacked Laurence with equal vigor, deploring his appeals for Christian charity as "fulsome nonsense; . . . the ways of God are not our ways; the Holy Ghost has told us that there is but *one* faith; . . . and that without it, it is impossible to please God."[61] The groundwork was being laid, even consciously, for the present-day tragedy of Ulster when the Anglican ministers took Laurence to task, declaring that they must "reconcile even the Archbishop of Cashel to the great and pious enterprise of diffusing the blessings of the Reformation throughout Ireland, and relieve him from his terrors lest the cause of Christianity should suffer in the conflict. It is true that a *fiery furnace* of persecution may even now be heating for many of those who shall turn their back upon the Church of their ancestors [the Irish Catholics]; it is true that fanaticism may lay a rude and violent hand on the standard of this great cause; . . . but, his Grace has not to learn, that in this world good and evil must ever grow up together; and that it hardly becomes a Christian warrior to sit down counting the cost, till the season of action is gone by! . . . He must acknowledge that there is something marvellous and awful in the present agitation of the public mind; and he will not surely be rash enough to deny that it *may possibly* be the sign of some great work which the Lord is about to perform in behalf of his Own truth."[62]

A century and a half later, the "great work" foreseen by a zealous clergy still goes on as a legacy of demoniacal hatred and bloodshed, and Richard Laurence stands vindicated not only as a champion of Christian charity but as one who has done more for the cause of Scriptural truth than all the rest of the clergy put together. For to him "belongs the honour of revealing to the world the treasure that had been hidden for so many ages, and which was almost universally supposed to be lost irrecoverably":[63] the book of Enoch. Obliged to do all his work in the dark and damp Bodleian Library, which begrudged lending him manuscripts in which it had not the slightest interest,[64] he produced in 1821 a translation under the title *"The Book of Enoch, an apocryphal Production, now first translated, from the Ethiopic Ms. in the Bodleian Library,* Oxford, 1821."

This work was reviewed by de Sacy in the *Journal des Savants* in 1822,[65] and a decade later A. C. Hoffman issued a Latin translation;[66] in 1840 A. F. Gfroerer included a translation of Laurence's English version in a Latin book of oddities.[67] Not until 1851 was an Ethiopian text published, edited by A. Dillmann, who in 1853 issued a German translation containing passages not found in Laurence.[68] The first French translation did not appear until 1856.[69] Laurence himself issued a revised version of his Enoch in 1833, 1838, and 1842; of recent years more translations have been available in English.[70] But the only book of Enoch available to anyone before 1830 was Laurence's translation of 1821. It called forth three studies in English, which, being by unknown scholars, "hardly attracted the attention of the learned world at all"; and even so, the tendency of these works was not to enhance but to minimize the importance of Laurence's Enoch.[71] After 1821 no translation was available to the public until 1833, when Joseph Smith's "Book of Enoch" was already three years old. Since we are to test that work by comparison with other versions since brought to light, it is important to ask at the outset just what other Enoch books Joseph Smith *could* have read. There is only one candidate: the Laurence translation of 1821. Could the Prophet have seen it before 1830? There would seem to be no possibility of that. Let us list the reasons for such a conclusion:

1. 1830 was a busy year for the Prophet Joseph; it saw the founding of the Church, the publication of the Book of Mormon, the sending of missionaries, much coming and going under persecution and pressure. It was also a banner year for revelation, including a sizable part of the Book of Commandments and the book of Moses. But for study? for research? for carefully digesting and critically exploiting a document like Laurence's Enoch, 214 pages long with a forty-eight-page introduction and footnotes? Any dealing with such a text would have left its mark on any work derived from it. All that work by a twenty-four-year-old farmer in upstate New York who had just produced a Book of Mormon without any footnotes at all? Hardly! Laurence's 1821 text only got into the hands of a few scholars in Europe and England, and they gave it scant notice; what would be the likelihood of a copy reaching Joseph Smith? By what grapevine? Who would transmit it and why? That is our next point.

2. Nobody in the learned world paid much attention to Laurence's Enoch. As we have seen, after its publication the "zeal for the cause of this long sought relic of antiquity appears to have expired for a long time in England. . . . In France the Book of Enoch scarcely awakened a sensation."[72] Even when the expedition of Napier to Magdala brought more Ethiopian manuscripts back to England, and the German missionaries whom he rescued brought yet more of them to Germany, those documents were promptly forgotten.[73]

3. More to the point, the Christian ministry of all denominations neither liked Laurence's Enoch nor wanted it. It was not circulated by them but suppressed. Just as Peiresc's treasure, on the authority of Ludolf, was thrown out as "nothing more than a worthless tract, replete with fable and superstition,"[74] so it was assumed from the first that the book of Enoch could only be full of "incantations and bestialities."[75] In 1828 the very learned Algernon Herbert observed, "It has been supposed that the authour of that epistle [Jude] received and cited, as a holy scripture, that which is called the Book of Enoch, being an ignorant and ridiculous effusion. . . . The book in question is so monstrously absurd, that no person citing it, . . . could have obtained credit with Tertullian. . . . A man so profoundly ignorant of criticism, as to receive the said book for divine revelation, and so nearly allied to the errours of gnosticism, as to believe in its contents," could, he avers, never have written the Epistle of Jude.[76]

One of the best studies ever made on the book of Enoch was written way back in 1840 by Michael Stuart, professor of sacred literature in the Theological Seminary at Andover College, where in 1882 the first and only translation of the Ethiopian Enoch to appear in America was to be published.[77] He was excited by the discovery, but for the message of the book of Enoch he had only contempt: "To what purpose is an appeal to a book confessedly *apocryphal,* and therefore of *no authority?* . . . I have not the most distant intention to refer to the book of Enoch, as a book of *authority.* I can never be brought to believe that the Ethiopians had any good right to place it in their Canon. . . . My full belief is, that 'our present Scriptures are the *only* and the *sufficient* rule of faith and practice.'"[78] He recognizes the gulf between the book of Enoch and the doctors of the Church who condemned it, noting that what is found in *their* writings is "less repugnant to sound reason and philosophy, than what is found in the book of Enoch."[79] "No one now pretends that the book of Enoch is an *inspired* book," he insists, though admitting that "time was, when individuals

probably thought so." Whereas the *early* Jewish writers and
Christian fathers "quoted it as a *holy* book . . . almost all
later fathers reject its claims to a place in the canon: as well
they might. . . . No claim to any *authority* on the part of the
book will now be made by any intelligent man."[80]

There it is again—and in America's most staid and respected school of divinity 135 years ago: the authentic,
original early Christians just didn't have the intelligence
and sophistication to understand things as they really
were. The *later* fathers were all right: they were educated
men who understood things the way we do—but those
primitive Christians and Jews! Take just one example: "The
very basis of the first part of his book, viz. the alleged carnal
intercourse of angels with the daughters of men, is an actual impossibility, not to say absurdity."[81] What could the
writer of the book of Enoch have had in mind? Instead of
asking that question, the churchmen of every denomina-
tion simply threw the book out of the window. To this day,
in the official encyclopedias of the Lutherans and even in
the literature of such fundamental literalists as the
Seventh-day Adventists and the Mennonites, no articles
appear under the name of Enoch. Nor do we find any mention of Enoch in the contemporary *Vocabulary of Jewish Life*
or in the *Book of Jewish Concepts.* Though all the other great
patriarchs have places of honor in these works, Enoch is
out!

The Catholic clergy of Joseph Smith's day fully shared
the scorn of Protestants and Jews for the new discovery.
"To him [Enoch] in the first centuries of the Church," wrote
the Abbé Glaire in 1846, "was attributed a work full of
fables about the stars, the descent of the angels to earth,
etc. But it appears that this production was fancied by the
heretics, who, not content with falsifying the holy Scriptures, took advantage of the credulity of their stupid followers in spurious and fabulous works. Some critics pre-
tend that this work, really by Enoch, has been disfigured
by the hand of infidels; they base this claim on St.

Jude. . . . But St. Jude cites Enoch without any mention of his book."[82]

Later Catholic authorities deplore Enoch on the same grounds as they object to the Dead Sea Scrolls and other more recent discoveries, namely, that if taken seriously they would deprive Christianity of its sovereign claim to absolute originality: "To attribute great influence on the New Testament ot the Book of Enoch as Charles does, is to ignore the powerful originality and divine inspiration of those to whom we owe the New Testament."[83] "Christ and the Apostles did not draw their doctrines from the Apocryphal works." Who says they did? There are other explanations for the resemblance—and no one today any longer denies that resemblance. But it annoys the clergy no end.

In a recent and important book, Klaus Koch has shown how Protestant and Catholic scholars alike through the years and right down until 1960 (when new discoveries forced them to change their attitude) resolutely steered clear of the basic apocalyptic works, of which Enoch is by all odds the most important,[84] and C. P. Van Andel, in his survey of the Enoch literature, notes that no one has been willing to touch the vital question of Enoch and the New Testament since 1900.[85] As recently as 1973, a writer in *Scientific American* pointed out how new manuscript discoveries, especially Enoch, are now for the first time requiring drastic revision of the conventional Christian and Jewish views regarding the nature of the early Christian and Jewish communities and their teachings.[86]

4. Freethinkers might have exploited the so-called absurdities of Enoch against the Christians, but the latter had beaten them to the punch by promptly and vigorously disowning the book. Who, then, would have an interest in the book of Enoch? One might expect it to appeal to Masons or Rosicrucians, but it did not; Enoch is not found among the books favored by mystic or gnostic groups, and his name does not occur in their lists of inspired prophets.[87] No library in America had a more representative collection of

the works of the ancients than that of Thomas Jefferson, "for in his book-collecting no subject was overlooked by him."[88] Book No. 1 in Jefferson's library was "Ancient History, Antwerp, including texts of Berosus, Manetho, etc.," and the books that follow show an equal concern for getting at the truth and the whole truth where the ancients were concerned. The collection was systematically and diligently continued, with careful concern for the latest and best information,[89] up until 1826. If one expected to find a copy of Laurence's 1821 Enoch anywhere in America it would be in this library; but it is not. It was simply unknown in America.

5. This is thoroughly borne out in Michael Stuart's long and careful study of 1840. The text Stuart uses is the 1838 edition of Laurence, whose work comes to him, nineteen years after the first version, as a novelty. Indeed, his aim in writing his long studies is to make American clergymen aware for the first time of the existence of the book: "The possession of this work, in our country, is *rare;* and our public, so far from being acquainted with the contents of the work are in general not at all aware, as I have reason to believe, that the book has even been recovered and published to the world."[90] If this applies to the larger and far more widely publicized edition of 1838, who would have known anything of the 1821 edition, which Stuart does not even mention, and which went unremarked even in Europe by all but a few specialists?

Of the later edition, Stuart writes: "The reader, who is not in possession of it, and may not be able to procure it [he is writing for ministers rather than the general public], will naturally be desirous to know something more particular respecting so curious and interesting a relic of antiquity; and for his sake I shall proceed to give a more enlarged summary of its contents."[91]

The thing was virtually unobtainable in this country. And why not? Its only appeal was as a religious book, but the religious were all against it. "Curious and interesting" it may have been for Stuart, but not to be recommended to the untrained in its original form: "It is in vain for any one to derive much from it which is intelligible. . . . For readers at large, the *Book of the Luminaries* is at present a sealed book."[92] The historical part is written "in a very obscure and sometimes even repulsive manner" with some of the principal chapters an "insipid and almost monstrous production."[93] This was no book "for readers at large"!

And now comes a surprise. The same edition of Laurence was reviewed in the same year by another critic, who thought it was simply wonderful! The name of the critic was Parley P. Pratt, at that time, 1840, in England editing the official Latter-day Saint publication *The Millennial Star*, in which his review appeared. Thus the Latter-day Saints first heard of Laurence's Enoch in England, and greeted it with joyful surprise.

Far from being insipid, repulsive, and monstrous, for Elder Pratt, "this book carries with it indisputable evidence of being an ancient production. It steers clear of modern sectarianism, and savors much of the doctrine of the ancients, especially in regard to things of the latter day. . . . It seems plainly to predict the coming forth of the Book of Mormon, and the mission of Elders . . . together with the late persecution befallen our people in America . . . and the final result of that matter, and the complete triumph of the Saints."[94] Extravagant as such conclusions may seem at first glance, recent studies of Enoch by non-Mormon scholars show it, as we shall see, to be surprisingly near the mark, for the book of Enoch was handed down through the centuries with the avowed intention of bringing comfort to the persecuted saints in every dispensation of the gospel.

Note that the 1838 edition of Laurence's book of Enoch is brought to the attention of the Saints as an exciting novelty. It does not occur even to the alert and searching Brother Pratt to compare the writing to Joseph Smith's 1830 book of Enoch, buried as it was in the book of Moses, to be published eleven years later in England under the title *Extracts*

from the Prophecy of Enoch. What catches the eye of Parley P.
Pratt are the parallels to the Book of Mormon and to the
condition of the Church and the world in the last days. "We
give the following extract, commencing at p. 156 [chapter
93:2ff], without further comment, and leave our readers to
form their own judgment in regard to this *remarkable* Book."
And he proceeds to quote passages peculiarly fitted to the
condition of the Latter-day Saints at that time: "To the righteous and the wise shall be given the books of joy, of integ-
rity, of great wisdom. To them shall books be given, in
which they shall believe: in which they shall rejoice."[95]

Well might they be impressed, and they should have remembered that Joseph Smith's book of Enoch was given to
them as a reward for their receiving and believing in the
Book of Mormon. But the parallels escaped them as they
have been overlooked by Saints ever since. In 1951 when
Elder John A. Widtsoe presented the writer with a copy of
the same text of I Enoch (the R. H. Charles edition of 1912),
it was with the regretful comment that he had never found
time to read it and wondered if it contained anything of interest. At that time this writer himself had never read it—
who had? It is only since about 1950 (with the discovery of
Enoch texts among the Dead Sea Scrolls), as Koch and Van
Andel point out, that anybody has begun to take this
Enoch seriously. Pratt read the 1838 edition in England,
and there is no indication that any Church member in
America owned a copy. The 1846 Inventory of Church Records includes no such title in the books of the Church Library taken across the plains.

6. This laboring of the only too obvious point, that
Joseph Smith could not have used or known about the 1821
edition of Laurence's book of Enoch, has been very necessary because: (a) that was the *only* translation of any ancient
Enoch text available to anyone at the time he dictated
Moses chapters 6 and 7, and (b) the two books are full of
most significant parallels. If such parallels are to have any
significance as evidence supporting the Prophet's claims,
we must of course rule out his use of the Laurence text.

Aside from the astronomical remoteness of such a probability, we have some useful positive "controls" that definitely show that such parallels are not dependent on the Laurence text. For many other manuscripts of the book of Enoch have come forth in various ancient languages since 1830, adding a great deal to the standard text that is *not* found in the 1821 version but that *is* found in the Joseph Smith Enoch. One of the most remarkable parallels, for example, is between some verses of Moses 7 and chapter 11 of the Ethiopian book of Enoch; yet that particular chapter was not included in the Laurence translation, and so could have been known to no one at the time.

7. Finally, even if Joseph Smith had had the rich apocryphal literature of our own day at his disposal, with the thousands of pages of Enoch, or even the 1821 text of Laurence, how would he have known how to handle the stuff? The Prophet's book of Enoch is less than three chapters long; how was he to know from all that what to put in and what to leave out to produce a text that most nearly corresponds to what modern scholars view as the authentic original material of Enoch's book? He did just that; he put together in a few hours the kind of text most closely corresponding to what specialists, after years of meticulous comparison of texts, come up with as the hypothetically essential text of Enoch. Let us now turn to the Enoch texts they have been using for their diligent comparative studies and see how the Enoch story has emerged through the years.

I Enoch

As recently as 1937 Professor C. Bonner could write: "No part of the original writings, Hebrew or Aramaic, which entered into the composite work, has survived in the original language. The Greek version, in which the early church read Enoch, also disappeared. . . . Modern knowledge of the work has been derived from the Ethiopian version," coming from a time "when all Christendom except Egypt had dropped Enoch from the list of sacred writ-

ings."[96] I Enoch has long been recognized as "the largest
and, after the canonical book of Daniel, the most important
of the Jewish apocalyptic works which have so recently
[this in 1916] come to be recognized as supplying most important data for the critical study of NT ideas and phraseology."[97] The work was translated into Ethiopic about A.D.
500, [98] but the twenty-nine Ethiopian Enoch texts used by
R. H. Charles in 1912 all date from the sixteenth and seventeenth centuries.[99] All agree that the Ethiopic Enoch is a
composite work, and the dating of its various elements is
still entirely a matter of conjecture.[100]

While only guesses are possible regarding the process
and steps by which the thing was brought together, Plöger
would assign what he considers the oldest parts to Essene
origin of the second century before Christ.[101] Bonner finds
that, compared with the Greek version, the Ethiopic translation "while faithful in intent . . . has many faults, omit-
ting here, expanding there, and in general committing
numerous errors. Yet there are not a few places in which it
preserves a reading better than that of the Greek
papyrus";[102] indeed, the text as a whole "may perhaps
be . . . truer to the [Hebrew] original than the Greek."[103]
However, "the Ethiopic text is more general and therefore
more imaginative and free as a literary work" than the
others,[104] and such freedom has been bought at a price, for
the work of the sixteenth- and seventeenth-century natives
"has been on the whole disastrous," according to Charles;
"by far the best" of the manuscripts "exhibits much strange
orthography and bad grammar, and many corruptions."[105]

Here it is proper to call attention to the lesson drilled
into his students by A. E. Housman: There is no such thing
as a *"beste Handschrift"*—the worst manuscript may contain
priceless bits of an ancient text in their purest original form,
while a manuscript that is notable for its convincing and
demonstrably correct readings may without warning come
up with unbelievable howlers. So it happens that the
Ethiopic Enoch, "though teeming with every form of

error . . . additions, corruptions, and omissions," contains for all that a number of "unique, original readings" that can be exceedingly valuable.[106]

II Enoch, the Secrets of Enoch

II Enoch was unknown to the Western World until Robert Henry Charles suspected in 1892 that a Slavonic manuscript published by A. Popov in 1880 was no mere re-hash of the Ethiopic Enoch, "but a different document. His suspicions proved correct when William Richard Morfill translated the Slavonic manuscript into English in 1896."[107] Plöger concludes that the Slavonic Enoch originated in a Jewish sect in Egypt and was translated into Slavonic at the beginning of the early Middle Ages.[108] S. Terrien notes that it "includes many beliefs of popular Judaism of the 1st century A.D."[109] Others dispute this; H. F. Weiss maintains that the Slavic Enoch is from a Greek original and does *not* go back to Palestine.[110] Others have it a reworking of the Ethiopic Enoch based on a Greek text, originally written in Palestine before the fall of the temple (A.D. 70), noting that its Hellenistic flavor suggests a Judaeo-Alexandrine author.[111] Recently, David Winston has called attention to strong Iranian influence in II Enoch.[112] The standard edition of the Slavonic Enoch is that of A. Vaillant, who brings together "a dozen different Slavonic manuscripts" for his text.[113] According to Vaillant, the Slavonic Enoch was first noticed in 1859.[114] R. H. Charles bases his version on the German translation of Bonwetsch and the English Morfill translation of 1896.[115]

The Slavonic Enoch comes to us in a long and short version, with the experts unable to agree on which has priority.[116] Vaillant finds the longer version "imputable to the fantasy of the 15th and 16th centuries,"[117] while they and the five Slavonic manuscripts of the short version (translations from the Greek),[118] once stripped of the late fantasies that so embarrassed Charles, present "a perfectly coherent ensemble, which without the slightest disparity falls into

place as a work of primitive Christianity."[119] Vaillant calls
the Slavic Enoch "this Christian imitation of a Jewish apocrypha" in which "Christian thought is expressed in terms
of the Old Testament, into which borrowings from the
Gospel seem to be transposed."[120] Though the first major
revision took place in the thirteenth century, the manuscript in which it reaches us is from the sixteenth century;
the language is Bulgaro-Serbian. Its writer borrows from
the Chronicle of Harmatole and belonged perhaps to the
circle of Vladislav the Grammarian.[121] A second major revision, which corrects the "mediocre Slavonic" of the first,
was by an unknown Moldavian scholar.[122]

III Enoch, the Greek Enoch

Greek excerpts from the book of Enoch have always
been available in Jude 14b-15 (quote I Enoch 4:14); the
Epistle of Barnabas 4:3, 16:5-6; Clement of Alexandria,
Eclog. Prophet. 53:4; Origen, *C. Cels.* 5:52; Comm. in John
VI, 42 (25); and the long ninth fragment in George Syncellus' *Chronicle.* (Dindorff, p. 24:2-11.) R. H. Charles lists no
fewer than 128 citations from Enoch in the New Testament![123] Yet these passages could not be identified until an
actual Enoch text of some sort was available; as late as 1912,
the Greek Enoch was known only through the tenth century Slavic tradition.[124]

A Greek Enoch fragment matching a section of the
Ethiopian (I Enoch 89:42-49) "was found in the Vatican Library by Angelo Mai in 1832 and deciphered by Johann Gil-
demeister in 1885. A considerable part of the same Greek
translation was discovered in Akhmîm in Upper Egypt in
1886-1887 and published in 1892."[125]

Thus, an important, though limited, control of the late
Ethiopian and Slavic texts was becoming possible, as the
much older Greek stuff emerged. In 1893, Charles made an
exhaustive comparison of the Ethiopic and newly discovered Greek texts, which are given in the original in the appendix of his 1912 translation of I Enoch (pp. 318-70).

Charles found that the Ethiopic was translated from the parent manuscript G^g, a very corrupt Greek text, though each contains original material not found in the other.[126] The important Akhmîm text was discovered "during the winter of 1886-1887 by the French Archaeological Mission" and "was thought at the time of its publication [by Bouriant in 1892] to be of the eighth century, but is now assigned to the sixth."[127]

When in 1930 the University of Michigan got six leaves of papyrus Codex of Enoch in Greek, Professor Bonner discovered that they belonged in a batch of papyri residing in the famous Chester Beatty collection; and sure enough, in 1931 Frederick Kenyon found more leaves of the same text in the Beatty collection, making a total of fourteen pages[128] written by a single scribe in a handwriting of the fourth century—by far the oldest Enoch text discovered up to that time.[129] "Written in a large and coarse hand, which is certainly not that of a trained scribe," the Michigan codex is "full of mistakes in spelling . . .";[130] "almost every page exhibits errors of a more serious sort which show that the scribe was often drowsy or inattentive, and suggest that he understood his text imperfectly. . . . The manuscript from which he copied was itself corrupt or else almost illegible in some places."[131] In form it is not a roll or scroll, but a book,[132] bound with a text of Melito. The Beatty Enoch is to be viewed, Van Andel suggests, as typical of that "edifying literature in Christian circles from the 3rd to the 6th (?) centuries,"[133] showing in what high esteem Enoch was held by the early Christians, having been taken into the church with full honors from earlier times.[134]

The Greek Enoch offers another example and warning to those who would rest arguments on silence. As late as 1910, no less eminent a scholar than C. Schmidt had "attempted to show . . . that the strange silence of all Patristic writers as to this remarkable book, whose Christian coloring, at least in its present form, would have been especially tempting to them, renders it doubtful whether it was ever translated into Greek."[135] Indeed, Schmidt could write in 1922, "No manuscript of the Greek text has yet been found, and it seems to have left no important traces in Byzantine literature, though it must have been read in Constantinople as well as in Alexandria."[136]

But once a book of Enoch came forth, Charles could supply, not only 128 citations from Enoch in the New Testament, but a list of over thirty important apocryphal (Jewish and Christian) and patristic works *quoting* Enoch.[137] Quite recently M. Philonenko has called attention to a Manichaean Greek text with an important excerpt from Enoch.[138] Mathew Black has brought together all available and reconstructed Greek Enoch texts into a single hypothetical "Apocalypsis Henochi Graeci,"[139] but still the big Greek text is missing.

The Hebrew-Aramaic Enoch

It has always been suspected that the oldest version of Enoch would turn out to be Aramaic or Hebrew. "The book of Zohar, in which are various allusions to Enoch, seems to speak of it as an important Hebrew production which had been handed down from generation to generation. The Cabbalists . . . thought that Enoch was really the author."[140]

One can follow Jellinek's unfolding of Hebrew Enoch texts in the pages of the *Bet ha-Midrash*. In 1859, Jellinek suggested that "a Hebrew Book of Enoch resembling the Ethiopian" had once circulated among the Jews: "The Karaite Salmon b. Jerucham in the 10th century, Moses of Leon [12th century] and the Zohar toward the end of the 13th century all cite from a Book of Enoch";[141] but as early as 1853, Jellinek had suggested some Hebrew sources for the Book of Enoch, and even posited that Enoch was an *Essene* creation.[142]

Large fragments of the lost book of Enoch are included, moreover, in the Pirke R. Elieser and the Hechalot, which in the Oppenheim Manuscript is actually labelled "Book of

Enoch."[143] In volume 2 of the *Bet ha-Midrash*, Jellinek gives the text of a "Book of Enoch" as preserved in Moses of Leon's "Book of the Dwelling of the Secrets,"[144] and in the next volume he notes that the Great Hechalot (meaning the Chambers, that is, of initiation in the temple) was a type of writing that combined Essenism and Sufism, and had great influence on poets and mystics. The Great Hechalot, he said, was actually a secret book of the Essenes dealing with the origin of the universe and the divine throne of Ezekiel. Parts of it appear in the Book of Enoch, that provided the source of Christian-Essene and Jewish-Essene literature. [145]

In *Bet ha-Midrash*, volume 4, Jellinek provides the text to a Life of Enoch from the *Sefer ha-Yashar*, using older sources, and announced that this provided "a new confirmation that the entire Enoch saga and the Enoch books were known to the Jews, and were only allowed to fall into neglect after the time when a growing Christianity displayed a dogmatic preference to this cycle (Sage)," that is, it was adoption by the Christians that soured the Jews on Enoch.[146]

In volume 5, in 1872, Jellinek joyfully announced the vindication of his long search: "In [*Bet ha-Midrash*]III, 1855, p. xxiii, I suggested that several versions of the Hechalot themes attributed to the Wisdom of Enoch must be in existence. And so also the primitive . . . Book of Enoch was put together from various smaller works, which had been traced back to Enoch!" The final proof is a text that Jellinek reproduced at this place, taken from Recamatic, commentary on the Pentateuch, Venice, 1545.[147] The study of Jewish apocalyptic literature in general was initiated in 1857 by M. Lilgenfeld, and it soon appeared, thanks to citations by the XII Patriarchs, Jubilees, and so on, that Enoch was "the first" and "most important" of all the Palestinian apocalypses.[148] "Of all the Palestinian writings," wrote the Catholic scholar J. B. Frey, "the Book of Enoch seems to have surpassed all the others in antiquity and in importance."[149]

N. Schmidt concluded that "it is possible that Pico's collection [in the 15th century], therefore, contained a copy of the Hebrew Enoch"[150] that the prejudice of the scholars allowed to pass by unnoticed. Besides the *Hechalot* published by Jellinek in 1873, Schmidt mentions as a Hebrew Enoch source the *Sefer Hechalot of R. Ishmael* (Lemberg, 1864), but insists that "the Hebrew Enoch contains material that appears to have been drawn from both Ethiopic and Slavonic Enoch . . . as well as from other sources," thus regarding it, as S. Zeitlin does the Dead Sea Scrolls, as a Medieval production.[151]

What fixes the Hebrew Enoch as the original is the discovery among the Dead Sea Scrolls of sizable fragments of the book of Enoch. It will be recalled that Jellinek suggested way back in 1853 that Enoch was an Essene production.[152] In this he was vindicated almost exactly a hundred years after.

In 1956, Father J. T. Milik mentioned eight different fragments in the Dead Sea Scrolls of I Enoch in Aramaic, and an Aramaic book III, which was superior to the Ethiopian section on astronomy. There was also an epistle of Enoch to Shamazya and his friends, a manuscript dating before A.D. 70.[153] F. M. Cross reported in 1954 that the Pesher or commentary on Habakkuk, one of the first works to be discovered at Qumran, was "an unknown work related to the Enoch Literature."[154] Between 1952 and 1973, however, only two of these Aramaic fragments had been published, and in 1970, M. Black had to send his book to press without the benefit of the larger fragments.[155]

All the Enoch fragments found in Cave I, according to Milik, were deposited there in the first century A.D.[156] "Fragments of I En. from QCave 4 found in 1952, are all in Aramaic, and show affinities with the Ethiopian version. They contain hitherto unknown Enoch material, such as a letter of Enoch to Shamazya." In three of these manuscripts Enoch's journey on the earth is given "in a longer recension."[157] But for all their importance, the old Aramaic Enoch texts are still being withheld from the world after more than twenty years. The important Genesis Apocryphon from Qumran begins with five columns that "deal with the birth of Noah in a manner that has no direct relationship at all to the brief biblical account in Genesis V, 28-29," but "resembles Chapter cvi of the *Book of Enoch* in most essential points."[158]

Appraisals of the Book of Enoch as a Whole

It was Laurence himself in his first two editions who suggested that "different parts of this book may have been composed at different times and by different persons."[159] Acting on such an assumption, E. Murray went overboard and saw in Enoch nothing but a jumble of separate treatises on disconnected subjects, clustered around an· original book of only thirty verses![160] From the mid-nineteenth to the mid-twentieth century, dismantling ancient writings into many original components was a favorite game of the learned; so J. B. Frey, while hailing the book of Enoch as a work of supreme age and importance, still insists that it is really not a book of Enoch but rather an Enoch literature consisting of very disparate works that have only the name of Enoch in common, as if "Enoch" could not have written on more than one subject.[161]

Carl Clemen in 1898 found no less than twelve separate traditions in Enoch and made much of the changes of person "as betraying the composite character of the work."[162] Charles suggests that Enoch is "built up on the debris" of an older Noah saga and insists that "the Parables are distinct in origin," as are the cosmological sections.[163] Every possible theory has been suggested by the experts to account for the book. As R. H. Charles notes, every scholar divides up the Books of Enoch differently and assigns different dates to them.[164] As early as 1840, M. Stuart had the perspicacity to note that "the tone and tenor of the book has many resemblances to passages in the Zend Avesta";[165] while Sieffert sees part of it by a Chasid of the age of Simon Maccabbee and part by an Essene before 64 B.C., Philippi finds it written entirely "in Greek by ONE author, a Christian, about A.D. 100."[166]

The *Dictionary of the Apostolic Church* declared Enoch to be "a work of curious complexity and unevenness. . . . In fact, it is quite a cycle of works in itself," though "in this medley we find certain recurring notes."[167] The *Interpreter's Dictionary of the Bible* (2:103) confesses that "the extent to which the compiler reworked his sources cannot be determined. He certainly made little effort to harmonize them. . . . To some extent he interwove his sources. . . . More typically, however, one source is followed by another, with little or no attention to the chronological or logical sequence or to consistency of thought."[168] In 1960, J. E. H. Thomson could still report that there is still as much disagreement as ever among the experts on the structure of Enoch and the nature and priority of its various parts.[169] C. P. Van Andel reported in 1955 that no overall study of any aspect of the book of Enoch had ever been undertaken.[170] He gives the Greek Enoch clear priority, since it is intelligible where I Enoch is often incomprehensible.[171] We shall note below important instances in which the Joseph Smith Enoch "follows" the Greek and not the Ethiopian versions.

The Ethiopian Enoch, Van Andel holds, comes from Jewish sources of about the time of Christ; though its "Stitz in Leben" remains to be determined, all the Enoch literature is recognized as being the work of sectaries. R. H. Charles sees a Hasidic origin, that is, Pharisee; while Leszynski thinks it is Sadducee, and Lagrange, Essene—all of which have been related in one way or another to the Qumran community.[172] That part of I Enoch known as the Wisdom of Enoch (91-107) belonged to a separatist group, according to Van Andel, who were without friends in the world and stood in sharp opposition to the ruling classes in Israel.[173] Van Andel concludes that the ultimate source of the Ethiopian Enoch was a book circulated among related Jewish sects of the second and first centuries B.C. who took Enoch as their model in denouncing a degenerate world.[174]

This "book" in turn came from the same source as Jubilees, but is older,[175] while the "Wisdom of Enoch" part has the same origin as the XII Patriarchs and the Zadokite Fragment of the Dead Sea Scrolls, with their emphasis on priesthood and the strict keeping of the Law.[176]

All scholars agree that the ultimate beginnings of Enoch or its several parts remain completely unknown, while insisting that the book of Enoch *must* have been derived from earlier writings. Yet the oldest sources we have claim to go back to Enoch and know of none earlier but Adam. Instead of ever seeking for sources to Enoch, which never turn up, why not do the sensible thing and accept Enoch himself as the source, as the writers of Jubilees and the XII Patriarchs do?

Van Andel, who rightly accuses Albert Schweitzer of paying no attention to Jewish Apocalyptic writings in reconstructing his concept of Jesus and his followers,[177] is guilty of the same sort of shortsightedness when he traces everything back to the Jewish writings of the third century B.C. and there comes to a dead halt, as if all were a vacuum before that. But Rudolf Otto asks why we cannot go much farther back than that, since the Seer with his view of the heavenly Zion and the Ancient of Days is a stock figure in very ancient writings indeed.[178]

A much debated issue has always been, How *Christian* are the Enoch writings? "There is a possibility that the latest wording of I Enoch has been written by Christian hand [sic], but nowhere do the various parts give cause to deem it of Christian origin or interpolation," is Van Andel's conclusion.[179] In such Jewish works as the XII Patriarchs, James II, Peter, Jude, Didache, Barnabas, and Hermas, he finds it "seldom possible to make a clear distinction between Christian and non-Christian elements."[180] J. Z. Werblowsky holds that II Enoch "incorporates the messianic concepts of Alexandrian Jewry as well as many Christian additions . . . in circulation during the 2nd Temple Period."[181]

Christian scholars exercised to preserve the "original-

ity" of Jesus in the case of Enoch, as with the Dead Sea
Scrolls, have leaned over backward in insisting that Enoch
is a work totally alien to the New Testament. In 1840,
M. Stuart finds that "the reader who has never pursued
at much length the study of sacred criticism, cannot well
imagine how much light is cast by it [I Enoch] on various
parts of the New Testament; particularly on the Apocalypse. . . . And yet—how *different* are the two composi-
tions, although partial and even general resemblances are
so frequent!"[182] He assures us that Enoch and the book
of Revelation were written by "two Jews writing at the
same period, having the same general theme and object. . . . Both authors . . . deal altogether in visions and
symbols."[183] To rescue the originality of the New Testament, he explains that the two books are independent inventions, as "both authors . . . range the world of imagination" and freely fabricate.[184]

Still, Stuart is amazed to find what looks like true Christology *before* the time of Christ![185] How could he account for
it? It *must* be a Christian work: "The whole contour of the
Messianic part of the book indicates more knowledge of
Christology than any uninspired Jew can reasonably be
supposed to have possessed . . . at any time before Christianity was published."[186]

How about an *inspired* Jew then? That, of course, is out
of the question: "My full belief is, that 'our present Scriptures are the *only* and the *sufficient* rule of faith and practice,'[187] a position that obliges him, no matter what, to announce: "I have not the most distant intention to refer to
the Book of Enoch as a book of *authority*. I can never be
brought to believe that the Ethiopians had any good right
to place it in their Canon."[188] Yet he frankly admits that the
early Christians, including the first of the Fathers, placed it
in *their* canon![189] His conclusion: "The author was a Christian Jew,"[190] Christian, because "no merely Jewish usage,
which is known to us, would, at so early a period, have led
the writer in the path that he has trodden";[191] Jewish, be-

cause he was "unusually familiar with the Old Testament scriptures, and probably having some acquaintance with those of the New. It was composed in all probability in the latter half of the first century of the Christian era."[192]

In 1860, G. Volkmar, moved by the same arguments, insisted that Enoch was a purely Christian work, the idea that it was pre-Christian resulting from faulty translation; it had nothing to do with the sectaries of the first century B.C.[193] Then in 1864, the purely Jewish Hebrew Enoch texts began to appear,[194] but A. Vaillant, as a good Catholic, meets the challenge: While the Hebrew Enoch is "badly constructed, confused, and murky, the Christian Enoch is reasonable, orderly, and clear." So it was the Christians who really organized the old Jewish materials and in the process "invented another history," which lets the Jews out.[195] In the same spirit, Weisse, Hofmann, and Philippi all insisted that Enoch was a Christian work, on the "dogmatic principle," according to Charles, that Christianity had to be vindicated "in its pure originality."[196]

This is a question that has exercised all the students of early apocalyptic writings of recent years—what can we do when an undeniably Jewish work is full of undeniably Christian elements? That, of course, was one of the major stumbling blocks of the Book of Mormon—how could Jews before the time of Christ speak and act so much like Christians and vice versa? The apparent anomaly has led both Jews and Christians to restrain their enthusiasm for the Dead Sea Scrolls and even to discourage their publication.[197]

After listing a dozen references to Enoch in the New Testament, the *Encyclopaedia Britannica* minimizes the tie-in on the theory that "the recurrence of similar ideas and phraseology need indicate no more than indebtedness to a common tradition."[198] Van Andel insists that the New Testament community that invented Enoch followed Christ, who was not an invention: "The real Enoch is lost in the mists of myth, while the real Christ is a historic figure."[199]

And how did they invent Enoch? How much of the story came down to them beside the name? Nobody knows, and theories are cheap. Even R. H. Charles, to avoid giving too much credit to Enoch, has introduced things into his translation, according to Black, without "the slightest support from manuscript tradition. . . . He has in fact practically rewritten the end of the *Similitudes* 'in accordance with his view of what Enoch ought to have said.'"[200]

But P. Batiffol, with his usual insight, observed long ago that such works as Enoch are both a prolongation of the canonical prophets, and "at the same time a prologue to the Gospel. So and so alone can one explain the favor with which they met in the Primitive Church, and how, neglected by the Jews of the Talmudic tradition, they have been preserved for us by Christian hands."[201]

The purpose of this dull and sketchy summary is to make clear at the outset that when Joseph Smith produces pages of a book of Enoch for our perusal he cannot be borrowing from any known ancient source, whether Ethiopian, Greek, Slavonic, Hebrew, Aramaic, Arabic, or anything else, for none of them were available to him in 1830.

Of all the momentous concepts brought to the attention of mankind through the ministrations of the Prophet Joseph Smith, none has met with greater derision or merits greater respect than his account of how certain sacred records have been kept and transmitted to the Saints of every dispensation down through the ages. He tells us how a depository of sacred writings has been preserved and expanded from the beginning of man to the present time; and if he is right, there exists somewhere on earth at this time, if only we knew where to find them, the equivalent of thousands of tapes and films recalling crucial events in human history. The equivalent? Better than that! The old science-fiction dream of some day recapturing the waves of sight and sound propagated by great historical events of the past turns out to be a mistake—physicists assure us that waves of light and noise have a way of losing definition and damping out soon after they begin their ambitious voyage

in all directions, and it can be shown that the most powerful instruments conceivable can never unscramble their
confused and mazy impulses.

This means that the skill of writing, a technique as old
as history, still remains and probably always will remain,
the most effective means of binding time and space. "But
of all other stupendous inventions," wrote the stupendous Galileo, "what sublimity of mind must have been his
who conceived how to communicate his most secret thought
to any other person, though very far distant either in time
or place, speaking with those who are not yet born, nor
shall be this thousand or ten thousand years? And with no
greater difficulty than the various arrangement of two
dozen little signs upon paper? Let this be the seal of all the
admirable inventions of man."[202] The sublimity of the
thing brings its human invention into question—men
never invented anything else like that before or since, and
the idea that "primitive man" insensibly floundered into it
inch by inch over tens of thousands of stumbling years is
simply hilarious.[203]

Well, Joseph the Seer doth a tale unfold which when
you put it together is as splendid as it is audacious. And it is
not hard to put together, for it runs through all of the inspired scriptures of which he is the purveyor; the Book of
Mormon in particular spells it all out for us. This is how it
goes.

Enoch of old declared that in the days of Adam "it was
given unto as many as called upon God to *write by the spirit
of inspiration*," that "a book of remembrance" was kept "in
the language of Adam," and handed down to his own
time, "written among us, according to the pattern given by
the finger of God." (Moses 6:5, 46; italics added.) At the
end of his life, Adam "predicted whatsoever should befall
his posterity unto the latest generation," and that information was carefully preserved: "These things were *all written
in the book of Enoch,* and are to be testified of in due time."
(D&C 107:56-57; italics added.)

Thus there is a written record that bridges all of human

experience from the beginning to the end. And in between
comes a busy operation of bookkeeping to fill out the record, bring it up to date, condense and abridge where necessary, and transmit it into the proper hands for still further
transmission. "For I command all men, both in the east and
in the west, and in the north, and in the south, and in the
islands of the sea, that they shall write the words which I
speak unto them; . . . I shall also speak unto all nations of
the earth and they shall write it." (2 Nephi 29:11-12.)

As writing bridges space, so it bridges time—as the
bronze plates that Lehi took from Jerusalem "go forth unto
all nations, kindreds, tongues, and people who were of his
seed," we are assured that they "should never perish;
neither should they be dimmed any more by time." (1
Nephi 5:18-19.) The world by this account is covered with a
sort of mesh of communications, something like Teilhard
de Chardin's mesh of organic life, by which the righteous
regardless of time or place can share in a common universe
of discourse: "He surely did show . . . unto many concerning us; wherefore, it must needs be that we know concerning them . . . that they might know concerning the doings
of the Lord in other lands, among people of old." (1 Nephi
19:21, 22.)

Even the angels enter into the game: a bit of cross-
referencing will show that when Gabriel came to put
Zacharias and Mary "into the picture," as it were, his
whole discourse to them was simply a pastiche of ancient
prophetic writings that were about to be fulfilled (Luke 1);
and when Moroni inaugurated a subsequent dispensation,
he did so in the same way, "quoting the prophecies of the
Old Testament . . . about to be fulfilled," and others both
properly corrected and "precisely as they stand in our New
Testament," with the necessary explanations. (Joseph
Smith History 1:36, 40.)

In the handing down of the sacred record, everything is
under strict control from on high, "given by inspiration,
and . . . confirmed . . . by the ministering of angels, . . .

proving to the world that the holy scriptures are true, and that God does inspire men and call them to his holy work in this age and generation, as well as in generations of old." (D&C 20:10-11.) Everything is timed to the hour, done in "the own due time of the Lord." (2 Nephi 27:10, 21; Ether 4:16-17; esp. Joseph Smith History 1:53-59.) The perfect matching of the records from widely scattered times and places attests their authenticity, for "these last records . . . shall establish the truth of the first." (1 Nephi 13:40.) And from first to last, all is done "by the spirit of inspiration." (Moses 6:5.)

The Prophet is good enough to tell us just how the thing operates. As the material is passed down from one hand to another, it snowballs as only libraries can, so that an abridged version must be made from time to time if the main message is to be kept to the fore, with the editor selecting for special attention what he deems primary and preserving the rest under various categories.

"And there had many things transpired which, in the eyes of some, would be great and marvelous; nevertheless, they cannot all be written in this book; yea, this book cannot contain even the hundredth part of what was done. . . . But behold there are records which do contain all the proceedings of this people; and a shorter but true account was given by Nephi [an earlier editor]. . . . I [Mormon] have made my record . . . according to the record of Nephi . . . on plates which I have made with mine own hands." (3 Nephi 5:10-11; see 1 Nephi 1:16-17.)

The last phrase is the standard colophon by which an ancient editor certifies the accuracy of the record both as he received it and as he is passing it on: "And we know our record to be true, for behold, it was a just man who did keep the record . . . if there was no mistake made by this man." (3 Nephi 8:1-2); the editor himself certifies, "I make a record of my proceedings in my days . . . and I know that the record which I make is true; and I make it with mine own hand; and I make it according to my knowledge." (1

Nephi 1:1-3, see 3 Nephi 5:17.) Jacob the brother of Nephi tells us that he took notes from the older records, of the things that might be of particular interest to his people, jotting down "the heads of them" (ancient *kephalaia*), to "touch upon them as much as it were possible . . . for the sake of our people." (Jacob 1:4.) For relevance is the keynote: "for I did liken all scriptures unto us, that it might be for our profit and learning." (1 Nephi 19:23.)

Methods of handling sacred writings are conditioned by the hostile world in which they find themselves. There are those who have sworn "in their wrath that, if it were possible, they would destroy our records and us, and also all the traditions of our fathers." (Enos 1:14.) Failing that, they can damage and corrupt them: "They have taken away . . . many parts which are plain and most precious; and also many covenants of the Lord have they taken away," with the disastrous effect that "an exceeding great many do stumble." (1 Nephi 13:26, 29.)

Why should anyone want to do that? For whatever reason, the burning of the books is a stock motif of real history. Ray Bradbury's novel *Fahrenheit 451* tells of a time in the future when the government and people of the United States systematically destroy all books, which are the disturbing element in a world dedicated to TV and the avoidance of serious thinking. But the author misses the main point: the books that are burned are not the sacred depository of which we have been speaking, but the books in the college "Survey of Western Civilization," a second-growth at best, a covering of beautiful fire-weed that sprang up on the ashes of the holy books that had been burned by the very schoolmen who now sponsor their successors. The question right now is not whether the sad and moving chorus of the "Great Books," all admittedly groping in the dark, can answer the great questions of life (by their own admission they cannot), but whether there ever were books that could do so, a lost library that they replaced. Joseph Smith was aware of the blank emptiness that exists between modern man and any such writings. "You may think this order of things to be very particular," he said to the brethren when he introduced them to the record-keeping system of the Church (D&C 128:5); and Moroni, the editor-in-chief of the Book of Mormon, despairs of approaching or even describing the inconceivable power and grandeur conveyed by the written word in the hands of such inspired masters as the brother of Jared. (See Ether 12:23-25.) The point is that such writing operates on a different wavelength from the ordinary; from it the receptive reader can get something that no other writing will give. The last dispensation was inaugurated by such a communication: "Never did any passage of scripture come with more power to the heart of man than this did at this time to mine." (Joseph Smith History 1:12.) The passage was familiar, but until then the power had been shut off.

Because the world is touchy and resentful of what it does not understand—"Dogs bark at strangers," says the immortal Heracleitus—the keeping of the record is much concerned with hiding, withholding, dissembling, rationing, and disguising: "Having been commanded of the Lord that I should not suffer the records which had been handed down by our fathers, which were sacred, to fall into the hand of the Lamanites, (for the Lamanites would destroy them) therefore I . . . hid up in the hill Cumorah all the records which had been entrusted to me by the hand of the Lord." (Mormon 6:6); "Those who have dwindled in unbelief shall not have them, for they seek to destroy the things of God." (2 Nephi 26:17.) Such things are "sealed up" and "shall not be delivered in the day of the wickedness and abominations of the people. Wherefore the book shall be kept from them." (2 Nephi 27:8.)

The safest way to preserve a book from destruction, and the *only* way to protect it from the inevitable corruption of contents that comes with copying and handling, is simply to bury it: "sealed up to come forth in their purity" (1 Nephi 14:26); "then shalt thou seal up the book again, and hide it up unto me, that I may preserve the words which thou hast not read, until I shall see fit in mine own wisdom to reveal all things" (2 Nephi 27:22, see Ether 4:4-6, D&C 6:26-27). The problem of finding the thing again raises no difficulty, of course, since they are hid up "unto God" by his instruction: "Touch not the things which are sealed, for I will bring them forth in mine own due time. . . . Wherefore, when thou hast read the words, . . . then shalt thou seal up the book again, and hide it up unto me." (2 Nephi 27:21-22.) And when they are found again, they are to be shown "only to those to whom [the finder] should be commanded to show them," on pain of the finder's own destruction. (Joseph Smith History 1:42.) When they are "had again among the children of men," it is only "among as many as shall believe. . . . Show them not unto any except them that believe." (Moses 1:41-42.) Some things are never to be circulated publicly, but are only "to be had in the Holy Temple of God" (Abraham, facsimile 2, figure 8); others may not be written down save by a special agent at a special time. (1 Nephi 14:25, 28.)

Sacred writings are often secured from unworthy eyes by the device of recording in code. In a sense, all writing is codified and can be read only by those who have received special instruction; to "read" means to "riddle" or decipher. King Benjamin had to learn a special language before he "could read these engravings," and he had his sons learn the language so they could keep the record (Mosiah 1:4); and the brother of Jared was ordered to guard the teachings, to "write them and . . . seal them up, that no one can interpret them; for ye shall write them in a language that they cannot be read." (Ether 3:22.)

To bridge the cultural and linguistic gap between the hider and the finder, thousands of years apart, special *gifts and implements* are provided, notably the seer-stones and Urim and Thummim. (Ether 3:23.) These are no mere mechanical gadgets, but "work not among the children of men save it be according to their faith" (2 Nephi 27:23), requiring far greater moral and intellectual qualifications than the manipulation of grammars and dictionaries. They work by "the same power . . . and the same gift" as those by which men wrote the words in the beginning. (D&C 17:7, 9:2, 8:11; Moses 6:5.)

It all begins on earth with the "Book of the Generations of Adam," a complete record of names and events and of God's dealing with his children on earth. (Moses 6:8.) He requires the Saints in every age to keep such a book, or rather to continue the original, adding their own names and histories to it, as they "arrange by lot the inheritances of the saints whose names are found, and the names of their fathers, and of their children, enrolled in the book of the law of God" (D&C 85:7), which is the same as the "book of remembrance" (D&C 85:9), which goes back to Adam (Moses 6:45-46) and is also "the genealogy of the sons of Adam" (Moses 6:22). Enoch reads from the books to remind his people of "the commandments, which I [God] gave unto their father, Adam" (Moses 6:28) when he "called upon our father Adam by his own voice" (Moses 6:51), and ordered them to pass it on: "Teach these things freely unto your children" (Moses 6:58), and in time they are to reach us! (D&C 107:56.) The rule is that "many books . . . of every kind" are "handed down from one generation to another . . . even until they [the people] have fallen into transgression" (Helaman 3:15-16), at which time they disappear until another prophet brings them forth.

Next to Enoch himself, the greatest transmitter of records would seem to be Moses, by whose hand we receive the records that came through Enoch and his successors. And it is Moses who gives us the key to the whole thing: "And now, Moses, my son, . . . thou shalt write the things which I shall speak. And in a day when the children of men shall esteem my words as naught and take many of them from the book which thou shalt write, behold, I will raise up another like unto thee; and they shall be had again among the children of men—among as many as shall believe." (Moses 1:40-41.)

Each time the records come forth, they are brought to-

gether in one with such scriptures as have survived among
men, making possible the correction and the understanding of the latter. Being the source and author of all, Jesus
Christ among the Nephites "expounded all the scriptures
in one, which they had written," and "he commanded
them that they should teach the things which he had expounded unto them." (3 Nephi 23:14.) This was after he
had personally examined all the records, corrected defects,
and brought them up to date. The same thing happened in
the Old World, where, "beginning at Moses and all the
prophets, he expounded unto them in all the scriptures the
things concerning himself," that being what all the writings were about. (Luke 24:27.) The fact that the Lord himself reads to men out of the ancient books, "for . . . they
are they which testify of me" (John 5:39), even though he
is personally present among them as the risen Savior ad-
dressing them with his own lips, gives awesome testimony
to the authority of the written word.

What the books testify of, after all, is the reality of the
Lord and his mission: "We labor diligently to engraven
these words upon plates, hoping that our beloved brethren
and our children will receive them. . . . For, for this intent
have we written these things, that they may know that we
knew of Christ, and we had a hope of his glory many
hundred years before his coming." (Jacob 4:3-4.)

"And a book of remembrance was written before him
for them that feared the Lord, and that thought upon his
name. And they shall be mine, saith the Lord of Hosts, in
that day when I make up my jewels" (3 Nephi 24:16-17),
that is, when I gather them all together and put them in
proper order. So whoever are in this book are "numbered
among the people of the first covenant," no matter when
they live (Mormon 7:10), for the writings themselves are
"proving to the world . . . that he is the same God yesterday, today, and forever." (D&C 20:11-12.)

To the Saints, the sacred record is a source of joy and
delight as well as of instruction and guidance; it is a joy to

read, a treat to the mind and spirit, "for my soul delighteth in the scriptures, and my heart pondereth them, and writeth them for the learning and profit of my children" (2 Nephi 4:15); "and if my people are pleased with the things of God they will be pleased with mine engravings" (2 Nephi 5:32). Their discovery is always exciting news to those who know how to value them, like the king who said, as he "rejoiced exceedingly, . . . Doubtless a great mystery is contained within these plates. . . . O how marvelous are the works of the Lord!" (Mosiah 8:19-20), and was "filled with joy" when he learned that somebody could read them. (Mosiah 21:28.) Intellectual curiosity and esthetic feeling are nothing to be ashamed of.

We must understand that the Spirit of God tells men both what and when to write—"you cannot write that which is sacred save it be given you from me" (D&C 9:9, 76:115), what records to translate—"Touch them not in order that ye may translate; for that thing is forbidden you" (Ether 5:1; 1 Nephi 14:28), and the imperative behind the operation: "Wherefore, the Lord hath commanded me to make these plates for a wise purpose in him, which purpose I know not." (1 Nephi 9:5.) "I do this for a wise purpose; for thus it whispereth me, according to the workings of the Spirit of the Lord which is in me." (Words of Mormon 7.) They are to serve "for the instruction of my people . . . and also for other wise purposes, which purposes are known unto the Lord." (1 Nephi 19:3.) The writings are placed completely outside of men's economy, and "no one shall have them to get gain; . . . and whoso shall bring it to light, him will the Lord bless. For none can have power to bring it to light save it be given him of God." (Mormon 8:14-15.) As to the implements and instructions, "whosoever has these things is called seer" (Mosiah 28:16), and his power "is a gift from God. . . . And no man can look in them except he be commanded, lest he should look for that he ought not and he should perish" (Mosiah 8:13). All of which does not exonerate the seer from using his own wits (see D&C 9:7-8; Mosiah 1:2-4) and learning all he can of "the language of his fathers" and "concerning the records . . . that thereby they might become men of understanding" (Mosiah 1:2-3).

The economy of the books is no mere toy for the weak minds of men to play with; it follows a pattern that extends to other worlds. The books that men keep on earth are matched by books kept in heaven: Adam's heavenly Book of Remembrance is duplicated on earth by a Book of Life, "the record which is kept in heaven; . . . or, in other words, . . . whatsoever you record on earth shall be recorded in heaven. . . . It may seem . . . a very bold doctrine that we talk of—a power which records or binds on earth and binds in heaven. Nevertheless, in all ages of the world, whenever the Lord has given a dispensation of the priesthood . . . this power has always been given." (D&C 128:7-9.) What is above is projected and recorded below: "Thou [the scribe] shalt write for him [the prophet]; and the scriptures shall be given, even as they are in mine own bosom." (D&C 35:20.) And what is below is projected above and recorded there: "The alms of your prayers have come up into the ears of the Lord of Sabaoth, and are recorded in the book of the names of the sanctified, even them of the celestial world." (D&C 88:2.)

The record is the source of all else, and from it come those writings that have ever been the cornerstone of civilization, a weak terrestrial reflection of the sublime. Aside from their holy offices, "they have enlarged the memory of this people" and preserved them from "incorrect tradition," thus keeping civilization on the track. (Alma 37:8-9.) They check the corruption of the language and the loss of religion (Omni 1:17), and though a great leader like Zarahemla might be able to give "a genealogy of his fathers, according to his memory" (Omni 1:18), still "it were not possible that our father, Lehi, could have remembered all of these things, to have taught them to his children, except it were for the help of these plates" (Mosiah

1:4), without which, says Mosiah, "even our fathers would have dwindled in unbelief . . . like . . . the Lamanites" (Mosiah 1:5).

The kings and leaders of the people, as the trustees of the heritage of culture and dominion, are the regular keepers of the record, "which is had by the kings" (Omni 1:11), handed down from father to son, with special preparation and instructions (Omni 1:1, 4, 9), along with the national treasures of which they are a part—the Liahona, seerstones, sword of Laban; the whole thing is summed up in Alma 37:2-3 and comes down to our own time when the Whitmers were promised a view of these things (D&C 17:1). Others besides the prophet were encouraged to ask for the gift to look into "all those ancient records which have been hid up, that are sacred" (D&C 8:11) and "to obtain a knowledge of history, and of countries, and of kingdoms" (D&C 93:53), as the Prophet was of "all good books, . . . languages, tongues, and people" (D&C 90:15), that they might not approach the sacred depository with vacant minds.

If one lightly assumes that Joseph Smith got these ideas from the Bible, where they are indeed implicit but by no means obvious, let us bear in mind that his contemporaries shrieked in derision when they heard him; and what scandalized them most of all was the idea of a second or third witness to place beside the Bible, in spite of "the divine law of witnesses." But the young prophet, far from simply running on about ancient plates and parchments, angels and seerstones ("the jibberings of a crazy boy," writes one Harvard don), actually went ahead and produced the wonderful volumes of which he spoke—full-length texts, broad fabrics of immense detail, enough rope to hang any imposter twenty times over. If the hypothetical house of books is a wonderful creation, with what astonishment must we view the real and solid structure erected singlehanded by the youthful prophet in the midst of countless distractions and afflictions?

According to the Latest News

The foregoing brief survey of a theme long familiar to Latter-day Saints and odious to others is to prepare our patient reader for a visit to the strange and wonderful edifice that houses the emerging Enoch literature, for it is built on precisely the same plan as that set forth by the Prophet Joseph to explain the holy books that he gave us.

We begin with Enoch keeping the books of Adam, recalling that the words and prophecies of Adam were "all written in the book of Enoch" (D&C 107:57), who reminded his people, "the first of all we know, even Adam. For a book of remembrance we have written among us" (Moses 6:45-46). Now according to the Zohar, "Enoch also had a book, which came from the same place as the book of the generations of Adam."[204] Rabbi Eliezer said that Adam hid the book that the angel Raziel, the purveyor of the heavenly secrets, gave to him, and that Enoch later found it, and that it was next delivered to Noah by Rafael and so passed on to Shem and hence from one generation to the next.[205] It is implied in Genesis 5:1-2 that the human race was fully launched when the book of the generations of Adam was inaugurated, since Adam and Eve were set apart (barā), and given a name and a blessing. A very old tradition equates true humanity with Enoch the record-keeper, a more complete man than Adam himself.[206] The early Christians were fond of the Book of Adam, according to Epiphanius,[207] and A. Vaillant, the authority on the Slavonic Enoch, maintained that the Christian Enoch book was not taken from Jewish sources but from an old lost Book of Adam and Seth.[208]

But everywhere Enoch is credited with being the scribe and transmitter par excellence, "the Righteous Scribe, the Teacher of heaven and earth, and the Scribe of Righteousness."[209] The "Joseph Smith Enoch" brings forth the books, including Adam's, as a testimony and a witness to his generation (see Moses 6:46); even so, according to Jubilees, "[Enoch] was the first to write a testimony, and he testified . . . among the generations of the earth. . . . He understood everything [compare Moses 6:37, 7:67], and wrote his testimony" (Jubilees 4:18f); and the Testament of Abraham reports that God "gave him [Enoch] the task to write down all the good and bad deeds that a man's soul would commit."[210]

In the secretarial line, preeminence goes to Enoch, "to whom the angels "showed everything which is on earth and in the heavens . . . and he wrote everything" (Jubilees 4:21), "the man of intelligence, the great writer, whom the Lord took to be a seer of the life above" (2 Enoch, Intd.), who was commanded by God to "take the books which I have written back to earth to your children . . . that they will read them and will know me for the Creator of all things, and distribute the books of the handwriting children to children, generation to generation, nation to nation." (2 Enoch 33:5-9.) Inevitably the saying went abroad in the land that it was that man who "first learned and taught writing, and was deemed worthy to reveal the divine mysteries."[211]

What is behind these Jewish and Christian traditions? The idea that there *was* such a man as Enoch, the "Enoch figure" whom we shall get to know much better, is as old as the oldest human records. We go back to the proposition, clearly set forth in the book of Moses (6:5, 6:46; D&C 128:5), that, in the words of N. Tur Sinai, "the miracle of writing was one which the Ancients regarded as a gift from heaven."[212] It is apparent from the earliest records of the Sumerians that they "were not ignorant of the concept of a 'sacred book,' that is, of a divinely inspired, even dictated text, which contains the only correct and valid account of the 'story' of deity," according to A. L. Oppenheim, who further observes that the transmitter of the record, according to the ancient doctrine, was not its originator, but only "a kâṣir kâmmé, 'one who collects/arranges/prepares the tablets' without interfering with the wording"—he is merely the transmitter of divine words; yet to function as such, he himself must be inspired. He is "the collector of the tablets," but his information comes to him in a vision of the night, which he faithfully writes down in the morning.[213]

Such is the office of Enoch: "Bring out the books from my store house," says God to his angels in the Slavonic Enoch, "and a reed of quick-writing [shorthand], and give it to Enoch, and deliver to him the choice books out of my hand." (2 Enoch 22:12.) Thus instructed, the seer wrote down the glories of the celestial throne on the one hand, and the endless combinations of the elements on the other. (2 Enoch Intd.)[214]

This introduces the cosmological element that is so conspicuous in the Enoch literature, Enoch being "the first among men that are born on earth who learnt writing and knowledge and wisdom and who wrote down the signs of heaven." (Jubilees 4:17.) God shows him "the book of the courses of the luminaries of the heavens." (1 Enoch 72:1.) The emphasis on cosmology, very prominent in the "Joseph Smith Enoch," was highly distasteful to the doctors of the Jews and Christians alike and was their strongest argument for rejecting it;[215] but the close affinity between the earliest writing and the signs of the heavens is undeniable.[216] Both among the Egyptians and the Chaldaeans, Clement of Alexandria reports, "writing and the knowledge of the heavens" go hand in hand;[217] the proper study of those apocalyptic writings so disdained by the doctors of the schools was, as H. Gunkel sums it up, eschatology, angelology, cosmology, and prehistory—all disturbingly tangible subjects.[218] The handing down of such records is nowhere more clearly stated than in the book of Abraham, 1:31: "But the records of the fathers, even the patriarchs, . . . God preserved in mine own hands; therefore a knowledge of the beginning of the *creation*, and also of the *planets*, and of the *stars*, as they were made known unto the *fathers*, have I kept even unto this day . . . for the benefit of my posterity that shall come after me." (Italics added.)

This literal-minded concern with the stars in their courses is a mark of antiquity and authenticity in the Enoch literature, as is the repeated reference to the heavenly *tablets*. "Observe, Enoch, these heavenly tablets," says the angel, "and read what is written thereon. . . . And I observed the heavenly tablets, and read everything . . . and understood everything, and read the book of all the deeds of mankind . . . to the remotest generations." (1 Enoch 81:1, 2, see Moses 7:67.) Here we meet the fusion of the heavenly and earthly books—are they one and the same?—as in the Joseph Smith writings. "I know a mystery; and have read the heavenly *tablets*, and have seen the holy *books* and have found written therein and inscribed regarding them." (1 Enoch 103:2, italics added.) "And after that Enoch . . . began to recount [or read] from the *books* . . . '[what] I have learnt from the heavenly *tablets*.'" (1 Enoch 93:1; italics added.) The impression is that the books were the earthly copies of the heavenly tablets: "the Lord has shown me and informed me, and I have read them in the heavenly tablets."[219] In Moses 7:67, "the Lord showed Enoch all things," and after a vision of heaven and earth he placed before the people "a book of remembrance . . . written among us, according to the pattern given by the finger of God." (Moses 6:46.) In this they recall the Tablets of the Law.[220] (Exodus 31:18.)

Indeed, "few religious ideas in the Ancient Near East have played a more important role than the notion of the Heavenly Tablets or the Heavenly Book";[221] "in the literature of early Judaism," in particular, they "play a considerable role."[222] The idea is at home in classical literature and hence it is assumed was taken over by the early Christians with their Book of Life.[223] In Rabbinic tradition, Abraham, "'being found faithful,' is declared a 'friend of God' on the 'heavenly tablets,' and every righteous keeper of the Covenant . . . is registered in the same Book of Life";[224] the antiquity of this is supported by the Battle Scroll of the Dead Sea Scrolls: "And the covenant of thy peace hast thou engraved for them with a stylus of life, to rule over them in all appointed times of eternity,"[225] where the situation is closely parallel to one in the Book of Mormon, Mosiah chapter 5.[226]

Noah, after Enoch, reports, "The Lord has showed me and informed me, and I have read . . . in the heavenly tablets, and I saw written on them that generation upon generation shall transgress" (Enoch 106:19, 107:1); and after him Jacob, when "an angel descended from heaven with seven tablets in his hands . . . he read them and knew all that . . . would befall him and his sons . . . and he showed them all that was written on the tablets" (Jubilees 32:21f). Next, Moses yielded up to an angel "the Tablets of the Divisions of the years . . . from the day of the creation to the time when the heavens and the earth shall be renewed." (Jubilees 1:29.) Thus the same tablets are handed down.

The books of Enoch contain information from all holy sources: "I Enoch will declare unto you, my sons, according to that which appeared to me in the heavenly vision, and which I have known through the word of the holy angels, and have learnt from the heavenly tablets. And Enoch began to recount from the books." (1 Enoch 93:2-3.) In the Slavonic version, Enoch, accompanied by two angelic guides, brings to earth "the books of handwriting" to be handed down from "generation to generation." (2 Enoch 88:6-9.)

The heavenly tablets may be traced back as far as the Babylonian Tablets of Destiny: "These tablets express the law of the whole world . . . and they are truly the mystery of heaven and earth."[227] At the coronation, rehearsing the great creation rite of the New Year, the king was thought to be caught up into heaven, there to receive his copy of the tablets with which he returned to earth as his badge of divine authority.[228] On a like occasion in Egypt the monarch, according to the oldest of books, the Pyramid Texts, is hailed as "the King who is over the spirits, who unites the hearts—so says he who is in charge of wisdom, . . . who bears the god's book, even Sia, who is at the right hand of Re."[229]

Back to the books of Adam for a moment, please. A very early Christian source reports that while God was contemplating putting the breath of life into Adam, He took a book, and wrote therein [the names of] those who should come forth from him and who should enter into the kingdom which is in the heavens. . . . 'These are they whose names are written in the Book of Life from the foundation of the world.'"[230] This is certainly close to the idea that the Saints, whose names are in the Book of Life, are "numbered among the people of the first covenant." (Mormon 7:10.) The members of the Qumran community are they whose covenant is "engraved with a stylus of Life."[231] After he had come to earth, Adam was given a Book of Knowledge by an angel sent to instruct him, giving him a knowledge of the mysteries—the ordinances—surpassing that of the angels.[232] According to the Zohar, Adam lost such a book upon leaving Eden, and when he "supplicated God with tears for its return . . . it was given back to him, in order that wisdom might not be forgotten of men."[233] Another version has it that a holy book of seventy-two letters was given to Michael, who gave it to Adam (those two are constantly being confused in the early writings), who based all his knowledge upon it.[234] When God ordered him to register all the animals, he inspired Adam invisibly so that he could read aloud, and on the first tablets he read out the names of the animals as they passed before him. After Adam and Eve had thus been drilled in reading, "God transported his school to the Garden of Eden."[235]

Abraham, when he set up his model Garden of Eden at Hebron, also established a school in the midst of it;[236] in the preexistence Abraham had already learned the art of writing and was given the Book of Creation, but on earth he was not able to read it without assistance, and so his teacher Shem helped him at it.[237] Recalling that Abraham possessed "the records of the fathers" containing "a knowledge of the beginning of the creation" according to the book of Abraham 1:31, one is interested to learn that "the writings of Seth and Idrisi were handed down to the time of Noah and Abraham," Idrisi being usually identified with Enoch himself, but in this Mandaean source is called "the first after Enoch son of Seth son of Adam to write with a reed."[238]

The valuable Apocalypse of Adam claims to be taken from a book handed down from Adam himself, containing an exposition of the gospel of salvation but dwelling with particular emphasis on the baptism of Adam;[239] this is particularly intriguing since the wonderfully condensed and powerful presentation of the gospel plan in the Joseph Smith book of Enoch devotes a whole page to the baptism of Adam. (See Moses 6:51-68.) Beginning with the reminder that God "called upon . . . Adam by his own voice" (Moses 6:51), all the words of Enoch's great sermon in the Joseph Smith Enoch are direct quotations from Adam and the Lord, Enoch's own calling being to hand on "the commandments, which I gave unto their father, Adam" (Moses 6:28).

The Pistis Sophia claims derivation from the two books of Jeu, "which *Enoch* has written as I spoke with him out of the Tree of Knowledge and out of the Tree of Life in the paradise of Adam."[240] As he was praying, an "angel . . . appeared to Adam, . . . saying, . . . 'Thy prayers have been heard and I am come to bring thee words of purity and much wisdom. I will make thee wise through the words of this holy book, from which you will learn whatever shall befall. . . . Whoever, even to the last generation makes use of this book, must be pure and faithfully observe what is written in it,'" and so on. [See Moses 1:35!] Then Adam fell upon his face before the angel who bade him rise, stand up, and be strong, and receive the book from his hand, concealing its contents from the unworthy. Then the angel departed in a roar of flame.[241] Adam's prostration reminds us of the Joseph Smith version, when Enoch presented the Book of Adam, "written . . . according to the pattern given by the finger of God" before the people, and they "trembled, and could not stand in his presence." (Moses 6:46-47.)

This book of Adam story is also told in the old book of Noah, which traces the record from Adam and Enoch to Noah; it begins with Adam's prayer after the fall, when the angel came to instruct him and gave him the book, which Adam hid in the ground and which was later dug up by Enoch.[242] Another account tells how Enoch was shown in a dream where Adam's book was buried and how he should obtain it; he went to the place early the next morning and hung around until noon, lest he excite the suspicion of the people in the fields; then he dug up the book, whose characters were interpreted to him by divine revelation, learned from it the fulness of the gospel, and was so set apart by his knowledge that he withdrew from the society of men.[243] C. J. Van Andel finds it significant that the Enoch writings of the Jews are not based on the Torah but go back to unknown works of great antiquity dealing with heavenly tablets.[244]

Recording sacred matters has been a prophetic function since Adam labored diligently to provide holy books for his descendants. Enoch carried on that tradition, busily arranging and editing the documents, as his grandson Methuselah reports: "After . . . Enoch gave me the teaching of all the secrets in the book and in the Parables which had been given to *him*, he . . . put them together for me in the words of the Book of Parables." (1 Enoch 68:1; italics added.) Here we must bear in mind that all the long-lived patriarchs from Adam to Enoch were contemporaries and knew each other. The situation is vividly brought home in D&C 107:53-57: "Three years previous to the death of Adam, he called Seth, Enos, Cainan, Mahalaleel, Jared, Enoch, and Methuselah . . . with the residue of his posterity who were righteous, into the valley of Adam-ondi-Ahman," and there "predicted whatsoever should befall his posterity unto the latest generation," and "these things were all written in the book of Enoch." Thus Rabbi Eliezer refers to the Book of Enoch as identical with the book of the Generations of Adam mentioned in Genesis 5:1.[245] Adam's book already contained the story of his family "unto the latest generation." (D&C 107:56.) "The Lord had his servants come down [to Adam], saying to them, 'Go ye and testify of me this day. Give to the Man Adam your hand [in covenant], and covenant with him by law.'" Then the Lord put it down in writing, which the three witnesses all signed. "If you ask: 'Could not the Lord have done without the written document, witnesses, and handclasp?' the answer is that it is the Lord's will that this shall be the proper procedure among the children of Adam forever."[246] So Joseph Smith is quite right in having Adam's book come down through Enoch to Abraham, Moses, and us.

It went first to Methuselah, who received from Enoch a charge exactly like that later given to Moses:

Moses 1:40—"Moses, my son, . . . thou shalt write the things which I shall speak."	1 Enoch 82:1—"preserve, my son Methuselah, the books from thy father's hand."
Moses 1:41—"the children of men shall esteem my words as naught and take many of them from the book which thou shalt write."	2 Enoch 47:2; 48:8—"Take these books of your father's [Enoch's] handwriting" the foolish ones "understand not the Lord . . . accept not, but reject."
	3 Enoch 104:10—"Sinners will alter and pervert the words of righteousness in many ways, and will speak wicked words, and lie."

Then comes Noah, who has the same experiences with the books and passes on the same information as Enoch.[247] "My grandfather Enoch," says Noah, "gave me the teaching of all the secrets in the book . . . which had been given to him" (1 Enoch 68:1), and indeed the Joseph Smith Enoch makes both Methuselah and Noah the heirs of his teachings and promises (Moses 8:2-3, 5-12). Next there is Abraham who, in the Testament of Abraham, has almost the same visions and makes the same heavenly journey as Enoch, and at the end of his celestial visit gives his source away: "I, Abraham, said to the archangel Michael, 'O Lord, who is this honorable old man who has this book in his hand, who comes near to the judge [Adam]?' . . . He replied, 'It is *Enoch*. . . . God gave him the task to write down all the good and bad deeds a man's soul would commit.'"[248]

Like Abraham, Isaiah is introduced to a venerable old man with a book at the end of his journey to heaven, and the man is Enoch.[249] The Lord himself says to Isaiah, "'No mortal has ever seen what you have!' Saying this, he placed a book in my hands and said to me: 'Take this and know . . . that there is nothing hidden of all the works in that world, good or bad.' And I took the book from his hand and read it, and behold everything was written down about every man from the beginning to the end of the world."[250]

This gives substance to the Lord's words to the Nephites as he turned the books over to them: "Search these things diligently; for great are the words of Isaiah. For surely he spake as touching *all things* concerning my people." (3 Nephi 23:1-2; italics added.) After Abraham, Jacob became the holder of the heavenly tablets, which told about the premortal existence, the eternal nature of Jacob's own promise and calling, and the deeds of his posterity to the remotest times, according to a very old Jewish work called the Prayer of Joseph.[251] Next Moses receives "the complete history of the creation" (Jubilees 2:1), which he transmitted to us. "The whole burthen of Moses' message," wrote C. L. Woolley, "is the restatement of Abraham's message," an appeal to the past.[252] Ezra too was commanded to "write down everything that has happened in the world from the beginning . . . that men may be able to find the path, and that those who live in the last days may live."[253] And how like Moroni's situation is that of Ezra's friend Baruch (both were associates of Jeremiah and Lehi) in a work "lost sight of for quite 1200 years" and discovered in 1866:[254] "'Earth, earth, earth, hear the word of the mighty God and receive what I commit to thee, and guard them until the last times, so that, when thou art ordered, thou may restore them, so that strangers may not get possession of them . . .' So the earth opened its mouth and swallowed them up."[255] The personification of the earth is a motif that goes back to Enoch. (See Moses 7:48.)

According to many recently discovered documents, it was during the forty-day mission of the Lord after his resurrection that he handed on the books to his disciples exactly as he does in the Book of Mormon during the same period. The important Epistle of the Apostles, concerning which "whoever knows and observes what is written therein shall be like the angels," was by the Lord "entrusted to Peter, John, Matthew, and to others at Jerusalem, that copies might be sent to [certain carefully chosen disciples], and by them to all the branches [*mansiones*]."[256] The newly discovered Apocryphon of James tells in detail how the books were entrusted by the Lord to Peter, James, and John for careful rationing; and in other new finds both Peter and Paul ascend to heaven and there receive holy books and are introduced to Enoch, the venerable scribe. Of particular interest is the emphasis on John, whose writings are now shown by the Dead Sea Scrolls, according to F. M. Cross, to be significantly "related to the Enoch literature."[257] Nowhere do we find fuller instructions for the guarding and transmitting of the records than those given by the Lord to John in the three newly found Apocryphons of John. And it was Joseph Smith who first apprised the world that there was a "record made on parchment by John and hidden up by himself." (D&C 7, section heading.)

The ever-attentive reader may have noticed how no matter who the bookkeeper is, Enoch is somehow lurking in the background. After all is said, he is the supreme scribe, and nowhere is that marvelous economy of book-keeping better described than in the Slavonic Enoch: "Take thou the books which thou hast written thyself . . . and go down to earth and tell thy sons all that I have told thee. . . . And give them the books of thy handwriting, and they will read them and will know me the creator of all . . . and let them distribute the books of thy handwriting—children to children, generation to generation, nation to nations. . . . Thy handwriting and the handwriting of thy fathers Adam and Seth shall not be destroyed till the end of time, as I have commanded my angels . . . that it be preserved, and that the handwriting of thy fathers . . . perish not." (2 Enoch 12.)

The injunction proceeds in words much like those of the book of Moses:

2 Enoch—"I know the wickedness *of men*, but I shall leave over *one just man with all his house* . . . ; and that race shall reveal the books of thy handwriting, and of thy fathers, . . . *among the children of men*; the guardians of the earth shall show them that race."

Moses 1:41—"When the *children of men* shall esteem my words as naught . . . I will raise up *another like unto thee*; and they *shall be had again among the children of men— among as many as shall believe*."

Need we point out that the Slavonic Enoch was not known at the time of Joseph Smith?

The attentive reader will also have noted the frequent reference to the last days whenever the writings of Enoch were mentioned. This is an important key. A. L. Davies makes the generalization that a "feature . . . common to this apocalyptic literature, is the reserving of the visions and the books of Enoch for the last days, for the elect to read and understand";[258] instantly bringing to mind the Lord's promises to Enoch in Moses 7:60, 62: "As I live, even so will I come in the last days, in the days of wickedness and vengeance. . . . Truth will I send forth out of the earth, to bear testimony . . . to sweep the earth as with a flood, to gather out mine elect," and so on. It is Enoch who presides when all things are gathered in one; the book that is to be revealed to them of the last days is that very same perfect book that existed from the first in the mind of God.[259] "I may write all that has happened in the world," says Ezra, "that they who would live at the last [days], may live."[260]

"This book," declares the newly discovered Gospel of Truth, "is to be revealed to the Eons [all the other dispensations?] in the End-time. It is secret, . . . known only to the initiated. It is a perfect book which existed first in the mind of God, by which it is conveyed to men."[261]

Contrary to what one might expect, and what has been taught for generations in colleges and seminaries, the ancient sectaries were not simply illiterates confined to an "oral gospel." On the contrary, Pere Lagrange notes with stern disapproval, "These visionaries are the most book-bound (libresque) of men,"[262] laying no claim to originality, but uniformly preoccupied, as J. Leipoldt has noted, with initiation rites, sacraments, baptism, common meals, secret books handed down from ancient times, and ordinances and doctrines alien to conventional Christianity. In all of this they resemble "late Judaism in general" and betray ancient connections with Babylonia and Iran.[263]

So the call goes forth in the Chester Beatty Enoch papyrus: "Prepare, ye righteous, and present records of your doings as a remembrance, give them as a testimony before the angels." (Gk. 91:3.) The chosen prophet who raises up a generation of righteousness is also chosen to "reveal to them the books of thy [Enoch's] handwriting, and of thy fathers" and to be the leader of God's word in that dispensation, "to the faithful . . . and they shall tell another generation," and so on.[264] In short, Enoch is writing for the church, and the idea of the church is nowhere more clearly stated than in the Enoch literature. Like the

Apocryphon of James, it "is for those blessed ones who will be saved by their faith in it."[265] When Enoch places restrictions on his works with the command, My sons, hand these books "to all who *want* them, and instruct them, that they may see the Lord's . . . works,"[266] he is giving the same orders as the Lord gives the disciples in the Apocryphon of John: "I tell you this that you may write it down and give it secretly to those who are of one heart and one mind [*homopneuma*] with you; it is reserved for the breed who do not vacillate."[267] So Enoch again: "Distribute the books . . . amongst the nations *who shall have the sense to fear God;* let them receive them, and may they come to love them . . . read them and apply themselves to them."[268]

Part of the book's appeal is its necessary *secrecy,* "revealed to the Eons in the End-time." It is a secret, a special writing, only for the initiates.[269] "'It is given to you to write it down,'" says the Lord to John, "'and it must be put in a safe place.' Then he said to me, 'Cursed shall be whoever gives it away as a gift or in return for food, drink, clothing, or anything of that nature.'" Then he handed the mysterion to John and immediately vanished.[270] Such writings as are made known are carefully rationed: "Some things thou shalt publish, and some thou shalt deliver in secret to the wise";[271] or, in another Ezra text, "These words shalt thou publish openly, but those thou shalt hide,"[272] twenty-four books being published and seventy withheld.[273]

The tradition of secrecy begins with Enoch: When Enoch found the Book of Adam and read it, "he knew that the human race would not be able to receive it. So he hid it again, and it remained hidden until Noah."[274] But the practice began with Adam, who received a golden book from Michael and "hid it in the crevice of a rock."[275]

The Torah itself was buried when Israel sinned, to be dug up in later times.[276] The Copper Scroll of the Dead Sea Scrolls shows us how in times of dire peril all those sacred things that had been dedicated, including the holy writings, were buried for safety,[277] a practice clearly set forth in the Book of Mormon. (Helaman 13:18-20.) From early Babylonian sources comes the report of Berossus, that Kronus ordered Xisuthros (Noah) "to inscribe in writing the beginning, middle, and end of everything, and to bury the records in the city of Sippar," to be exhumed after the Flood.[278]

So when we are told that the writing of Moses "because of wickedness . . . is not had among the children of men" (Moses 1:23), the claim is confirmed by the tradition that the sons of Moses had a book that their father entrusted to them, but when *their* children lightly leaked its contents to the world, "the angel returned, took the book, and carried it up with him to heaven."[279]

The oldest Sumerian epic shows that Mesopotamian theologians knew about a "sacred book" that is of divine inspiration, "which contains the only correct and valid account of the 'story' of the deity."[280] This was the book of all knowledge possessed by the king in both Egypt and Babylonia.[281] Through a Christian channel comes the well-known and very early Babylonian tradition that the Fish- or Flood-god Oannes taught men all the arts and sciences and wrote all knowledge down in a book, and "nothing since that time has ever been added to human knowledge."[282] This is the book that the Babylonian Noah was commanded to bury at the time of the flood, and it is not surprising that scholars have on philological and other grounds often identified Oannes with Enoch.[283]

When Enoch and the others saw everything and wrote everything down such as pertains to this world, they were all writing the same book—and they knew it. In Revelation 5:1-2 there *is* such a book, "a 'revelation' from the Spirit of the Father into the 'Heart of Man.'"[284] Yet in the recently discovered reality of the hologram, we have something akin to the paradox of the book each of whose letters contains all of its parts: "each letter is a perfect truth, like a perfect book in itself, for they are letters written in the Oneness."[285]

In the Joseph Smith Enoch, all the writings from Adam
on down have one central perennial theme—the atoning
mission of Jesus Christ, which emerges full-blown in a succession of dispensations. (Moses 7:39, 47, 54-67.) In the
book of Enoch "the Lord, the Father, wrote with his own
fingers ten words," which were "teachings regarding the
Son," to whose earthly ministry Enoch looked forward.[286]
"The limited mysteries . . . which God caused Enoch to
write" were later "revealed in their fullness by Jesus," says
the Pistis Sophia.[287] It is the Savior, according to the Mandaeans, who "brings to mankind the primordial revelation
contained in the heavenly books."[288] The tradition of the
perennial gospel was known to the early church and is confirmed by Athanasias, who explains that the gospel is not
new but was preached and known to Adam, Abel, Enoch,
Noah, Abraham, and Moses, before the time of Christ.[289]
Later Christianity, however, down to the present, lays
great emphasis on the originality of Christ, and Pico della
Mirandola, while translating a newly discovered manuscript of Ezra, reported with amazement, "I see in it (as
God is my witness) the religion not so much of Moses as of
Christ!"[290]

The idea of doubled sets of books, one on earth and one
in heaven, is also widespread and very ancient. Of Enoch's
writings we are told, "some of them are written and inscribed above in the heaven, in order that the angels may
read them" (1 Enoch 108:7), while Enoch's own writings
are transcripts from a book kept in heaven, and made
known in sundry portions to the Fathers,[291] all of whom,
but most notably Enoch, report having got their information by "reading it in the heavenly tablets" (for example,
Jubilees 4:1). Thus by the books above and below, brought
together like the sticks of Joseph and Ephraim in perfect
agreement as perfectly agreeing witnesses, the world will
be judged.[292]

Enoch's writings are above all else a *warning* to the
wicked, particularly in the last days, in the days of wicked-

ness and vengeance,[293] to the end "that they who live at the last days may live."[294] His book is "for those who . . . keep the law in the last days, and equally for those who break it: "In those days Enoch received books of zeal and wrath, and books of disquiet and expulsion."[295] Enoch's book is both a threat and a comfort, "an exhortation not to be troubled on account of the times," but to be vigilant and never overconfident.[296]

Whenever the sacred writings come forth, they are greeted by the righteous with glad surprise and eager enjoyment: "Then books will be given to the righteous and the wise to become a cause of joy and uprightness and much wisdom . . . and they shall believe in them and rejoice over them." (1 Enoch 104:10-13.) They "will be shown to faithful men," and "shall be glorified thereafter more than the first." (2 Enoch 12.) "They who have the wisdom to receive them . . . will be nourished by them and become attached to them." (2 Enoch 12, p. 48.) "This hope," comments R. H. Charles, "was to a large degree realized in the centuries immediately preceding and following the Christian era,"[297] until the doctors of the church threw the treasure away. At a time when the church will be "oppressed and suffering and has no place to set its foot," the sacred writings, having "evaded the hands of the wicked," finally come into the hands of the Saints, properly witnessed and certified and "written in exceeding plainness"; "the Saints will kiss them and say: O Wisdom of the Great One! O armor of the Apostles!"[298]

The Curtain Rises

The Pearl of Great Price should be read as a single work, an epitome of world history, summarizing and correlating in the brief scope of less than sixty pages the major dispensations of the gospel, past, present, and future. The story is told largely by excerpts, which announce themselves as fragments of original books written by Adam, Enoch, Abraham, Moses, and Joseph Smith, all centering about the figure of Christ and his mission in the meridian of time, with a preview of the millennium thrown in. Enoch's proper place in that story is best known by those who see the big picture. Thus, the following section deals with the *type* of story that Enoch's history belongs to, the visions from Creation to Judgment.

The recent flowering of comparative studies that look into long-neglected or newly discovered apocryphal writings makes it clear that the concept of recurrent dispensations of light and darkness, restoration and apostasy, is valid for every age of recorded history. Nowhere is the patttern set forth more clearly than in the epic sweep of the Pearl of Great Price. Surprisingly, the perennial pattern presented there is not limited to Jewish and Christian traitions but extends to the oldest ritual literature—epic and dramatic—of the human race; chapter 1 of our book of Moses is as much an introduction to world literature in general as to our conventional scriptures. Daring as such a claim may seem, the more carefully the text is studied the more impressively it is confirmed. Consider the episodes in the order given by this remarkable prologue to the study of man.

A. The story opens (verse 1) with Moses speaking with God face to face on "an exceedingly high mountain," wrapped in the divine glory, sharing the light of divinity. This situation, including the mountain, is the well-known epic and dramatic "prologue in heaven," with the hero receiving a special calling and assignment to a work in this lower world; like the audience, he is being prepared for the blows that follow.

B. Next the lights go out, the glory departs, and we find Moses lying helpless upon the bare earth, cut down to size; he slowly regains his strength until he is able to utter his first commentary on life: "Now, for this cause I know that man is nothing, which thing I never had supposed." (Verses 9-10.) Man begins his earthly career at the bottom of the ladder. Then the hero's next remark puts a different

face on things: "But now mine own eyes have beheld
God; . . . his glory was upon me; and I beheld his face, for I
was transfigured before him." (Verse 11.)

And this is the human predicament, man's condition in
its most stark and elementary terms, *la misère et la gloire*, that
besetting contradiction that is the constant concern of early
Christian and Jewish writers and the subject of countless
philosophical and Gnostic texts, endlessly restated as a pe-
rennially new discovery in all the great literature of the
world: "How weary, flat, stale and unprofitable" is the
earthly life of man, the "quintessence of dust," and yet
"how noble in reason" is that same man, "how infinite in
faculty! . . . in action how like an angel! in apprehension,
how like a god." (*Hamlet* 1, ii, 133; 2, ii, 303-8.) Yet Moses
declares that man is nothing, even while in the same breath
calling attention to the clouds of glory still remembered
from his native condition.

C. In this state of weakness and suspense, of trials and
contradictions, he is the ideal target for the Adversary, who
with his usual evil methodology chooses precisely this moment to attack, taking full advantage of his enemy's im-
periled condition. With the appearance of this sinister
figure the drama begins in earnest. Satan wants to be ac-
knowledged as the ruler of the world—that is the theme—
and Moses promptly challenges his claim. Moses, remem-
bering his own high calling, questions his adversary, asking again and again: "Who art thou? For behold, I am a son
of God, in the similitude of his Only Begotten; and where is
thy glory, that I should worship thee?

"For behold, I could not look upon God, except his
glory should come upon me. . . . But I can look upon thee
in the natural man. Is it not so, surely?" (Verses 13-14.)

Note that the contest is not between God and the
devil—that was never a contest. It is Moses himself who
here proclaims his own advantage over Satan, as he goes
on: "Where is thy glory, for it is darkness unto me? And I
can judge between thee and God." (Verse 15.) In the next

three verses he repeats that he shares the nature of the
Only Begotten and finds Satan a fraud: "Satan, deceive me
not," ending by summarily ordering him off the premises.
(Verses 16-18.) These are stinging blows, for Satan has always claimed the earth as his own special precinct and the
role of the Only Begotten as his exclusive vehicle. Moses'
repeated reminders of his own intimacy with the Only Begotten drives the pretender into a screaming rage.

D. Casting off all pretense to his celebrated subtlety
and cunning, the Adversary resorts to an all-out frontal attack, and the battle is on—the ritual combat that meets us
so often in the earliest dramatic and epic literature of the
race: "Satan cried with a loud voice, and rent upon the
earth, and commanded, saying: I am the Only Begotten,
worship me." (Verse 19.) Moses was terrified by the ferocity and passion of the attack; in fact he was quite overcome.
Paralyzed with fear, "he saw the bitterness of hell." (Verse
20.) It is the well-known theme of the hero-king reduced to
the last extremity, calling with his last ounce of strength
out of "the bitterness of hell": "Nevertheless, calling upon
God, he receives strength" (verse 20), and at the last moment is delivered.[299]

And now the tables are turned: It is the dark opponent
who is down; he trembles and the earth shakes as he
retreats in uproar and anguish. Here it is in order to note
that the Adversary who relentlessly assails the hero in the
earliest epics is none other than the "Earth-shaker,"
Enosichthōn.

E. Next in order, according to the established pattern,
the hero, having met and survived the onslaughts of the
Destroyer, should be hailed as victor and king, and this is
exactly what happens in our story; God proclaims him
blessed, endows him with divine strength, and declares
him chosen to be the leader and deliverer of his people,
his own representative on earth: "I, the Almighty, have
chosen thee, and thou shalt be made stronger than *many
waters*; . . . as if thou wert God . . . for thou shalt deliver

my people." (Verses 25-26; italics added.) As we have
shown elsewhere, the king must emerge victorious at the
moment of passing through the waters of life, death, re-
birth, and purification, and the ancients always understood Moses' leading his people through the Red Sea as the
type and similitude of a baptism, symbolizing at one and
the same time death, birth, victory, and purification from
sins.[300]

F. In the scene that follows, Moses is shown the extent
of his "kingdom," in other words, his field of labor; viewing the vast display, he is filled with wonder and asks the
Epic Question: "Tell me, I pray thee, why these things are
so, and *by what* thou madest them?" (Verse 30; italics
added.) What is behind it all? Let us recall how the ancient
epic poet, after stating his basic proposition in the opening
lines, launches into his story by asking for revelation in the
same terms: "Say first *what cause* moved our Grandparents
in that happy state . . . to transgress. . . . *Who* first
seduced them?" Thus Milton in *Paradise Lost*, borrowing
from Vergil in his *Aenead: Musa mihi* Causas *memoro*, quo
numine laeso, quidve *dolens*, and so on—why, who, how?
Who borrows in turn from Homer: Ex hou *de ta prōté* . . . tis
t'ar' sphōe theōn—for what cause, who was responsible?

G. The epic question really invites the poet himself to
come onto the stage and tell his whole story. Having asked,
we cannot begrudge him the long hours needed for a full-
scale epic recital. In Moses' case, we are spared, for the
Lord will give him "only an account of this earth" (verse
35), still with the reminder that he must never lose sight of
the vast cosmic perspective that forms the background to
the story and without which human history becomes a
rather pointless and parochial tale.

All of that is familiar literary ground in our story's great
prologue, and that with a minimum of biblical prompting.
Those who wish to credit Joseph Smith with a comprehen-
sion of comparative literature and ritual far beyond his time

and training are free to do so. They may even insist, as they have with the Book of Mormon, that this is the way any un-educated rustic would tell the story. Today, however, we have several very ancient and significant parallels to Moses 1, which lie far beyond the reach of coincidence or day-dreaming. The number of details and the order in which they occur make it perfectly clear that we are dealing with specific works of great antiquity that come from a common source. To show what we mean, let us compare Moses', Abraham's, and Adam's confrontations with Satan; these stories themselves contain pointed references to Enoch, with whom each hero is duly compared. These accounts are not scripture, but are simply ancient records that help us understand the Enoch story.

First the Apocalypse of Abraham, an Old Slavonic ac-count discovered in 1895 and first published by Bonwetsch in 1898.[301] K. Koch has recently ranked it as one of the five definitely authentic early Hebrew Apocalypses.[302] Let us place it in parallel columns against our book of Moses, chapter 1.

Moses, Chapter 1	Apocalypse of Abraham, Chapter 9 (Chapter 1 of the Apocalypse Proper)
The Setting	
1:1. The words of God . . . unto Moses . . . when Moses was caught up into an exceedingly high mountain.	9:8. [Abraham, in order to receive the vision, must] "Bring me the sacrifice . . . upon a high mountain."
God Will Show Him Everything	
4. I will show thee the workmanship of mine hands: but not all, for my works are without end. . . .	6. In this sacrifice I will show forth to thee the ages of the world,

5. Wherefore, no man can behold all my works, . . . and no man can behold all my glory. [See Abraham 2:12: "Thy servant has sought thee earnestly; now I have found thee."] . . .

and show thee that which is hidden. Thou shalt behold great things, which thou hast never seen before,

because thou delightest to seek after me,

6. And I have a work for thee, Moses, my son. . . .

and I have called thee my friend.

8. And . . . Moses looked, and beheld the world upon which he was created . . . and all the children of men which are, and which were created. . . .

9. And I will show unto thee, the ages of the world fixed and created by my word, and show thee what is going to happen to the children of men as they shall do good or evil.

The Hero Is Helpless after the Vision

9. And the presence of God withdrew from Moses, . . . and . . . he fell unto the earth.

10:1. [Hearing a voice] I looked here and there.

2. It was not a human breath, and so my spirit was afraid, and my soul departed from me. And I became as a stone, and fell to the earth, for I had no more strength to stand;

10. And . . . it was for the space of many hours before Moses did again receive his natural strength. . . .

3. And as I lay with my face to the ground I heard the voice of the Holy One say,

4. Go, Jaoel, in the power of my name, and raise that man up! Let him recover from his trembling.

Satan Takes Advantage of His Weakness

[Chapters 11 & 12 are a detailed description of Abraham's sacrifice, during which, in chapter 13]:

12. Behold. Satan came tempting him, saying: Moses, son of man, worship *me*. [Italics added.]

13:1. I carried out everything according to the angel's instructions . . .
3. Then an unclean creature with wings alighted upon the sacrificial victims . . . 4. The unclean bird said to me: What are you doing, Abraham, in this holy place . . .where . . . you yourself may perish in the fire! 5. Leave the man [angel] standing beside you and flee!

13. And . . . Moses . . . said: Who art thou? . . .

6. . . . And I asked the angel, "Who is this, my Lord?"

15. I can judge between thee and God. . . .
16. Get thee hence, Satan; deceive me not. . . .

7. He said: This is ungodliness: this is Azazel [Satan]!

Satan Put to Shame by Humiliating Contrast with the Hero

13. I am a son of God, . . . and where is thy glory, that I should worship thee?

8. . . . [Michael:] Shame upon you, Satan!
9. For Abraham's part is in heaven, and thine is upon this earth.
10. (God has placed thee upon this earth as the Adversary, to lead dishonest spirits and practice deception.)

14. For behold, I could not look upon God, except . . . I were transfigured before him. But I can look upon thee in the natural man. Is it not so, surely?
15. . . . Where is thy glory, for it is darkness unto me? And I can judge between thee and God. . . .

12. Listen, my friend, and I will put you to shame.

13. Thou hast not the power to tempt all the righteous.

16. Get thee hence, Satan; deceive me not:

14. Depart from this man! Thou canst not lead him astray, for he is thine enemy and enemy to all those who follow thee and love after thy desire.

for God said unto me: Thou art after the similitude of mine Only Begotten.

15. For behold, the garment [of glory] which once fitted you in heaven, is now laid up for him. And the decay to which he was fated now goes over to thee!

The Hero is Strengthened for the Contest

17. And he also gave me commandments . . . saying: Call upon God in the name of mine Only Begotten, and worship me.

14:3. Take heart, exercise the power that I give thee over this one, who hateth truth . . .

4. . . . who rebelled against the Almighty . . .

18. . . . I have other things to inquire of him: for his glory has been upon me, wherefore I can judge between him and thee. Depart hence, Satan.

5. Say to him: . . . Depart, Azazel . . . 6. Thy lot is to rule over those who are with thee . . . 7. Depart from me . . . 8. And I spoke as the angel instructed me.

The Hero Is Overcome but Calls Out and Is Saved

19. And . . . Satan cried with a loud voice, and ranted upon the earth, and commanded, saying: I am the Only Begotten, worship me.

9. He [Satan] spoke: Abraham! And I said: Here is thy servant.

20. And . . . Moses began to fear exceedingly; and . . . saw the bitterness of hell. Nevertheless, calling upon God, he received strength, and he commanded, saying, Depart from me, Satan. . . .

10. [But] the angel said to me: O, do not reply to him! For God has given him power over those who answer him. 11. . . . no matter how much he speaks to thee, answer him not, lest his will overpower thine.

21. And now Satan began to tremble, and the earth shook; and Moses received strength, and called upon God, saying: In the name of the Only Begotten, depart hence, Satan.

12. For the Eternal One has given him a powerful will. Answer him not! [See Testament of Abraham (Falasha p. 100ff.), where he says to Isaac approaching the altar: "Come near, my son, so that thou mayest perceive the one . . . who frightened me and because of whom I was afraid . . . " referring to his own jeopardy on the altar.]

[This detail is found in *Enoch's* meeting with Satan in Gizeh 13:1-3. "And Enoch said to Azazel, Depart! Thou shalt have no peace, a great sentence has gone forth against thee to bind thee. 2. And there will be no further discussion or questioning with thee, because of thy dishonest and deceitful and sinful works among men."]

22. And . . . Satan cried with a loud voice, with weeping, and wailing, and gnashing of teeth; and he departed hence, even from the presence of Moses, that he beheld him not. . . .

Gizeh 13:3. Then he departed and spoke to all of them [his followers] and they all feared, and trembling and terror seized them.

The Hero Is Borne Aloft

24. And . . . when Satan had departed . . . Moses lifted up his eyes unto heaven, being filled with the Holy Ghost. . . .

15:2. The angel in charge of the sacrifice . . . took

3. me by the right hand, and set me on the right wing of the dove while he sat on the left side.

25. And calling upon . . . God, he beheld his glory again. . . .

4. So it bore me to the limits of the flaming fire . . . then on into heaven, as if on many winds, which was fixed above the firmament.

[See 2 Nephi 4:25—"Upon the wings of his Spirit hath my body been carried away upon exceeding high mountains. And mine eyes have beheld great things, yea, even too great for man."]

24. And . . . when Satan had departed from the presence of Moses, . . . Moses lifted up his eyes unto heaven, being filled with the Holy Ghost. . . .

25. . . . And he heard a voice, saying: Blessed art thou, Moses, for I, the Almighty, have chosen thee, and thou shalt be made stronger than many waters; for they shall obey thy command as if thou wert God. [Here Moses is hailed as the victorious sacral king.]

27. And . . . Moses cast his eyes and beheld the earth. . . . 28. And he beheld also the inhabitants thereof, and there was not a soul which he beheld not . . . and their numbers were great, even numberless.

Bet ha-Midrash 5:170. R. Ishmael (double for Enoch): When I went up to the mountain top . . . arriving at the seventh temple, I stood to pray before God; and I lifted up my eyes and said. . . . deliver me from Satan. And the Metratron [also Enoch!] came who [served?] the angel, even the Prince of the Presence, and spread his wings and came to meet me with great joy . . . and he took me with his hand and raised me up.

17:1. And while he was speaking, fire surrounded us and a voice . . . like the voice of many waters like the raging of the sea in the surf.

15:6. And I saw . . . a mighty light . . . and in the light a mighty fire in which was a host, even a great host of mighty beings [forms] constantly changing shape and appearance, moving, changing, praying, and uttering words I could not understand.

He Is Shown the Field of His Mission

In the "Testamentary" literature, each Patriarch takes a journey to heaven and is given a view of the entire earth, an account of which then becomes an integral part of his missionary message upon his return. (Compare 1 Nephi 1:4-15; Abraham 3:15; Moses 1:40.)

27. As the voice was still speaking, Moses cast his eyes and beheld the earth, yea, even all of it; and there was not a particle of it which he did not behold. . . .

21:1. He said to me: Look beneath thy feet upon the Firmament. Recognize at that level the creation there presented, the creatures that are in it, and the world that has been prepared for them.

28. And he beheld also the inhabitants thereof, and there was not a soul which he beheld not, . . . and their numbers were great, even numberless as the sand upon the sea shore.

2. And I looked down, and behold . . . the earth and her fruits, and all that moves upon her . . . and the power of her people . . . 3. the lower regions . . . the pit and its torments . . .

29. And he beheld many lands; and each land was called earth, and there were inhabitants on the face thereof.

4. I saw there the sea and its islands, the beasts, its fishes, leviathan and his sphere . . . 5. the streams of water, their sources and their courses . . .

9. I saw there a mighty host of men, women, and children half of them on the right side of the picture and half on the left.

Confrontation with God

31. And . . . the glory of the Lord was upon Moses, so that Moses stood in the presence of God, and talked with him face to face. . . .

16:1. I said to the angel: . . . I can see nothing. I have become weak, my spirit leaves me!
2. He said to me: Stay with me; be not afraid. He whom thou now beholdest coming towards us . . . is the Eternal One, who loves thee.

3. But He himself you do not see . . . 4. But do not be overcome, I am with you to strengthen you.

30. And it came to pass that Moses called upon God. . . .

17:5. So I continued to pray . . . 6. He said: Speak without ceasing!

7-10. [Abraham calls upon God naming his attributes.] 11. Eli, meaning My God . . . El! El! El! El Jaoel!

33. And worlds without number have I created; and I also created them for mine own purpose. . . .

13. Thou who bringest order into the unorganized universe, even the chaos which in the perishable world goes forth from good and evil.

38. And as one earth shall pass away, . . . even so shall another come; and there is no end to my works, neither to my words.

Thou who renewest the World of the righteous.
14. O light, that shone upon thy creatures before the morning light . . .

The Epic Question and Answer

30. And . . . Moses called upon God, saying: Tell me, I pray thee, *why* these things are so, and by *what* thou madest them? [Italics added. Compare Abraham 1:2. "I sought for the blessings of the fathers, . . . desiring also . . . to possess a greater knowledge."]

16. Hear my prayers!
17. Look with favor upon me: Show me, teach me. Give thy servant all that which thou hast promised him.
26:1. . . . Eternal, Mighty, Only One! *Why* hast thou so arranged things, that it should be so?

31. . . . And the Lord God said unto Moses: For mine own purpose have I made these things. Here is wisdom and it remaineth in me.

26:5. . . . As thine own father's [Terah's] will is in him, and as thine own will is in thee, so the resolves of mine own will are set in me for all the future, before you knew there even was such a thing . . .

33. And worlds without number have I created; and I also created them for mine own purpose. . . .

35. But only an account of this earth, and the inhabitants thereof, give I unto you. For behold, there are many worlds . . . that now stand, . . . but all things are numbered unto me, for they are mine and I know them.

19:3. . . . Look upon the places beneath the firmament, upon which thou standest [Compare this formula in Abraham 3:3, 4, 5, 7, etc.!] Behold there is not a single place nor any spot at all but what is occupied by Him whom thou seekest. . . .
4. As he spoke the place opened up and beneath me there was heaven. 5. And upon the seventh Firmament on which I stood I saw . . . the splendor of invisible glory investing all living beings.

Left Alone a Second Time

9. And the presence of God withdrew from Moses, that his glory was not upon Moses; and Moses was left unto himself. And as he was left unto himself, he fell unto the earth.

30:1. And as he was still speaking I found myself upon the earth.
2. I spoke: Eternal, Mighty, Only One!
3. Behold I am no longer in the glory in which I was above! And what my heart sought to know I did not understand.

[Abraham 2:12: "Now, after the Lord had withdrawn from speaking to me, and withdrawn his face from me, I said in my heart: Thy servant has sought thee earnestly; now I have found thee."]

4. And he said to me: What in thy heart thou didst so desire, that I will tell thee, because thou hast sought diligently to behold, etc.

These parallel accounts, separated by centuries, cannot be coincidence. Nor can all the others. The first man to have such a confrontation with Satan was Adam. A wealth of stories about it closely matches the accounts of Abraham, Moses, Enoch, and other heroes. Perhaps the oldest Adam traditions are those collected from all over the ancient East at a very early time, which have reached us in later Ethiopian and Arabic manuscripts under the title of "The Combat of Adam and Eve against Satan."[303] It contains at least thirteen different showdowns between Adam and the Adversary, of which we present a few of the most striking. Since the motif was characteristically repeated with variations (the monkish mind could not resist the temptation to work a good thing to death), it will be necessary to repeat some passages from the book of Moses.

Moses, Chapter 1	Combat of Adam and Eve
	(Direct quotations from the documents are indicated with quotation marks)
9. And the presence of God withdrew from Moses, that his glory was not upon Moses; and Moses was left unto himself. . . . He fell unto the earth.	Pp. 297-98. Leaving the glorious garden, they (Adam and Eve) were seized with fear and "they fell down upon the earth and remained as if dead."
10. And it came to pass that it was for the space of many hours before Moses did again receive his natural strength like unto man; and he said unto himself: Now, for this cause I know that man is nothing, which thing I never had supposed.	P. 299. While Adam was still in that condition, Eve, stretching high her hands, prayed: "O Lord . . . thy servant has fallen from the Garden" and is banished to a desert place. (Genesis 3:18f.)
11. But now mine own eyes have beheld God; but not my natural, but my spiritual eyes, for my natural eyes could not have beheld; for I should have withered and died in his presence; but his glory was upon me; and I beheld his face, for I was transfigured before him.	P. 299. They say: "Today our eyes having become terrestrial can no longer behold the things they once did."

12. And it came to pass that when Moses had said these words, behold, Satan came tempting him, saying: Moses, son of man, worship me.

P. 306. Satan, seeing them at prayer, appears to them in a great light and sets up his throne on the site, thus claiming the earth as his kingdom while his followers sing hymns in his praise.

13. And it came to pass that Moses looked upon Satan and said: Who art thou? For behold, I am a son of God, in the similitude of his Only Begotten; and where is thy glory, that I should worship thee?

P. 307. Adam, puzzled, prays for light, asking: Can this be another God here hailed by his angels? An angel of the Lord arrives and says: "Fear not, Adam, what you see is Satan and his companions who wish to seduce you again. First he appeared to you as a serpent and now he wants you to worship him so he can draw you after him away from God."

15-18. . . . Where is thy glory, for it is darkness unto me? . . . Get thee hence, Satan; deceive me not; . . . I can judge between thee and God. Depart hence, Satan.

Then the angel exposed and humiliated Satan in Adam's presence and cast him out saying to Adam:

13. I am a son of God. . . . 14. . . . I could not look upon God, except . . . I were transfigured before him. [See verse 20: "Calling upon God, he received strength."]

"Fear not: God who created you will strengthen you!"

Pp. 307-8. The next morning as Adam prayed with upraised hands, Satan appeared to him, saying, "Adam, I am an angel of the great God. The Lord has sent me to you." It was his plan to kill Adam and thus "remain sole master and possessor of the earth." But God sent three heavenly messengers to Adam bringing him the signs of the priesthood and kingship.

P. 309. And Adam wept because they reminded him of his departed glory, but God said they were signs of the atonement to come, whereupon Adam rejoiced.

Pp. 323-24. After a forty-day fast Adam and Eve were very weak, stretched out upon the floor of the cave as if dead, but still praying. Satan then came, clothed in light speaking sweet words to deceive them saying, "I am the first created of God. . . . Now God has commanded me to lead you to my habitation . . . to be restored to your former glory."

12. . . . Satan came tempting him, saying: Moses, son of man, worship me.
19. . . . I am the Only Begotten, worship me.

P. 325. But God knew that he planned to lead them to far-away places and destroy them. Adam said, Who was this glorious old man who came to us? Answer: He is Satan in human form come to deceive you by giving you signs to prove his bonafides but I have cast him out.

13. . . . Moses looked upon Satan and said: Who art thou?

P. 326. Adam and Eve, still weak from fasting and still praying, are again confronted by Satan, who, being rebuffed, "is sore afflicted" and weeping and wailing says, "'God has wrecked my scheme . . . he has rendered worthless the plan which I contrived against his servants.' And he retired in confusion."

21. Now Satan began to tremble. . . . 22. And it came to pass that Satan cried with a loud voice, with weeping, and wailing, and gnashing of teeth; and he departed hence.

18. . . . I have other things to inquire of [God]: for his glory has been upon me, wherefore I can judge between him and thee. Depart hence, Satan.

P. 327. Adam asked, Why is this? Answer: "God wanted to show you the weakness of Satan and his evil intentions for since the day you left the Garden he has not let a day pass without trying to harm you, but I have not let him have the victory over you." [Adam thus learned to distinguish between good and evil.]

5:6. And after many days an angel of the Lord appeared unto Adam, saying: Why dost thou offer sacrifices unto the Lord? and Adam said unto him: I know not, save the Lord commanded me.

7. And then the angel spake, saying: This thing is a similitude of the sacrifice of the Only Begotten of the Father, which is full of grace and truth. 9. . . . As thou hast fallen thou mayest be redeemed, and all mankind, even as many as will.

P. 329. Again Adam and Eve were sacrificing with upraised arms in prayer, asking God to accept their sacrifice and forgive their sins. "And the Lord said to Adam and Eve: As you have made this sacrifice to me, so I will make an offering of my flesh when I come to earth, and so save you. . . . And God ordered an angel to take tongs and receive the sacrifice of Adam."

10. . . . Adam . . . was filled, . . . saying: . . . In this life I shall have joy, and again in the flesh I shall see God.

At this Adam and Eve rejoiced. God said: When the terms of my covenant are fulfilled, I will again receive you into my Garden and my Grace. So Adam continued to make this sacrifice for the rest of his days. And God caused his word to be preached to Adam.

P. 330. On the fiftieth day, Adam, offering sacrifice as was his custom, Satan appeared in the form of a man and smote

1:20. Moses began to fear exceedingly; and as he began to fear, he saw the bitterness of hell. Nevertheless, calling upon God, he received strength. [See Book of Abraham, Facsimile No. 1!]

5:7. This thing is a similitude of the sacrifice of the Only Begotten of the Father, which is full of grace and truth.

him in the side with a sharp stone even as Adam raised his arms in prayer. Eve tried to help him as blood and water flowed on the altar. "God . . . sent his word and revived Adam saying: 'Finish thy sacrifice, which is most pleasing to me. For even so will I be wounded and blood and water will come from my side; that will be the true Sacrifice, placed on the altar as a perfect offering.' . . . And so God healed Adam."

Surprisingly enough, the best documented story of a clash between Adam and Satan is the scene in heaven. One old writing with unusually good credentials that trace back to books deposited by the apostles in the archives of the early church in Jerusalem is the Coptic "Discourse of the Abbaton, a sermon based on the text delivered by Timothy the Archbishop of Alexandria."[304]

The book belongs to the forty-day literature; and as it opens, the Lord on his last day on earth with the apostles just before his ascension asks them if there is any final request they would like to make of him—exactly as in 3 Nephi 28:1. What they want most is to understand the role of death and its horrors in God's plan for his children.[305] To explain this the Lord tells them of the council in heaven in the preexistence where the plan of the creation is being discussed. There was great reluctance among the hosts to proceed with the creation of the earth, the earth itself complaining, exactly in the manner of Moses 7:48, of the filthiness and corruption that would surely go out of her and begging to be allowed to rest from such horrors. (Fol. 10a-b.) Because of the council's reluctance to proceed, God allows the lifeless body of Adam to lie upon the earth for forty days, unwilling, without the council's approval, to let

his spirit enter. (11b.) The Son of God saves the day by offering to pay the price for whatever suffering will be en-
tailed, thus permitting "God's children to return again to
their former condition." (12a.) Christ alone thus becomes
the author of our earthly existence; amid joy and rejoicing
God calls for a book, in which he registers the names of all
the "Sons of God" who are to go to earth. (See Genesis
5:1ff; Fol. 12b.) This of course is the heavenly book of the
generations of Adam opened at the foundation of the
earth, the book to which Enoch refers so explicitly in Moses
6:46, 8.

In the presence of all the hosts, Adam is next made
ready to take over his great assignment. He is placed on a
throne and given a crown of glory and a scepter, and all the
sons of God bow the knee first to God the Father and then
to Adam the Father in recognition of his being in God's
exact likeness and image. (13a.) Satan, however, refuses to
comply, declaring that he is willing to worship the Father
but not Adam: "It is rather he that should worship me for I
arrived before he did!" (13a-b.) (See Moses 1:19: "I am
the Only Begotten, worship me.") God saw that Satan,
because of his boundless ambition and total lack of humil-
ity, could no longer be trusted with celestial power and
commanded the angels to remove him from his office. This
ordinance they performed with great sorrow and reluctance: They "removed the writing of authority from his
hand. They took from him his armor and all the insignia of
priesthood and kingship." Then with a ceremonial knife, a
sickle, they inflicted upon him certain ceremonial blows of
death which deprived him of his full strength forever after.
(14a.) Other accounts say that after these cuts he retained
only one-third of his former power, even as he was followed by one-third of the hosts.

Next Adam was escorted to earth to enter his mortal
body, and for a hundred years thereafter he was often visited by angels. (14b.) Thereafter, for two hundred years he
lived happily in innocence with Eve, taking good care of

the animals in his charge. Eventually Satan succeeded in getting possession of a mortal creature, which enabled him to carry on an extensive campaign aimed at Eve. (16a-17a.) Adam was greatly upset; but when Eve, the victim of a trick, took all responsibility, he joined her. (17b.)

Satan stopped Adam outside of the Garden and gloatingly told him that this was his sweet revenge for Adam's victory in heaven: Adam had got him expelled from heaven and now he had paid him in kind; what was more, he intended to continue his project—"I will never cease to contend against thee and against all those who shall come after thee from out of thee, until I have taken them all down to perdition!" (21a-b.) With the threat of death before him, Adam saw the bitterness of hell (19a, 21b), but calling upon God he received not only the assurance of salvation for the dead through the atonement of Christ (20b), but was told that death shall be sweet to those whose names are in the Book of Life (24a-b). Fear of death (the angel Mouriel) is wholesome and necessary to remind the human race of its fragility and constant need of repentance. This has the salutary effect of countering Satan's plan by providing a constant check on the tendencies of men to misbehave, a sobering and, if necessary, frightening lesson.

What comes after the showdown between our first parents and the Adversary? Our sources obligingly go right on with the story and follow Satan from his attempts to win Adam's obedience to his highly successful interviews with Cain, tracing the steady spread of wickedness among mankind down to its culmination in the days of Enoch. There is no better summary of the story than that given in the book of Moses, which is surprisingly close to the "Combat of Adam" version on every point. Let us briefly survey events leading up to the call of Enoch, as given in the Joseph Smith account.

Having been instructed by an angel of the Lord, Adam and Eve enjoyed a fulness of the gospel, "and they made all things known unto their sons and their daughters." (See

Moses 5:1-2.) Enter Satan, the negative one, with his non-gospel: "Believe it not!" and his countergospel: "I am also a son of God." (Moses 5:13.) He gains a following by pushing downhill, in the direction of what is "carnal, sensual, and devilish." (Moses 5:13.) This called for much preaching of repentance (Moses 5:14-15), as Adam and Eve remained true and faithful, and "ceased not to call upon God" (Moses 5:16). Into this world was born Cain, who rejected his parents' teachings as irrational—"Who is the Lord that I should know him?" (Moses 5:16.) The Lord gave Cain every chance to be wise and save himself, showing him in all reasonableness the dangerous course he was taking, and warning him that he would be in Satan's power to the degree that he refused obedience: "And thou shalt rule over him." (Moses 5:23; see also Genesis 4:7.) Cain rule over Satan? Yes, that is the arrangement—the devil serves his client, gratifies his slightest whim, pampers his appetites, and is at his beck and call throughout his earthly life, putting unlimited power and influence at his disposal through his command of the treasures of the earth, gold and silver. But in exchange the victim must keep his part of the agreement, following Satan's instructions on earth and remaining in his power thereafter. That is the classic bargain, the pact with the devil, by which a Faust, Don Juan, Macbeth, or Jabez Stone achieve the pinnacle of earthly success and the depths of eternal damnation.

The Lord held forth the fatherly invitation to Cain: "If thou doest well, thou shalt be accepted," along with the solemn warning, "Satan desireth to have thee." (Moses 5:23; see also Genesis 4:7.) He is admonished against the folly of "reject[ing] the greater counsel" (Moses 5:25), and the door of repentance is held open right to the last moment, when it is Cain himself who breaks off the conversation and angrily stamps out, refusing to listen "any more to the voice of the Lord" or to his brother's remonstrances (Moses 5:26). Cain married "one of his brother's daughters" not necessarily Abel's), and together "they

loved Satan more than God" (Moses 5:28), quite satisfied
with their religion and quite defiant about it.

What could one do in such a situation? Nothing:
"Adam and his wife mourned before the Lord, because of
Cain and his brethren." (Moses 5:27.) Having deliberately
severed all connection with his Heavenly Father, Cain was
free to enter a formal agreement with Satan, by which he
would receive instruction in the techniques of achieving
power and gain: "Truly I am Mahan, the master of this
great secret [The language is that of ancient colleges or
guilds where the secret is the mystery of the trade or pro-
fession; in this case, his secret is how to convert life into
property], that I may murder and get gain." (Moses 5:31;
see also Moses 5:49.) Cain "gloried" in the power of his
new-found skill and dialectic, declaring that it made him
"free." (Moses 5:33.) He put his knowledge to work in a
brilliantly successful operation in which "Abel . . . was
slain by the conspiracy of his brother" (D&C 84:16), and
gleefully congratulated himself and "gloried in that which
he had done, saying: I am *free*; surely the flocks of my
brother falleth into my hands." (Moses 5:33; italics added.)
This new light on Cain's behavior is confirmed in the *Combat of Adam and Eve,* where we learn that, after killing Abel,
Cain "felt no inclination to repent of what he had done," a
detail pointed out also by some of the early church
fathers.[306]

Plainly this is not the conventional novel of Cain and
Abel, in which an impetuous adolescent loses his head
and brains his spoiled brother in a fit of jealousy; it is a carefully planned and executed operation in which Cain slew
"his brother Abel, for the sake of getting gain" (Moses
5:50), dismissing his conscience with the thought that all
was fair and square since Abel was quite capable of taking
care of himself: "Am I my brother's keeper?" (Moses 5:34).
This was the philosophy by which Satan seduced the
human race, teaching them that "every man fared in this
life according to the management of the creature; therefore

every man prospered according to his genius, and that every man conquered according to his strength; and whatsoever a man did was no crime." (Alma 30:17.) When God took a different view and called him to account, he still pleaded the profit motive as an excuse: "Satan tempted me because of my brother's flocks." (Moses 5:38.) Being "shut out from the presence of the Lord" (Moses 5:41), Cain started his own establishment, the main line of his descendants being Enoch (who built *a* city of Enoch), Irad, Mahujael, Methusael, Lamech the father of Jubal and Tubal Cain. (Moses 5:42-46.) Lamech like Cain "entered into a covenant with Satan," and like him "became *Master Mahan.*" (Moses 5:49; italics added.) When Lamech heard that Irad the son of Enoch was violating the secrecy of these terrible things, he "slew him for the oath's sake" (Moses 5:50), since "Irad began to reveal . . . unto the [other] sons of Adam" these top-secret signs of recognition (Moses 5:49). All those who covenanted with Satan were excluded from the holy covenants of God, though they pretended that everything was the same as before. The dirty business spread as such things do once started; Lamech became an outcast like Cain, not because of the murder but because his wives started spreading his secrets—the very ones he had murdered Irad for divulging. "And thus the works of darkness began to prevail among all the sons of men. And God cursed the earth with a sore curse." (Moses 5:55-56.)

Is there no relief in the terrible picture? There is: all this time the gospel was "being declared by holy angels . . . and by the gift of the Holy Ghost" (Moses 5:58), while "all things were confirmed unto Adam, by an holy ordinance," in the assurance that "the Gospel . . . should be in the world, until the end thereof" (Moses 5:59). Adam, having lost Abel, got another son, Seth, to carry on his work. (Moses 6:2.) From him comes that line of successors in the priesthood, duly registered in the Book of Life, from which the wicked were excluded. (Moses 2:5-8.) After Seth came Enos, who decided to make an important move. Since "in

those days Satan had great dominion among men, and
raged in their hearts," causing "wars and bloodshed . . .
in administering death, because of secret works, seeking
for power" (Moses 2:15)—exactly as in the modern
world—Enos gathered "the residue of the people of God"
and with them migrated out of the country "and dwelt in a
land of promise," named Cainan after his son (Moses 2:17).
The line is Seth, Enos, Cainan, Mahalaleel, Jared, Enoch,
Methuselah, Lamech, and Noah. (Moses 6:16-21; 8:2, 5-11.)

In *The Combat of Adam and Eve,* as Migne observes, "the
author depicts the descendants of Adam as divided into
two separate and distinct branches: the Cainites dedicated
to following Satan, who lived in a fertile country but very
far distant from Eden, and who devoted themselves to all
the pleasures of the flesh and all manner of immorality,"
and the Sethites who "dwelt in the mountains near the
Garden, were faithful to the divine law and bore the name
of the Sons of God."

The occurrence of like names in the two genealogies
should not surprise anyone who does much genealogy,
where the same family names keep turning up in an endless round. The thing to notice is that there are two lines
and that Enoch is seen as a stranger and a wild man only
when he leaves his native colony in Cainan, "a land of righteousness unto this day" (Moses 6:41), to sojourn as a missionary among the wayward tribes. And so the stage is set
for Enoch.

The Wicked World of Enoch

The wickedness of Enoch's day had a special stamp and
flavor; only the most determined and entrenched depravity merited the extermination of the race. In apocryphal
Enoch stories we are told how humanity was led to the ex-
tremes of misconduct under the tutelage of uniquely competent masters. According to these traditions, these were
none other than special heavenly messengers who were
sent down to earth to restore respect for the name of God
among the degenerate human race but instead yielded to

temptation, misbehaved with the daughters of men, and ended up instructing and abetting their human charges in all manner of iniquity. They are variously designated as the Watchers, Fallen Angels, Sons of God, Nephilim, or Rephaim, and are sometimes confused with their offspring, the Giants.[307] Other candidates for this dubious honor have been suggested by various scholars, the trouble being that more than one category of beings qualify as Fallen Angels and spectacular sinners before the time of the Flood.[308] The Bible uses the title *sons of God*—were they different from the Watchers of tradition?

"The sons of God saw the daughters of men that they were fair; and they took them wives of all which they chose.

"There were giants in the earth in those days; and also after that, when the sons of God came in unto the daughters of men, and they bare . . . to them . . . mighty men. . . . men of renown.

"And God saw that the wickedness of man was great in the earth." (Genesis 6:2, 4-5.)

The idea of intercourse between heavenly and earthly beings was widespread in ancient times. Thus, in the newly discovered Genesis Apocryphon, when Lamech's wife bears him a superchild (Noah), he assumes almost as a matter of course that the father is "one of the angels" and accuses her of faithlessness until his grandfather, Enoch, whose "lot is with the Holy Ones" and who lives far away, clears up the misunderstanding. Significantly, the name of the child's mother is Bit-enosh, that is, she is one of the "daughters of men."[309] The Cedrenus fragment avoids the problem of heavenly origin by identifying the sons of God and the daughters of men with the descendants of Seth and Cain respectively, and he specifically designates the sons of God as the Watchers.[310] Recently M. Emanueli has suggested that the various terms are merely "a figure of speech in order to express the depth of the deterioration of that generation."[311]

While the sons of God have been identified with both

angels and the Watchers, the Greek Enoch does not identify the Watchers with Satan's hosts who fell from heaven
from the beginning—they are another crowd.[312] It is the
Joseph Smith Enoch which gives the most convincing solution: the beings who fell were not angels but men who had
become sons of God. From the beginning, it tells us, mortal
men could qualify as "sons of God," beginning with Adam.
"Behold, thou [Adam] art one in me, a son of God; and thus
may *all* men become my sons." (Moses 6:68; italics added.)
How? By believing and entering the covenant. "Our father
Adam taught these things, and many have believed, and
become the sons of God." (Moses 7:1.) Thus when "Noah
and his sons hearkened unto the Lord, and gave heed . . .
they were called the sons of God." (Moses 8:13.) In short,
the sons of God are those who accept and live by the law of
God. When "the sons of men" (as Enoch calls them) broke
their covenant, they still insisted on that exalted title: "Behold, we are the sons of God; have we not taken unto ourselves the daughters of men?" (Moses 8:21), even as "the
sons of men," reversing the order, married the daughters
of those "called the sons of God," thereby forfeiting their
title, "for," said God to Noah, "they will not hearken to my
voice." (Moses 8:15.) The situation was, then, that the sons
of God, or their daughters who had been initiated into a
spiritual order, departed from it and broke their vows,
mingling with those who observed only a carnal law.

"Why have you left heaven [and] the Exalted One,"
says Enoch in a Gizeh fragment, "and . . . with the
daughters of men defiled yourselves? . . . Ye have be-
haved as sons of Earth and begotten to yourselves giant
sons. And you were once holy, spiritual, eternal beings . . . and have lusted after the flesh . . . as do mortal
and perishable creatures."[313]

What made the world of Enoch so singularly depraved
as to invite total obliteration was the deliberate and systematic perversion of heavenly things to justify wickedness. An early Christian writer, Hippolytus, says that the
Anti-Christ imitates Christ in every particular: each sends

out his apostles, gives his seal to believers, does signs and wonders, claims the temple as his own, has his own church and assembly, etc. Such is the method of "the great Deceiver of the World," against whom, says Hippolytus, "Enoch and Elias have warned us."[314] We are reminded how Satan put forth his claim. "I am also a son of God" (Moses 5:13), and commanded Cain to "make an offering unto the Lord (Moses 5:18-19) and to take his oaths "by the living God" (Moses 5:29), as if everything were still in the proper order. In the same spirit Noah's descendants in their wickedness still insisted that nothing had changed. The children of men said to Noah: "Behold, we are the sons of God; have we not taken unto ourselves the daughers of men?" (Moses 8:21.)

The apocrypha agree: "For in the days of Jared my father, they departed from the teaching of the Lord, from the covenant of heaven. And behold they commit sin and reject [parabainousin] the proper way [ethos] . . . and beget children not like spiritual but like carnal offspring." (Black, p. 44, 106:6, 13-14.)

Sophisticated deception is the name of the game. "Woe unto you who deliberately go astray [poiountes planemata]," cries Enoch, "who promote yourselves to honor and glory by deceitful practices. . . . Who misapply and misinterpret straightforward statements, who have given a new twist to the everlasting Covenant, and then produce arguments to prove that you are without guilt!"[315] Cold-blooded calculation is the keynote. The "Watchers" (using the Greek word) led away "myriads of myriads . . . with their Prince Satanel," says the Slavonic Enoch, "and defiled the earth by their acts. And the wives [instead of daughters!] of men did a great evil, violating the law . . . a great iniquity." [316] For "in secret places underground" we read in a very early Judeo-Christian source, "they wrought confusion; . . . They committed adultery, every man with his neighbor's wife. They concluded covenants with one another with an oath touching these things."[317] Such practices went back to the days of Cain:

Moses 5:52. . . . The Lord cursed . . . all them that had covenanted with Satan; for they kept not the commandments of God.

Gizeh 6:2. (The Sons of Heaven wished to break their covenants and join with the daughters of men) 3. but Seimizas [Satan] said "I am afraid you will not be willing to go through with this thing. . . . " 4. And they answered him all saying, We will all swear with an oath, and bind each other by a mortal curse [lit., anathemize each other], that we will not go back on this agreement [*gnome*] until we have carried it out; . . . 5. Then they all swore together and pronounced the doom of death on each other.

5:29. And Satan said unto Cain: Swear unto me . . . and swear thy brethren . . . that they tell it not; for if they tell it, they shall surely die.

5:51. For, from the days of Cain, there was a secret combination, and their works were in the dark, and they knew every man his brother.

5:29-30. Satan said unto Cain: Swear unto me by thy throat, and if thou tell it thou shalt die; and swear thy brethren by their heads, and by the living God, that they tell it not; for if they tell it, they shall surely die; and this that thy father may not know it. . . . And all these things were done in secret.

1 En. 69:13. Kasbeel, the chief of the oath . . . when he dwelt high above in glory . . . 14. . . . requested Michael to show him the hidden name, that he might enunciate it in the oath, so that those might quake before that name and oath who revealed all that was in secret to the children of men.

1 En. 69:6. It was Gadreel "who showed the children of men all the blows of death, and he led astray Eve."

5:16. And Adam and Eve . . . ceased not to call upon God. . . . But behold, Cain hearkened not, saying: Who is the Lord that I should know him?

Ethiop. Bk. Mysts. PO 6:431. "In the days of Cain evil . . . and deceitful practices increased. The wicked angels set themselves up in open and insolent opposition to Adam, and glorying in their earthly bodies learned a great sin. And

5:51. For, from the days of
Cain, there was a secret
combination, and their works
were in the dark.

openly exposed all the work
which they had seen in
heaven."

And so we find in a Greek Enoch text the Great Angels
returning from earth to report to God that they had found
"Azael teaching all manner of unrighteousness upon the
earth, and he has laid bare those mysteries of the age which
belong to heaven, which are [now] known and practiced
among men; and also Semiazas is with him, he to whom
thou gavest authority [over] those who go along with
him."[318]

As bad as breaking their oaths was divulging them to
those not worthy to receive them, thereby debasing and in-
validating them. One of the most widespread themes of
myth and legend is the tragedy of the hero who yields to
the charms of a fair maiden or *femme fatale* and ends up revealing to her hidden mysteries. The story meets us in the
oldest Egyptian epic (where the lady Isis wheedles out of
Re the fatal knowledge of his true name) and in like tales of
Samson and Delilah, the daughter of Jared, Lohengrin, and
so on, in which the woman is Pandora who *must* know
what is in the box. On this theme the Gizeh fragments offer
a significant parallel to the Joseph Smith version, in which
the common background of the text and the confusion of
the later scribes are equally apparent: "Lamech had spoken
the secret *unto his wives*, and they . . . declared these
things abroad, and had not compassion. . . . And thus . . .
darkness began to prevail among all the sons of men."
(Moses 5:53, 55.)

Compare this to: "And now concerning the Watchers,
[say to them,] You were in heaven and there you knew
every *mysterion* which had not been made known to you as
well as that mystery which God allowed; and that you dis-
closed to your wives in the hardness of your heart, and it
was through this mystery that women and men caused iniquities to abound upon the earth." (Gizeh 16:2-4.)[319]

Clement of Alexandria attributed to Musaeus, the founder of the Greek Mysteries, an account of "how the angels
lost their heavenly heritage through the telling of the secret
things [*mysteria*] to women," things, Clement observes,
"which the other angels keep secret or quietly perform
until the coming of the Lord."[320]

Rather surprisingly, the age of Enoch is consistently
described as the time of great intellectual as well as material
sophistication. "Azael . . . taught [men] to make knives
and breastplates and all kinds of military hardware; and to
work the ores of the earth, and how gold was to be worked
and made into ornaments for women; and he showed them
polishing [eye-paint] and cosmetics and precious stones
and dyes. . . . And the sons and daughters of men
adopted all these things and led the saints astray. And
there was great wickedness on the earth, and they became
perverted and lost in all their ways. . . . Along with that
their leader Semiazas taught them scientific formulas
(*epaodas kata tou nous*), and the properties of roots and
plants of the earth. The eleventh, Pharmakos, taught all
manner of drugs, incantations, prescriptions, formulas.
[Others] taught them stargazing, astrology, meteorology,
geology, the signs of the sun and moon. All of these began
to reveal the mysteries to their wives and children."[321]

The leaders of the people devoted most of their wealth
to all kinds of engineering projects for controlling and taming nature. But the Lord altered the order of creation, making the sun rise in the west and set in the east, so that all
their plans came to naught.[322] The idea of controlling the
environment independently of God was not so foolish as it
sounds, says the Zohar, "for they knew all the arts . . . and
all the ruling chieftains [*archons*] in charge of the world, and
on this knowledge they relied, until at length God disabused them by restoring the earth to its primitive state
and covering it with water."[323] Rabbi Isaac reports: "'In the
days of Enoch even children were acquainted with these
mysterious arts [the advanced sciences].' Said R. Yesa: 'If
so, how could they be so blind as not to know that God in-

tended to bring the Flood upon them and destroy them?' R. Isaac replied: 'They did know,'" but they thought they were smart enough to prevent it. "What they did not know was that God rules the world. . . . God gave them a respite all the time that the righteous men Jered, Methusaleh, and Enoch were alive; but when they departed from the world, God let punishment descend . . . , 'and they were blotted out from the earth' (Genesis 7:23)."[324]

A Book of Mormon text betrays the Enoch tradition (possibly contained in the brass plates) in a transparent parallel: "Priestcrafts are that men . . . set themselves up for a light unto the world, that they may get gain and praise of the world; but they seek not the welfare of Zion." (2 Nephi 26:29.)

Compare this to: "These men [of Enoch's time] erected synagogues and colleges, and placed in them scrolls and rich ornaments . . . but they did it to set themselves up for a light, and for the honors of men; and in such a way the powers of evil prevail over Israel." (Zohar. Bereshith 25b.)

Power and gain are two faces of one coin: "We are able to do whatever we please," said the people in Enoch's day, "because we are very rich!" To which Enoch replied: "You are wrong! Your riches will soon depart from you . . . "; but they went on seeking the power of gain more grimly than ever.[325]

An interesting connection emerges in the account of how "in the time of Enoch they committed murder, shedding of blood of the children of men; they enslaved them, they sold what did not belong to them, they entered homes without right, and took whatever they wanted . . . they rigged the laws in their favor, and imitated the abominable deeds of the rebellious angels of a former time in which, when Abel tried to check them they encompassed his death by a conspiracy."[326] For this confirms a bold statement found in the Doctrine and Covenants 84:16: "Abel . . . was slain by [a] conspiracy." Ambition was the motivating force in all this evil. "The giants," says Ben Sira 16:7, "were aspiring spirits who desired to be great in the manner of God on earth"; E. Kraeling has pointed out that the biblical term "men of name," means "men who aspired to be great, 'to make a name' for themselves."[327] The Slavonic Enoch version matches the book of Moses in taking us back to the beginning of the matter:

Moses 4:1. That Satan . . . came before me, saying— Behold, here am I, send me, I will be thy son, and I will redeem all mankind . . . wherefore give me thine honor.	Ms. R. Ch. 11: The Devil knew that I wanted to make the world . . . with Adam ruling as Lord of it. . . . he became Satan when he fled from heaven, before which time he was Satan-el. He
4:4. And he became Satan, . . . to lead them captive at his will, even as many as would not hearken unto my voice.	changed his nature and was no longer an angel; he preserved his identity, but his state of mind was altered, as when any righteous person becomes wicked . . . and he conceived the impossible idea of setting up his throne . . . to be equal to my power. [God has given him great power over such as listen to him.] [Apocalypse of Abraham 14:1-2; see also Dead Sea Thanksgiving Scroll VI [f] p.X.)

Almost all our sources, and especially the Joseph Smith book of Enoch, emphasize the point that the people did not drift imperceptibly into ways of folly. They were so constantly warned that only a high and determined willfulness brought destruction upon them:

Moses 6:28. And for these many generations . . . have they gone astray, . . . and have sought their own counsels in the dark; . . .	Beatty 99:89. And they shall go astray in the foolishness [aphrosyne] of their hearts, and the visions of their dreams [the dark] shall lead them astray.
6:29. Wherefore, they have . . . brought upon themselves death.	And the lying words you have made shall perish. 98:9. Woe to you foolish ones, for you shall perish through your own folly!

5:57. For they would not hearken unto his voice, nor believe on his Only Begotten Son.

Secrets 4 (Vaillant. p. 18). These are they who denied the Lord, and would not hear the voice of the Lord, but followed their own counsel.

6:29. . . . they have foresworn themselves, and, by their oaths, they have brought upon themselves death; and a hell I have prepared for them, if they repent not.

1 Enoch 63:9. We pass away . . . on account of our own works . . . descending . . . into Sheol [hell].

6:43. . . . why counsel ye yourselves, and deny the God of heaven?

Black 99:2. Wo unto you who pervert the eternal covenant and reckon yourselves sinless!

Bet ha-Midrash (*BHM*) 5:171. I am Enoch! When the generation of the Flood sinned and said of God: Turn away from him, and in the knowing of his ways do not rejoice. Then God delivered men.

Nothing could be more deliberate. All the wickedness and folly of the time is summed up in one simple phrase: "Behold, they are without affection!" On this theme there are striking parallels between the Joseph Smith and the Slavonic texts:

Moses 7:32. The Lord said unto Enoch:

Secrets 11 (Vaillant, pp. 100ff). The Lord said unto Enoch:

Behold these thy brethren; they are the workmanship of mine own hands, . . .

. . . Upon the earth I placed him as the second angel, in honor and great glory

Moses 7:32. . . . and I gave unto them their knowledge, in the day I created them; and in the Garden of Eden, gave I unto man his agency;

And I established him as King [lit., Caesar, Czar] over the earth, ruling by my authority [wisdom] . . . and I called his name Adam, and I gave him his agency [*volya yevo*]

7:33. And . . . also [have] given commandment, that they should love one another, and . . . choose

and I told him: This is good for thee and that is bad [gave him a choice],

me, their Father; but behold, they are without affection, and they hate their own blood.

in order to determine whether he would have love or hatred for me, by showing his love for me among those of his own race [*v rodye yevo*] . . . [but] all the earth is filled with blood. They will abandon their creator.

7:34. . . . and in my hot displeasure will I send in the floods upon them. . . .

Therefore I will command the abyss, and the deposits of the waters of heaven will descend

7:37. . . . and the whole heavens shall weep over them. . . .
7:41. . . . and all eternity shook.

. . . and the earth will be shaken and lose its stability.

Equally impressive is a parallel with 1 Enoch:

Moses 7:33. . . . they are without affection, and they hate their own blood;

1 En. 4 (99:15). Wo unto them who work unrighteousness . . . and slay their neighbors.

34. And the fire of mine indignation is kindled against them; . . .
[I will] send in the floods against them . . .

He . . . shall arouse His fierce indignation and destroy you all with the sword

37. . . . .and the whole heavens shall weep over them. . . .

and all the holy and righteous shall remember your sins.

6:15. . . . a man's hand was against his own brother, in administering death, . . . seeking for power.

For a man shall not withhold his hand from slaying his sons . . . , nor from his beloved to slay him
. . . nor from his brother.

These moving passages are to explain the Great Weeping. First, Enoch weeps:

Moses 7:41.
. . . wherefore Enoch knew, and looked upon their wickedness, and their misery, and wept. . . .
7:44. And as Enoch saw this, he had bitterness of soul, and wept over his brethren, and said unto the heavens: I will refuse to be comforted.

Secrets of Enoch 41. (Morfill). And I saw . . . and I sighed and wept, and spake of the ruin [caused by] their wickedness. 2. And I meditated in my heart and said: Blessed is the man who is not yet born [etc.].

Manichaean Frg.[328] Enoch the Just said: I have seen great sorrow, and an outpouring of tears from my eyes, having heard which vile things issue from the mouths of the wicked . . . My eyes are filled with tears and my tongue is tied . . .

Then, as we shall presently see, all nature weeps, and Enoch is dumbfounded to learn that God himself weeps! This bold concept (quite inadmissible to the Fathers of the fourth century)[329] is attested in other Enoch texts:

Moses 7:28-29. And . . . the God of heaven looked upon the residue of the people, and he wept; and Enoch bore record of it, saying, How is it . . . that thou canst weep, seeing thou art holy, and from all eternity to all eternity? . . .
31. . . . how is it thou canst weep?

Jewish Encyclopedia 8:519. "When God wept over the destruction of the Temple, Metatron [Enoch] fell on his face and said: I will weep, but weep not thou! God answered and said: If thou wilt not suffer me to weep, I will go whither thou canst not come and there will I lament."

The angels in heaven and all the other worlds join in the weeping:

Moses 7:37. . . . the whole heavens shall weep over them, even all the workmanship of

2 Baruch 67:2. Dost thou think that there is no anguish to the angels in the presence of

mine hands; wherefore should not the heavens weep? . . .

7:40. Wherefore, for this shall the heavens weep, yea, and all the workmanship of mine hands.

the Mighty One. . . . Dost thou think that in these things the Most High rejoices, or that his name is glorified?

With the Great Weeping the universe itself is shaken:

Moses 7:41. . . . Enoch . . . wept and stretched forth his arms, and his heart swelled wide as eternity; and his bowels yearned; and all eternity shook.

Zohar. Shemoth 8a. Then the Messiah lifts up his voice and weeps, and the whole Garden of Eden quakes, and all the righteous and the Saints who are there break out crying. . . . When the crying and weeping resound for the second time, the whole firmament above the garden begins to shake . . . and God sets about to destroy the wicked.

Equally shattering is the announcement that, while God sorrows, the Devil is laughing:

Moses 7:26. Satan . . . looked up and laughed, and his angels rejoiced.

7:28. And . . . the God of heaven looked . . . and . . . wept.

7:33. . . . they should choose me, their Father; but behold, they are without affection, and they hate their own blood.

34. . . . I will send in the floods . . .

41. And . . . Enoch . . . wept . . . and all eternity shook.

Secrets 22 (Vaillant).[330] . . . a man hates his neighbor . . . all the earth will be full of blood . . . and they shall abandon their Creator. . . . The Adversary will be in his glory [lit., will make himself great] and rejoice in their [his angels'] works, to my [the Lord's] great affliction. . . .

Then I will command the abyss, and the water reserves of heaven will descend upon the earth . . . and all the earth will be shaken and no longer have foundation.

It is in view of the infinite exaltation and glory of the Deity that Enoch is overwhelmed by his weeping. This is expressed both in a doxology and an aretology (i.e., a speech in which God describes his own glory).

Moses 7:29-30. How is it thou canst weep, seeing thou art holy, and from all eternity to all eternity? . . . Millions of earths like this . . . would not be a beginning . . . of thy creations. . . .
31. . . . and naught but peace, justice, and . . . mercy shall go before thy face and have no end. . . .

1 En. 71:14. And righteousness of the Head of Days forsakes him not. 15. . . . from hence hath proceeded peace since the creation of the world. 16. And . . . righteousness never forsaketh Him. With Him will be their dwelling-places, . . . forever and ever.

7:35. (Aretology). Behold, *I am God; Man of Holiness is my name*; Man of *Counsel* is my name.
. . . 36. Wherefore, I can stretch forth mine hands and hold *all the creations* which I have made; and mine *eye can pierce* them also.

Gizeh 9:4. [The Angels:] *Thou art the God* of Gods, and Lord of Lords, . . . and God of men [G[81] of the worlds, ages], and the throne of thy glory is for all generations [cycles] of the ages [eternities or worlds]; and thy name is Holy One and is praised unto all the ages. 5. For thou didst make all things and hast all authority, and all things are plain before thee and revealed, and thou seest all things.

7:24. . . . and behold, the power of Satan was upon all the face of the earth. 26. And [Enoch] beheld Satan; and he had a great chain in his hand, and it veiled the whole . . . earth with darkness; and he looked up and laughed, and his angels rejoiced.

1 En. 53:3. For I [Enoch] saw all the angels of punishment abiding and preparing all the instruments of Satan. . . .
54:3. and here mine eyes saw how they made these their instruments, iron chains of immeasurable weight. . . .
53:5. . . . for the kings and the mighty of this earth, that they thereby might be destroyed.

With the binding, of course, goes imprisonment, a temporary prison for such fallen mortals as repent, a permanent one for the others.

Moses 7:38. But behold, these which thine eyes are upon shall perish in the floods; and . . . I will shut them up; a prison have I prepared for them.

2 En. 5.[331] This place, Enoch, is prepared for those who practiced abominations on earth. . . . who would not know their Creator. . . . It is for all those that this place has been prepared as an eternal heritage.

6:29-30. They have brought upon themselves death; and a hell I have prepared for them, if they repent not. And this is a decree . . . from my own mouth.

Jubilees 10:5. Noah: And thou knowest how [the] Watchers, the fathers of these spirits, acted in my day; and as for these spirits which are living, imprison them and hold them fast. . . . [See 1 Pet. 3: 19-20. Jubilees does not borrow from the New Testament!]

Those in prison, chains, and darkness are only being kept there until the Judgment, which will liberate many, not only because of their repentance, but through the power of the Atonement. It is when Enoch reaches the lowest depth of despair that the revelation of God's plan of merciful redemption turns all to joy: "And as Enoch saw this, he had bitterness of soul, and wept over his brethren, and said unto the heavens: I will refuse to be comforted; but the Lord said unto Enoch: Lift up your heart, and be glad; and look." (Moses 7:44.) It was specifically the spirits who were disobedient in Enoch's day who were to enjoy the preaching of the Lord and promise of deliverance in the meridian of times. (See 1 Peter 3:19-20.)

Moses 7:67. And the Lord showed Enoch all things . . . and he saw the day of the righteous, the hour of their redemption; and received a fulness of joy.

1 En. 60:5. Why art thou [Enoch] disquieted . . . 6. that day is prepared . . . for sinners and inquisition . . . that the punishment of the Lord of Spirits may not come,

1 Pet. 3:18. For Christ also hath once suffered for sins . . . 19. By which also he went and preached unto the spirits in prison; 20. Which sometime were disobedient . . . in the days of Noah.

in vain . . . Afterwards the judgment shall take place according to his mercy and patience.

Black 10:6. Azael is bound in prison unto the Great Day of Judgment, when he is led to the *enpyrismon,* while 7. the earth will be healed. . . [of] the blow, that all the sons of man may not be destroyed by the mystery in which the Watchers stumbled and which they taught to their sons.

Moses 7:47. And behold, Enoch saw the day of the coming of the Son of Man, even in the flesh; and his soul rejoiced.

7:38. . . . these . . . shall perish in the floods; and behold, I will shut them up; a prison have I prepared for them. 39. And That which I have chosen hath pled before my face. Wherefore, he suffereth for their sins; inasmuch as they will repent in the day that my Chosen shall return unto me, and until that day they shall be in torment.

1 En. 45:2. Such shall be the lot of sinners . . . who are thus preserved for the day of suffering and tribulation. 3. On that day mine Elect shall sit on the throne of glory and shall try their works.

Another parallel on the same theme:

Moses 7:57. And as many of the spirits as were in prison came forth . . . and the remainder were reserved in chains of darkness until the judgment of the great day.

Beatty 103:7. . . . in Hades shall they be in great torment 8. and in darkness, and in chains and in burning flame, and your spirit will come unto a great judgment.

World in Upheaval

An unfailing aspect of apocalyptic literature in general and of the Enoch writings in particular is the reverberation through their pages of vast upheavals in the natural world. This aspect of apocalyptic has begun to be taken seriously only within very recent years, and it is the scientists rather than the theologians who are impressed by the ancient records.[332] Enoch, in fact, is one of their favorite references. They are impressed by the authentic ring of the catastrophic motif in the old apocalyptic writings while the ministry deplores and denounces them as unfortunate examples of a bogeyman mentality.[333]

What was the world like in Enoch's day? Joseph Smith places the action amidst pastoral nomads ranging the mountains and valleys—and so do the other sources. They show us the righteous and the wicked, sometimes designated as Sethians and Cainites, living respectively in the mountains and the lowlands.[334]

Moses 7:17. . . . the Lord blessed the land, and they were blessed upon the mountains, and upon the high places, and did flourish.	4 Ezra 6:51. And I gave to Enoch a dry part of the earth, that he might dwell therein, where there were a thousand mountains.

It was the archetype of Zions to follow:

D&C 49:24-25. But before the great day of the Lord . . . Zion shall flourish upon the hills and rejoice upon the mountains, and shall be assembled together unto the place which I have appointed.	Apocalypse of Adam, folio 85, lines 9-11 (p. 193). At the end of time the Saints will come to a high mountain, upon a stone of truth.

The other side of the picture shows us the wicked gathered together in great valleys. The image not only suits this world, but is projected into the next.

Moses 7:5. . . . I beheld in the valley of Shum, and lo, a great people which dwelt in tents, which were the people of Shum. . . .	1 Enoch 13:9. Enoch came to them [the Watchers], and they were all sitting gathered together weeping in Abelsjaîl, which is between [the mountains] Lebanon and Sênêsêr, with their faces covered.

7. And the Lord said unto me . . . the people of Shum . . . shall utterly be destroyed; and the people of Canaan shall divide themselves in the land, and the land shall be barren and unfruitful. . . . 8. For behold, the Lord shall curse the land with much heat, and the barrenness thereof shall go forth forever.

Secrets 13 (Vaillant, p. 42). I saw a certain plain, like a prison . . . and I sighed and wept . . . 8. Why is this hollow place separated from the other? 9. . . . that the spirits of the dead might be separated . . . 11. . . . set apart in this great plain until the day of judgment . . . 12. And this division has been made for the spirits . . . of those who were slain in the days of sinners.

Gizeh 10:11. . . . Go, Michael, and bind . . . all who have defiled themselves . . . 12. bind them for 70 generations in the valleys [*napas*] of the earth.

The first warning to hit the sinners in the plain is, following the ancient pattern, a terrible drought, of which Enoch literature gives us vivid descriptions.

Moses 7:7. And the Lord said unto me: Prophesy . . . the land shall be barren and unfruitful, and none other people shall dwell there but the people of Canaan. 8. For behold, the Lord shall curse the land with much heat, and the barrenness thereof shall go forth forever; and there was a blackness came upon all the children of Canaan, that they were despised among all people.

Gizeh 26:2. And I saw the holy mountain and water descending from the mountain . . .
4. and a deep dry valley, and another valley [see Shum and Canaan, Moses 7:5].
5. (Both valleys were utterly desolate and without a tree.)
27:2. This is a cursed land, reserved for the cursed forever . . .

Black, p. 6. 100:11. Every cloud and mist and dew and rain shall be withheld because of your sins. 100:12. Therefore offer gifts to the rain that it be not hindered from descending for you, and to dew, and cloud and mist. 101: For if He closes the window of heaven and hinders the dew and rain from descending because of you, what will you do?

1 Enoch 18:12. I saw a place which had no firmament. . . . There was no water upon it, and no birds, but it was a waste and horrible place. 22:3. These hollow places have been created for this very purpose, . . . that all the souls of the children of men should assemble there.

Bad times render men desperate. Obsessed by dread and guilt, they turn hysterically against each other, and soon find themselves locked in deadly combat to the point of extermination.

Moses 7:7. . . . Behold the people of Canaan, which are numerous, shall go forth in battle array against the people of Shum, and shall slay them that they shall utterly be destroyed.

Gizeh 10:9. Go, Gabriel, to the ill-begotten ones, the crooked ones, and the sons of adultery; and destroy the sons of the Watchers from among men. Set them to fighting each other in war and in wanton destruction.

The picture fits later dispensations as well:

D&C 87:6. And thus, with the sword and by bloodshed the inhabitants of the earth shall mourn . . . until the consumption decreed hath made a full end of all nations.

Black 7:6. The earth fell under the rule of the lawless, and [8:1] Azael [Satan] taught them the manufacture of weapons and how to work the treasures of the earth. 4. The

7. That . . . the blood of the saints, shall cease to come up into the ears of the Lord of Sabaoth, from the earth, to be avenged of their enemies.	cry of those slain of the people ascended to heaven. 9:1-3. The angels saw blood flowing upon the earth, and heard the voices of the slain crying out to God for vengeance.
D&C 1:35. . . . the hour is not yet, but is nigh at hand, when peace shall be taken from the earth, and the devil shall have power over his own dominion.	Secrets MS. R, 22 (Vaillant). Nation rises against nation for the devil has begun to reign . . . and there arose warfare and great trouble.

Besides the people of Canaan who extirpate those of Shum, seven other exotic tribes are named in the Joseph Smith Enoch, suggesting the familiar seven-pattern of tribal organizations. They are the people of the lands of Sharon, Enoch, Omner, Heni, Shem, Haner, and Hanan-nihah. (Moses 7:9.) What would ancient copyists thousands of years later on the other side of the world have made of such a list? They would handle it exactly as scribes have always done, by transferring it to a more familiar setting. The scribe of the Ethiopian Enoch puts in the place of those familiar tribes the names of what were *to him* the most distant and exotic of peoples on earth, and naturally treats the reference to lions as a familiar and highly conventional figure of speech:

Moses 7:5. . . . I beheld . . . a great people which dwelt in tents, . . . the people of Shum. 6. . . . and I looked towards the *north*, and I beheld the people of Canaan, which dwelt in tents. (Italics added.)	1 Enoch 56:5. To the *east* [I saw] Parthians and Medes [the two great tent-dwelling nations of antiquity]:
9. [Enoch beholds the seven other nations] 13. . . . and the roar of the lions was heard out of the	they shall stir up the [other] kings, . . . that they may break forth as lions and from their lairs.

wilderness: and all nations
feared greatly. . . .
16. And from that time
forth there were wars and
bloodshed among them.

One of nature's ironies is that not enough water usually
leads to too much. Enoch's world was plagued by flood as
well as drought; we are regaled by the picture of lowering
heavens ceaselessly dumping dismal avalanches of rain
and snow upon the earth. The constant weeping of Enoch
and all the saints is matched in the powerful imagery of the
weeping heavens and the earth veiled in darkness under
the blackest of skies: In the book of Enoch the same
imagery is applied to the meridian and the fulness of times
as well as the Adamic age.

Moses 7:28. [Enoch:] How
is it that the heavens weep,
and shed forth their tears as
the rain upon the mountains?

1 Enoch 100:11-13.
. . . because of their sins all
heavens weep and darkness
prevails, 13. with ice, hail,
cold and winds together.

1 Enoch 17:2, 4. I saw the
mountains of the darkness of
winter, . . . and the place
from which all the waters of
the deep flow.

7:37. . . . the whole heavens
shall weep over them, even all
the workmanship of mine
hands; wherefore should not
the heavens weep, seeing
these shall suffer?
38. But behold, these . . .
shall perish in the floods. . . .
40. Wherefore, for this shall
the heavens weep. . . .
56. [At the Crucifixion] the
heavens were veiled; and all
the creations of God mourned;
and the earth groaned. . . .

Miracles of Jesus.[335] [He
tells Peter that because the
world will reject the gospel it]
will cause the Sun and the
Moon to weep . . . and at the
corruption of the teachings the
hills and mountains will
weep.
Berayta, pp. 205-20.[336] The
waters under the earth are like
a small spring beside the
waters of creation, which in
turn are like a small spring
compared with the ocean; but

61. . . . before that day the heavens shall be darkened, and a veil of darkness shall cover the earth. . . . 62. And righteousness will I send down out of heaven; and truth . . . out of the earth . . . and . . . cause [them] to sweep the earth as with a flood.

the sea is like a small spring compared with the waters which weep.

7:26. [In the days of Cain] it veiled the whole face of the earth with darkness. . . .

Mysteries of Jesus.[337] God punished Cain with seventy-seven days of unmitigated rain.

7:28. And it came to pass that the God of heaven looked upon the residue of the people, and he wept; and Enoch bore record of it, saying: How is it that the heavens weep, and shed forth their tears as the rain upon the mountains?

1 Enoch 95:1. O that mine eyes were [a cloud of] waters that I might weep over you, and pour down my tears as a cloud of waters. [Passage very corrupt; reconstructed by Charles. This is also the most corrupted part of Gizeh, c. 28—the scribes don't understand it].

We find in a striking passage of the Joseph Smith account of Enoch a curious mixture of fire and water; the same oddity in the other Enoch text suggests scenes of volcanic activity with fumeroles, sulphurous vapors, rivers of fire, etc.: ". . . in darkness and in chains, and in burning flame. . . ." (Beatty 103:8.)

Moses 7:34. And the fire of mine indignation is kindled against them; and in my hot displeasure will I send in the floods upon them, for my fierce anger is kindled against them.

Secrets 13 (Vaillant). I could not support the fear of the burning fire—that is how the words of the Lord were.

bin Gorion 1:195. The rains of the Flood were intermingled with showers of fire from heaven.

> 2 Baruch 53:7. It rained
> black waters . . . and fire was
> mingled with them
> and . . . they wrought
> devastation and
> destruction. . . . 9. [The]
> lightning healed those regions
> where the waters had
> descended.

> 1 Enoch 17:4. And they
> took me to the living waters,
> and to the fire of the west, [the
> waters of creation and
> baptism]. . . .
>   5. And I came to a river of
> fire in which fire flows like
> water.

> 1 Enoch 67:5-7. And I saw
> that valley in which there was
> a great convulsion, and a
> convulsion of the waters. . . .
> 6. . . . from that fiery molten
> metal and from the convulsion
> thereof in that place, there was
> produced a smell of sulphur,
> and it was connected with
> those waters. . . . 7. And
> through its valley proceed
> streams of fire.

We are told that when the wicked tried to flee back to
the safety of the holy mountain as the waters of the flood
began to rise, they could not approach the ark because the
rocks were burning hot.[338] It is pictures like this that
convince the scientists that there may be something to
these old apocalyptic tales.

The most conspicuously and consistently reported of
all the evils in Enoch's day are the earthquakes, consistent
with the picture of plate tectonics that the whole thing
presents.

Moses 6:34. . . . and the mountains shall flee before you, and the rivers shall [accordingly] turn from their course. . . .

7:13. . . . the earth trembled, and the rivers of water were turned out of their course; . . . and all nations feared greatly.

Gizeh 1:5. And all the people shall fear . . . and trembling and great fear shall seize them to the extremities of the earth.

6. And high mountains shall be shaken and shall fall and be dissolved . . . and the mountains shall flow down [*diarrhynai*, "to slip through, to leak, to fall away like water"] and be turned into side-channels, and shall melt like wax before a flame.

7. And the earth will be rent with a splitting and a crackling [*rhagas*], and everything on the earth will be destroyed.

These events are correlated with the activities of Enoch, who does not, however, cause them; they are programmed to his purposes, and God stands behind him and speaks through his voice the words of power.

Moses 7:13. . . . Enoch . . . led the people of God, and their enemies came to battle against them; and he spake the word of the Lord, and the earth trembled, and the mountains fled, even according to his command; and the rivers of waters were turned out of their course; and the roar of the lions was heard out of the wilderness.

6:34. Behold my Spirit is upon you, wherefore all thy words will I justify; and the mountains shall flee before you, and the rivers shall turn from their course; and thou shalt abide in me, and I in you; therefore walk with me.

Psalms of Solomon 11:1. At the gathering of Zion . . . 5. Lofty mountains has he humbled, and made plain before them [the people of God] and the hills fled away before their entrance.

Black 102:1. And when he gives forth his voice . . . 2. the whole earth shall be shaken and trembling and thrown into confusion.

1 Enoch 52:6. These mountains . . . shall be in the presence of the Elect One as wax before the fire, and like the water which streams down from above. . . .

7:13. . . . all nations feared greatly, so powerful was the word of Enoch, and so great was the power of the language which God had given him.

Secrets 13 (Vaillant). I have heard the words of the Lord like a great thunder amidst ceaseless agitation of the clouds. The Lord of the Earth is terrible and most perilous. [Bonner, pp. 58f, Black 102:1.] And when he gives forth his voice against you, will not you be shaken and affrighted by the mighty sound? And the whole earth shall be shaken and trembling and thrown into confusion."

6:34. [God:] All thy words will I justify; and the mountains shall flee before you.

7:13. . . . he spake the word of the Lord, and the earth trembled, and the mountains fled, even according to his command.

The really spectacular show in the Enoch literature is the behavior of the seas. Like the alternating drought and flood from the skies, there is either too much sea or not enough. Before "the floods came and swallowed them up" (Moses 7:43), the sea first drew back in places, leaving its coastal beds high and dry in anticipation of the great *tsunami* (seawave) which came with the earthquake.

Moses 7:13-14. The earth trembled, and the mountains fled. . . . There also came up a land out of the depth of the sea, and so great was the fear of the enemies of the people of God, that they fled and stood afar off and went upon the land which came up out of the depth of the sea.

Secrets 6 (Vaillant 106:6). Enoch: Are not all the sea and its waters the work of the Most High, and did he not set their limits? 7. And by his wrath they are affrighted and dried up.

1 Enoch 60:16. Enoch: The spirit of the sea . . . draws back with a rein, and in like manner it is driven forward and dispersed amid all the mountains of the earth.

The sea misbehaved on other occasions in Enoch's day:

Moses 7:66. Before that . . . he saw great tribulations

Mid. Rab. 1:37. [Twice the sea invaded the earth.] Once

among the wicked; and he also saw the sea, that it was troubled.

was in the generation of Enosh, and a second time in the generation of the separation [The Tower].

bin Gorion 1:153. In the days of Enoch, the sea rose and flooded one-third of the land!

Combat of Adam and Eve, p. 361. The animals were urged on to the ark by the trembling of the earth; the sea rose in violent agitation, the winds were terrible, the sun disappeared and all the sky. . . . The sea cast mountain waves upon the land.

4 Ezra 6:49. And how thou hast saved two spirits: the one thou hast named Behemoth, and the other Leviathan, 50. And thou didst separate one from the other, for the seventh part, where the water was gathered together, was unable to hold them (both). 51. And thou didst give Behemoth one of the parts [of the earth], which had been dried up on the third day—that he might dwell therein, where are a thousand hills.

The terrors of the book of Enoch reach their culmination when the upheavals of nature extend to the entire cosmos. Many apocalyptic accounts of the disturbed heavens suggest to some scientists today an actual shifting of the earth on its axis (a phenomenon now well attested from the study of ancient magnetized ceramics) or a massive showering of meteoric particles.

Moses 7:61. . . . the heavens shall shake, and also the earth; and great tribulations shall be among the children of men.

7:41. . . . Enoch . . . wept and stretched forth his arms, . . . and all eternity shook.

Black 102:1. And when he gives forth his voice against you, 2. will ye not be shaken and affrighted by the mighty sound? And the whole earth shall be shaken, and trembling, and thrown into confusion. . . .

3. And the heaven and its lights be shaken and trembling, [and] all the sons of the earth.

Bonner, p. 58. "And all the earth was shaking and trembling, and thrown into confusion; and also angels having completed their assignments, and the heaven and the Lights [*phosteres*] were shaken and trembling, and all the sons of earth."

1 Enoch 60:1. I saw how a mighty quaking made the heaven of heavens to quake, and the host of the Most High, and the angels, a thousand thousands and ten thousand times ten thousand, were disquieted with a great disquiet.

But there is one concept which goes beyond the scope of astronomy in its exciting implications. It is the doctrine that when a world is destroyed, all the other worlds that have contributed to its existence join in a general mourning.[339]

Moses 7:36. . . . and among all the workmanship of mine hands there has not been so great wickedness as among thy brethren. . . .

37. . . . the whole heavens shall weep over them, even *all* the workmanship of mine hands; wherefore should not the heavens weep, seeing these shall suffer? (Italics added.)

40. Wherefore, for this shall the heavens weep, yea, and all the workmanship of mine hands.

41. Enoch . . . wept and stretched forth his arms, and his heart swelled wide as eternity; and his bowels yearned; and all eternity shook.

1 Enoch 60:3. And a great trembling seized me, and fear took hold of me, and my loins gave way and dissolved were my reins, and I fell upon my face, 4. For I had not been able to endure the look of this host, and the commotion and the quaking of heaven.

7:56. And the heavens were veiled; and all the creations of God mourned; and the earth groaned and the rocks were rent.

Apocryphon of John, p. 20. As I was thinking the heavens opened. . . . 21. . . . . And the whole cosmos shook; and I was afraid and fell upon my face. [And God appeared to him and spoke with him comforting him as he did Enoch.]

The peculiar nature imagery found in the Joseph Smith account of Enoch gets down to basics with the personification of the earth as *Terra Mater,* speaking as a living entity in a passage strikingly paralleled in the Greek fragments.

Moses 7:48. . . . Enoch looked upon the earth; and he heard a voice from the bowels thereof, saying: Wo, wo is me, the mother of men. . . . When shall I rest, and be cleansed from the filthiness which is

Gizeh 10:20. And cleanse thou the earth from all uncleanliness [*akatharsias*] and from all unrighteousness and from all sin and corruption [*asebeias*] and purge away [*exaleipson,* "flush, scour"] all gone forth out of me? When will my Creator sanctify me, that I may rest, and righteousness for a season abide upon my face?

impurities, which have come upon the earth.

22. And all the earth shall be cleansed from all pollution [*miasmatos*] and from all impurities. . . .

11:2. And then truth and peace will dwell together (*Koinonesousin homou*, "embrace, have all things in common") . . . for all the generations of men.

7:49. And when Enoch heard the earth mourn, he wept, and cried unto the Lord, saying: O Lord, wilt thou not have compassion upon the earth?

1 Enoch 7:5-6. "And they began to . . . devour one another's flesh, and drink the blood. Then the earth laid accusation against the lawless ones.

A man is called wicked [*rasha^c*] if he merely lifts his hand against his neighbor. . . . But only he is called evil [*ra^c*] who corrupts his way and defiles himself and the earth.

The rest and comfort that come after the flood will bring a new order of things.

Moses 7:48. . . . When shall I rest, and be cleansed . . . that I may rest, and righteousness for a season abide upon my face? 49. . . . Wilt thou not bless the children of Noah? [The name *Noah* means "rest."] 50. . . . have mercy upon Noah and his seed. 51. And the Lord . . . sware . . . that he would call upon the children of Noah.

Beatty 106:17b. [Enoch:] And he [Noah] shall cleanse [*praunei*] the earth from all the defilement [*phthoras*] which is in her. 18. And now tell Lamech that he is his son in truth, . . . [and] call his name [Noah]; for he shall be a remnant of you whereon ye shall rest for a season [*katapausete*] and his sons, also from the defilement [*phthoras*] of the earth and from all the wickedness [*hamartolon*, "pollution"] and from all the vileness [upon the earth].

A lengthy passage from The Book of the Combat of Adam and Eve in which that patriarch foresees the flood presents such an arresting correspondence to the Joseph Smith account as to provide a most instructive summary to this depressing part of our history. The Adam quotations are given in the order in which they occur; the matching quotes from the Joseph Smith Enoch are all from the same chapter and describe the same series of events.

Moses 7:66. And he also saw the sea, that it was troubled.	Combat of Adam and Eve 10.[340] At the sight of him the sea was troubled.
7:13. . . . the rivers of water were turned out of their course; . . . and the mountains fled, . . .	The Jordan reversed its course [lit., returned to its source] the mountains bounded like the stags and does of the valley.
7:17. . . . they were blessed upon the mountains, and upon the high places, and did flourish.	The hills resounded with hymns of adoration, the high peaks joined in a hymn of praise
7:41. . . . all eternity shook. 56. . . . and the earth groaned; and the rocks were rent.	Yea, the earth opened up and shook to its foundations,
7:14. There also came up a land out of the depth of the sea. . . .	The king of the sea saw me and fled. O sea, why hast thou fled? . . .
7:34. . . . I [will] send in the floods upon them. . . . 7:43. . . . the floods came and swallowed them up.	O depths of the abyss, why are you troubled? Currents [whirlpools] of the Ocean, why have you overflowed [swollen yourselves]?
7:13. Enoch . . . led the people of God, and their enemies came . . . against	The chariot of God rumbled in space . . .

them; and . . . [at] the word of
the Lord, . . . the earth
trembled, . . .

| and the roar of the lions was heard out of the wilderness; 7:37. . . . the whole heavens shall weep over them, even all the workmanship of mine hands; . . . 38. . . . these which thine eyes are upon shall perish in the floods. | and a great roaring arose from the midst of the terrified beasts. And everything on earth was overthrown. |

Being called, Enoch shrank back in fear and pleaded his unfitness, protesting among other things that he was "but a lad," although sixty-five years old at the time! (6:31.) How is that strange anomaly to be explained? Joseph Smith could have known of none of the writings below which also deal with it. Where did he get the idea? Certainly not from apocryphal sources, although it appears not uncommonly in them. Just a few examples:

bin Gorion 1:295f: The Metatron has 70 names, but the King calls me "the Lad." Why? 296. Because I act in the capacity of one who was before me, even Enoch, who was called "the Lad" 297. because he was the youngest of the hosts.

Book of Adam 1:165-66: Enoch: "I heard my brothers say when I was small how wicked the world is; how then can I all alone achieve anything? If only my brothers were here I could ask them! Yet youthful though I am, I am still older than my brothers, though the last to come into this world. . . ."

BHM 5:172: I am small [qatan, young] in the midst of them [the Watchers, of vast age, to whom he was sent], and am but a lad among them in days and months and years; in view of which they call me 'Lad.'"

Jewish Encyclopedia, 8:519: "In the Hebrew writings . . . and . . . the Apocrypha" Enoch is represented as a young man, "since both sources represent him as a youth"—nobody knows why.

Zohar, Beshalah 66b: "They saw the light of the Shekhinah, namely him who is called 'the Youth' [or Lad] Metatron-Henoch, who ministers to the Shekhinah in the heavenly Sanctuary." And the paved world of sapphire rock [Stone of Truth]. (See also Exodus 24:10.)

Book of Adam, 1:238: Enoch's grandfather, being called on a mission in the same way, made the same objection. When Adam sent the heavenly messengers to him with a mission call, "Seth said: 'O good teacher, for barely eight years [!] have I been in this world . . . I have not yet worn the male tiara [the round cloth cap of Exodus 28:40] nor borne the sword. Go back to Adam who is over 1,000 years old and tell him these things.' But they said: 'Seth, we have already told these same truths to your father Adam. He has been through all this.'" Then the winds bore Seth on high [as they later do Enoch], and he sat on the Throne of Light.

The patronizing title of "lad" reflected the general contempt in which Enoch was held—"All the people hate me," he said, "for I am slow of speech." (Moses 6:31.) The Ethiopian passage as rendered by Charles presents a peculiarly instructive parallel to the Joseph Smith version; both contain exactly the same ideas and expressions, but the African scribe has mixed them all up in an interesting way:

Moses 6:31. And when Enoch had heard these words, he bowed himself to the earth before the Lord, and spake before the Lord saying: Why is it that I have found favor in thy sight, and am but a lad, and all the people hate me; for I am slow of speech. . . .

32. And the Lord said unto Enoch: Go forth . . . open thy mouth, and it shall be filled. . . .

1 Enoch 15:24. And until then I had been prostrate on my face, trembling; and the Lord called me with his own mouth, and said to me: Come hither Enoch and hear my words. . . .

1 Enoch 103:9. Say not to the righteous and good who are in life: ". . . we have experienced every trouble, and

33. Say unto this people: Choose ye this day, to serve the Lord God who made you.

met with much evil . . . and have become few and small [*mikropsychos*, insignificant]. . . . 10. and have not found any to help us even with a word [i.e., in speech]. . . . 11. Sinners have laid their yoke heavily upon us; 12. They have had dominion over us; that hated us and smote us, and to those who hated us we have bowed our necks. 104:2. God answered: Be hopeful . . . ye shall shine as the lights of heaven . . . 3. and in your cry, cry for judgment. . . . 9. Be not godless in your hearts.

32. And the Lord said unto Enoch: Go forth and do as I have commanded thee, and no man shall pierce thee.

Book of Adam, p. xxi. And now, little Enoch, ["the Lad"] I have told you the mysteries of the wicked people of this world whose appearance has filled you with fear and distress . . . and that the wicked have conspired to do away with you but in vain. [See also xlvii: All the wicked plotted against Enoch, but in vain.] But fear not. I will return to deliver you from evil and sin . . . and I shall lead thee from this dark world to the dwelling of light.

Behold my Spirit is upon you, wherefore all thy words will I justify . . . and thou shalt abide in me, and I in you; therefore walk with me.

34. . . . all thy words will I justify; and the mountains shall flee before you, and the rivers shall turn from their course.

The angel of life said to little Enoch, Arise, take thy way to the source of the waters, turn it aside from its course . . . at this command Tavril indeed turned the running water from its course. . . .

As to being slow of speech, God will put his very words into Enoch's mouth, so that in a special way it will be the Lord speaking through him:

Moses 6:32. . . . Go forth and do as I have commanded thee, and no man shall pierce thee. Open thy mouth, and it shall be filled, and I will give thee utterance . . . and I will do as seemeth me good.

Secrets 13 (Vaillant). I have been sent by the mouth of the Lord to you to tell you what will be. . . . And now my children, it is not out of my own mouth that I speak to you today, but by the mouth of the Lord who has sent me to you. For you hear the words of my mouth, and I have heard the words of the Lord.

30. And this is a decree which I have sent forth in the beginning . . . from my own mouth, . . . and by the mouths of my servants, thy fathers, have I decreed it.

2 Enoch 29, p. 454. I am sent forth to you today from the Lord's mouth to speak to you. . . . not from my own mouth am I today informing you, but from the Lord's mouth, for you have heard my words from my mouth, but I have heard the Lord's words. . . .

Enoch was received by the public first with curiosity and surprise, then with resentment, then with fear, and finally with a measure of acceptance that was to produce a church and the city of Enoch. First we see Enoch, the mystery man, the alien, a great curiosity:

Moses 6:38. And they came forth to hear him, upon the high places, saying unto the tent-keepers: Tarry ye here . . . while we go yonder to behold the seer, for he prophesieth, and there is a strange thing in the land;

BHM 4:129. And all the people gathered together and went up . . . to Enoch to hear this thing.

Secrets 16 (Vaillant, p. 60). And they all came together, saying: Come, let us greet

Enoch, and they came to the place Azouchan.

a wild man hath come among us.

Iesous Basileus, 2:19ff, 107. John the Baptist was received as Enos [Enoch] returned to earth, preaching in the desert as a wild man.

Book of Adam, p. 17. There are false prophets who wander through the mountains and hills, wild men with wild hair and wild voices. They are called vagabond shepherds, live on herbs, and claim that God speaks mysteries by their mouths. 147. One of them, by the name of Marmon [!], led his followers to a place of filthy water.

40. And there came a man unto him, whose name was Mahijah, and said unto him: Tell us plainly who thou art, and from whence thou comest?

BHM 4:131. And Enoch went out [after his long hiding] and there came a voice saying: Who is the man who rejoices . . . in the ways of the Lord? . . . [See Mahujah and Mahijah, pp. 277-78 .] And all the people gathered together and came unto Enoch. . . . and Enoch taught all the people again to keep the ways of the Lord, . . . and gave them all his peace.

His answer:

Moses 6:41. And he said unto them: I came out from the land of Cainan, the land of my fathers, a land of righteousness unto this day. And my father taught me in all the ways of God.

Gizeh 12:1. . . . Enoch was taken, and no man knew where he went, where he is or what became of him. 2. But his works [i.e., missionary labors] are with the Watchers, while his days are with the Saints.

1 Enoch 12:1. And before [this] Enoch was hidden, and no one of the children of men knew where he was hidden, and where he abode and what had become of him. 2. And his activities had to do with the Watchers, and his days were with the Holy Ones.

BHM 4:129. Enoch . . . served God and shunned the ways of the wicked sons of men. And Enoch cleaved unto the Order of God in knowledge and intelligence. . . . And he separated himself in his wisdom from men and hid from them for many days. . . . 130. [After preaching] he withdrew again, as in the beginning, and hid himself, to serve the Lord.

This is the familiar theme of the holy man—Adam, Seth, Noah, Elijah, Abinadi, Ether, Mormon, etc.—who goes forth to admonish the wicked world from time to time, and then withdraws to the society of the righteous, usually in a vale or on a mountain. Such prophets are a disturbing presence among the people. Nowhere is the idea more movingly expressed than in this speech in the book of Moses:

Moses 6:37. And all men were offended because of him.

Book of Adam 1:170. And Enoch arose in joy and went forth to preach. But all conspired against him . . . and all the elements were thrown into confusion.

6:39. . . . when they heard him, no man laid hands on him; for fear came on all them that heard him; for he walked with God.

BHM 4:130. When he visited them, "the children of men feared Enoch greatly."

6:47. And as Enoch spake forth the words of God, the people trembled, and could not stand in his presence.

Gizeh 13:3. Then going forth I spoke to all of them, and they were all afraid, and trembling and terror seized them.
5. Because they could not speak, neither raise their eyes to heaven for shame. . . .
1 Enoch 13:3. Then I went and spoke to them all together, and they were all afraid, and fear and trembling seized them.

What caused them to tremble most of all was that Enoch produced a special book as a witness against them. He climaxes the story of his vision "by the sea east" by reminding them of a certain book.

Moses 6:46. . . . we have a book of remembrance we have written among us, according to the pattern given by the finger of God; and it is given in our own language [a book meant for them to *read*].

1 Enoch 93:2. I, Enoch, will declare . . . according to that which appeared to me in the heavenly vision . . . and have learnt from the heavenly tablets. 3. And Enoch began to recount from the books.

The purpose of the book, to witness their fallen state and betrayal of their ancient covenants, as given in the Joseph Smith version, finds striking confirmation in the ancient records:

Moses 6:45. . . . we know them [our ancestors], and cannot deny, and even the first of all we know, even Adam.
6:46. For a book of remembrance we have written among us, according to the pattern given by the finger of God; and it is given in our own language.

Testament of Abraham. Adam says: Tell me all its [the soul's] deeds that are written down. And immediately an old man [Enoch] came forth from behind the veil with a book in his hand. . . . Then the soul denied, thinking that its deeds would not be remembered. . . . But Adam said: No, there is no lie in this place!

Black 98:7. Think not in
your souls . . . that . . . your
wrongdoings are not observed
nor written down before the
highest. 8. From now on all
your transgressions are
written down day and night
until your judgment.

Black 97:6. And all . . .
your unrighteousness shall be
read out in the presence of the
Great Holy One and in your
own presence; because
(104:9ff) . . . you have got by
through juggling the books
and falsifying reports: that is
how you got your power,
influence, and wealth!

Beatty 98:15. Woe to you
who write false words . . . and
falsify the record. . . . 91:2.
Prepare, ye righteous ones,
and present the records of your
doings as a remembrance, give
them as a testimony before the
angels, that they may bring the
sense of righteousness before
the Most High, for a
remembrance.

Testament of Dan 5:6. (and
other Testaments of the
Twelve Patriarchs). For I have
read in the book of Enoch the
righteous that your prince is
Satan, and that all the spirits
of wickedness will . . . cause
[the sons of Levi] to sin before
the Lord.

While Charles finds passages in this part of the Ethiopian Enoch "very confused" and "clearly corrupt," all the

versions agree on a consistent story: Enoch, while journeying in the highlands passing by a certain sea, has a vision in
which the Lord talks with him and sends him to rebuke the
people; he finds them assembled in a high place and dis-
cusses with them a certain book—a *Hypomnemata*, or
memorial. As a result of what he tells them about the book,
they are completely overcome and cannot raise their eyes
to Enoch or to heaven for shame. The Joseph Smith account
is substantially like that of the Greek and Slavonic texts.

Moses 6:47. And as Enoch
spake forth the words of God
[confirmed by the book], the
people trembled, and could
not stand in his presence.

Gizeh 13:3. They
asked . . . me to read for them
the *Hypomnemata* (memorial,
remembrance) before the face
of the Lord, 5. because they
were in no condition to speak,
neither could they raise their
eyes to the heavens for
shame.

1 Enoch 13:3ff. [In this
version "the passage is very
confused," says Charles,
"clearly corrupt." (P. 30.) 7.
And I went off and sat down
at the waters of Dan, in the
land of Dan to the south of the
west of Hermon. I read their
petition [or memorial,
remembrance] till I fell asleep,
8. and behold . . . I saw
visions of chastisement, and a
voice came bidding me tell the
sons of Heaven and reprimand
them. 9. And when I awaked
I came unto them, and they
were all sitting gathered
together weeping in
"Abelsjail" . . . with their
faces covered.
10. [Then he begins to read
to them from] the book of the

> words of righteousness, and of
> the reprimand . . . in
> accordance with the command
> of the Holy Great One in that
> vision.

Enoch's Visions

Before dealing with the success of Enoch's mission, we must consider more closely the marvelous visions which prepared him for it and which are the most significant part of the Enoch literature and the principal reason for its rejections by the conventional Christian and Jewish scholars of the fourth and following centuries. We refer to the cosmological or astronomical teachings most widely associated with the name of Enoch, who, not content with describing a purely spiritual heaven or beatific vision, insists on bringing real stars and planets into the picture—a thing which medieval and modern theologians find unspeakably crass—the very antithesis of everything worthy of the ethereal name of religion. While the Jewish doctors rejected the old cosmological absorption because it turned out to be altogether too popular with the early Christians,[341] the Christian doctors in turn attacked them as too popular with the gnostic sectaries and even the heathen.[342] Both agreed in tracing back their origin to Enoch.

Thus, quoting Eumolpus (140 B.C.), Eusebius reports that Abraham taught astronomy to the Egyptians at Heliopolis (the great prehistoric Egyptian observatory), giving himself and the Babylonians credit for establishing the science while actually recognizing Enoch as its true discoverer.[343] Syncellus and Cedrenus hand down the tradition, on the authority of Enoch himself, that it was the angel Uriel who taught astronomy to Enoch.[344] To clinch their disapproval, the doctors of Alexandria—the great "spiritualizers"—follow Clement of Alexandria, who maintains that according to Enoch it was the fallen angels who taught "astronomy and divination [*mantiken*] and related sciences [*technas*]" to the human race.[345] Mystics and theologians thereafter rejected Enoch's cosmologies precisely because they were not mystic but scientific, sharing the Christian prejudice due to which "cosmogonic accounts are in fact exceedingly rare both in Israel and in Islam. . . . Mohammed warned that they would lead to atheism—an old Rabbinical idea."[346]

Modern theologians see in Enoch "a curious attempt to reduce the scattered images of the [Old Testament] to a physical system. . . . It seems to repeat in every form the great principle that the world, natural, moral, and spiritual, is under the immediate government of God."[347] And what, we may ask, is wrong with that? The Reverend Michael Stuart, foremost American theologian when the book of Enoch first came to America in the 1838-40 editions, protested that the scriptures "no where introduced such idle and Phantastic speculations about the natural phenomena of the heavens and earth, as we find in the Book of Enoch,"[348] and he speaks for conventional Christianity—even today—when he says, "Every science . . . is entirely foreign to the Scriptures, inasmuch as they were written purely for *moral* and *religious* purposes, and not to give lessons in science," for which reason Enoch's cosmology is at present a sealed book.[349]

The churches are changing their tune so fast today that we must make an effort to remind ourselves that only yesterday Joseph Smith's "cosmism" and literalism were viewed with universal horror and alarm. A leading Catholic theologian of our time assures us that the longing of the Christian is "to be rapt away from matter" and receive "the cup of the spirit which from heaven is held out to earth,"[350] while his eminent Protestant counterpart is pleased to note that, thanks to present-day demythologizing of old teachings, "redemption and the spirit are no longer thought of in the Gnostic manner as quasi-physical entities," in spite of Paul.[351]

It was among the early sectaries that the astronomical

parts of Enoch (72-82) enjoyed their greatest favor, according to Van Andel's study. (Pp. 53, 40.) He notes that the inclusion of the physical world in the story of redemption which was indeed inevitable in a history which is a prologue to the Flood—a very physical event indeed (p. 41)—and that the exponents of such literature very sensibly hold that the cosmos itself cannot very well be left out of the picture of God's dealings with men, beginning with the Creation, another physical event. Is it not a main purpose of the Bible to make the cosmos understandable? (P. 93.) In apocalyptic literature the greatest "emphasis is laid on the [historic personality] of Enoch" as the conveyor of cosmic knowledge. (P. 118.) Long ago J. P. Migne protested that it was the very literal and "scientific" tone of it that rendered such religious literature dangerous, and that the proper apocryphal writings for Catholics to read are those which are frankly popular fables, poetic fantasies, and moral and symbolic tales claiming in the end no historical or physical reality.[252]

It is not our purpose here to discuss Enoch's cosmological discourses, which would take us pleasantly afield but require too much paper. It will be enough to confine our attention to the cosmological passages that can be paralleled in the book of Moses. These parallels are surprisingly plentiful.

We begin with the declaration that Enoch was shown a vision of *everything:* indeed, receiving a total revelation of all things seems to have been a privilege of each of the great founding fathers of the dispensations, from Adam on.

Moses 1:27. . . . as the voice was still speaking, Moses cast his eyes and beheld the earth, yea, even all of it; and there was not a particle of it which he did not behold, discerning it by the spirit of God.

Gizeh 5. For thou hast made all, and hast all authority, and all things appear before thee and are revealed, and thou seest all things.

Secrets 17: (Vaillant, pp. 62f). If you lift your eyes to the heavens the Lord is there, because he made the heavens; and if you look upon the earth or the sea, or if you think of things under the earth, the Lord is there also, for he made all things.

7:67. And the Lord showed Enoch all things, even unto the end of the world.

1 Enoch 19:3. And I, Enoch, alone saw the vision, the ends of all things: and no man shall see as I have seen.

7:4. . . . and he [the Lord] said unto me: Look, and I will show unto thee the world for the space of many generations.

Gizeh 2:2. See the earth, and consider the works done in it from the beginning to the end, . . . and all the works of God will appear to you.

bin Gorion 1:251. The Lord showed Adam everything, including Abraham's story. . . . 253. And "he [Adam] took a leaf and wrote down his Testament, and sealed it up unto the Lord, the Metatron [Enoch], and Adam."

Apocalypse of Abraham 21:1. He said to me [Abraham] look! . . . 2. I look down and behold the six heavens and all that is in them, and also the earth and her fruits and all that moves upon her, and her spirits, and the power of her inhabitants [men] . . . 3. and the lower regions . . . 4. [and] the sea and its islands, the animals and its fishes . . . 9. [and] I saw a mighty host of men, women, and children. . . .

1:28. And he [Moses] beheld also the inhabitants thereof, and there was not a soul which he beheld not; and he discerned them by the Spirit of God; and their numbers were great, even numberless. . . .

Secrets, Ms. R., ch. 10. The Angel Braboil [umpire or scorekeeper] said to me [Enoch]: Sit down and write all the spirits of men, all those who have not yet been born . . . everything to the end of this world, even from the foundation thereof! . . . And I wrote down all the affairs of men.

1:29. And he beheld many lands; and each land was called earth, and there were inhabitants on the face thereof.

1 Enoch 33:1. I went to the ends of the earth and saw there great beasts, and each differed from the other; and (I saw) birds also differing . . . 2. and to the East . . . I saw the ends of the earth whereon the heaven rests.

Jubilees 4:19 (Charles) or 4:181 in Bekker, p. 17. And what was and what will be he saw . . . as it will happen to the children of men throughout their generations until the day of judgment; he saw and understood everything, and wrote his testimony.

6:42. . . . I [Enoch] beheld a vision; and lo, the heavens I saw, and the Lord spake with me.

Secrets 13 (Vaillant, pp. 40ff). And now my children, I know all things, some from the mouth of the Lord, others that I have seen myself. . . . I have written of the extremities of the heavens and what is in them; I have measured the movements of their hosts . . . I have explored the places of the clouds . . . I have written about the deposits of the snow and reservoirs of ice, . . . how all these things are controlled by the power of God.

Origen, "First Principles," in *P.G.* 11:409. In the same book attributed to Enoch is written: "*Universas materias perspexi*," which would imply that he had seen every category of matter, divided not separate and distinct species from a single universal substance, to wit, of men or animals, or heavens, or Sun, or of everything that is in this world.

6:36. And he beheld the spirits that God had created; and he beheld also things which were not visible to the natural eye.

BHM, 5:176. Enoch knows the names of the Sarim [lords, administrators] who administer every department of existence. . . . Enoch knew not only all the secrets of the Makrokosmos, but of the Mikrokosmos as well.

The ancients recognize that others, from Adam to Daniel, also had the great Universal Vision, but give Enoch a special rating. Enoch alone, says the Ethiopian Book of Mysteries, saw it all from the beginning to end, before it happened.[353] "The Lord has chosen thee more than any other man on the earth, and has appointed thee the Scribe of His Creations, both visible and invisible. . . ." (Secrets, Ms. R, Vaillant, p. 61, see n. 17.)

Joseph Smith's preoccupation with mountains in his Enoch account would appear suspicious were it not that the other Enoch texts have the same obsession:

Moses 7:2. . . . there came a voice out of heaven, saying—Turn ye, and get ye upon the mount Simeon. [n.b. Simeon means "place of hearing," hence "audience, assembly"] 3. And it came to pass that I turned and went up on the mount; and as I stood upon the mount, I beheld the heavens open, and I was clothed upon with glory; 4. And I saw the Lord; and he stood before my face, and he talked with me.

Gizeh 32:2. And thence I took my way along the tops of these mountains, keeping far from towards the East of the earth, and I passed above the Erythrean Sea, and went up to the peaks [akron] and from there passed on higher to Zoti-el. 3. And I went to the paradise of righteousness, and beheld from afar among its trees . . . two trees in particular, great and laden, . . . and the Tree of Knowledge [phroneseos], of whose fruit the holy one ate and received great understanding.

1 Enoch 17:2. And they brought me to the point of darkness, and to a mountain whose summit reached to heaven. 3. And I saw the place of the luminaries.

6:37. And . . . Enoch went forth . . . standing upon the hills and the high places. . . .

42. As I journeyed . . . by the sea east, I beheld a vision; and lo, the heavens I saw, and the Lord spake with me, and gave me commandment.

BHM 5:172. God raised me up . . . in the heaven above, to be a witness against them for all time to come . . . and the holy one, Blessed Be He, made me one with the high place as a prince and a ruler among the angels of the ministry.

The ancients were quite aware of how Enoch's mysterious departure to heaven and Moses' ascent of Mt. Nebo and his disappearance (Deuteronomy 32:49) resembled each other. Others have also found mountains to be places of special closeness to the Lord—for example, Elijah, Nephi, and the famous Rabbi Ishmael.

2 Nephi 4:24. My voice have I sent up on high; and angels came down and ministered unto me. 25. And upon the wings of his Spirit hath my body been carried away upon exceeding high mountains. And mine eyes have beheld great things, yea, even too great for man; therefore I was bidden that I should not write them.

BHM 5:170. R. Ishmael: When I went up to the mountaintop to contemplate the Markabah, I entered into the six temples, room by room. Arriving at the entrance to the seventh [the Holy of Holies], I stood to pray before God; and I lifted up my eyes and said: Lord of Eternity, . . . grant me in this hour the crown of the priesthood. . . . And deliver me from Satan. And the Metatron [Enoch] came who [served?] the angel, the Prince of the Presence, and spread his wings and came to meet me with great joy . . . and he took me with his hand and raised me up.

In these passages, as throughout the book of Enoch, imagery and reality seem to meet and fuse in a peculiar way. Reference to the Holy of Holies is unmistakable in the last passage cited, recalling the well-known Ziggurat concept of the ancients in which the temple itself was to represent a mountain by which one mounted to heaven and the presence of God. Let us return for a moment to Nephi's story of his father's vision, which in some ways parallels Enoch's:

1 Nephi 1:4. . . . in the commencement of the first year . . . 5. . . . my father Lehi . . . prayed unto the Lord, yea, even with all his heart, in behalf of his people. . . . 7. . . . he returned to his own house at Jerusalem; and he cast himself upon his bed, being overcome with the Spirit. . . . 8. And

2 Enoch 1:2. On the first day of the month I was in my house alone, and I rested on my bed and slept [BHM 4:127: "he was praying before God in (his) house and chamber"], 3. and as I slept great grief came upon my heart, and I wept with mine eyes in sleep. . . . 4. There appeared to me two men . . . 8. and these

being thus overcome with the Spirit, he was carried away in a vision, even that he saw the heavens open, and he thought he saw God sitting upon his throne, surrounded with numberless concourses of angels.

men said to me: Have courage Enoch, do not fear . . . the eternal God sent us to thee, and lo! Thou shalt today ascend with us into heaven.

The manner in which the prophet is caught up is of particular concern and interest to the ancients. What are "the wings of the Spirit"? Lehi was "carried away in a vision, even that . . . he *thought* he saw God sitting upon his throne, surrounded with . . . angels," to match which Enoch says, "My spirit was translated, and it ascended to heaven; and I saw the holy sons of God . . . 10. and with them the Head of Days . . . 11. and my spirit was transfigured." (1 Enoch 71:10, 11.) The old writers also treat the idea:

2 Nephi 4:25. Upon the wings of his Spirit hath my body been carried away upon exceeding high mountains. And mine eyes have beheld great things, yea, even too great for man.

BHM 5:170. R. Ishmael [a stand-in for Enoch] was on a high mountain when the Metatron [often equated with Enoch] came, who served the angels, the Prince of Presence, and he spread his wings and came to meet me with great joy to deliver me from the hands of Satan. And he took me by the hand and raised me up.

Moses 1:1. Moses was caught up into an exceedingly high mountain.

BHM 6:175. God laid his hand upon me and raised me and exalted me . . . and seventy-two wings raised me up, so many on one side and so many on the other; it was as if the world was filled with wings. . . .

Abraham 2:7. I cause the wind and the fire to be my chariot; I say to the mountains—Depart hence—and behold, they are taken away by a whirlwind.

1 Enoch 39:3. And in those days a whirlwind carried me off from the earth, and set me down at the end of the heavens. 4. And I saw another vision, the dwelling places of the Holy One, the resting-place of the righteous.

Book of Adam 1:238. So Seth arose and prayed, and put off his envelope of flesh. . . . Then the winds of heaven lifted him up in the midst of myriads of spirits . . . and placed him on a shining throne.

As everyone knows, the Hebrew *ruach* means both "wind" and "spirit," giving rise to much speculation. A typical example would be Enoch's declaration that Adam "was caught away by the Spirit of the Lord, and was carried down into the water," (Moses 6:64), or that Enoch's people "were caught up by the powers of heaven into Zion." (7:27.) The last indicates that we are dealing with forms of power yet unknown to men, for which the words "wind" and "spirit" may be taken to represent unknown quantities. Competent scientists have now begun to explore the reality of heretofore unknown forms of power,[354] with surprising results.[355] One of the special characteristics of the Enoch literature is the constant interplay between the physical and psychic, in which the Joseph Smith text leads the way.

Enoch and the Cosmos

Clement of Rome, in the opening lines of the *Recognitions*, says that what drew him to investigate the gospel and join the church was his burning desire to find answers to the great questions of life: "When was this world made? What was there before it? Was it always there? Is there a life after death?" He says that he wore himself out at school but could find no professor or philosopher who could give him a satisfactory answer.[356] It was such "constant seeking for knowledge," as H. D. Betz points out, that necessarily carried the early Christians "beyond history . . . into astronomy and astrology."[357] The later church fathers fought with "bitter polemic" against the tendency to ask such questions,[358] and the rabbis declared that "anyone who studies the subjects of the Creation or the Chariot, or who puts his mind to the questions What is above? What is below? What is beyond? What is in the eternities?—it were better for him had he not come into this world!"[359]

Enoch was one of the curious ones: "I raised my eyes and contemplated this universe, the sky with its glittering stars, the sun and the moon, . . . the angels [who] control the water, the wind, the fire, the earth and all that is in it, the mountains, the sea, the planets, and the trees. Who could tell me where all these powers take their rise? How do they operate? How do they keep going? Who can explain to me the alterations of dawn and dusk, day and night, moon and stars?" He summarizes: "Thus as I viewed the organizations of this world I was troubled." And prostrating himself, he prayed for enlightenment.[360]

The objection of the religious to the astronomical teachings of the book of Enoch is that they are not in the least bit spiritual: "Through all these chapters," writes Charles of 1 Enoch 72-79, "there is not a single ethical reference. The author has no other interest save a scientific one. . . . [We] have to deal with a complete and purely scientific treatise."[361] Moreover, the interest is in the sun, moon, and stars solely as regulators of the special calendar which set the Enoch-sectaries apart from the rest of the world in their observances.[362] And yet Van Andel recognizes that the Enoch cosmology was for those people something more than calendar: it was nothing less than the knowledge of the eternities, "before all else the secret of the Creation . . . God's plan for the entire universe, which had been revealed to the community of the righteous" as a fundamental and organic part of the gospel.[363]

This broader aspect of the higher knowledge is, however, conspicuously missing from the Ethiopian 1 Enoch, engrossed as it is in the meticulous business of counting and measuring times and cycles, which was to titillate the vanity and challenge the invention of generations of cabalists, cultists, astrologers, schoolmen, and pyramidologists for ages to come, and which indeed justified the doctors of the church and synagogue in their distaste for the whole business. But the cosmology of the Joseph Smith translation of Enoch in the book of Moses is something quite different—a sober concern with a few basic principles which differs so radically from the Ethiopian Enoch that Joseph's critics might well discover here a clear case of outright refutation of the latter-day scripture by the ancient sources were it not that his Enoch text is impressively vindicated by the closely matching concepts of the Slavonic Enoch. The reason for this particular affinity must be examined at a later time; for the present it is sufficient to recognize how strongly Joseph Smith's cosmology is supported by ancient texts known only long after his death. The main subjects common to these documents are the mystery of glory, the universal ongoing creation, the plurality of worlds, and the relationship of the worlds to God and to each other.

It is standard procedure in apocalyptic writings to have the hero introduced to cosmology in the course of his visit to the heavenly realms; in these accounts the leitmotif is *glory* in varying degrees, and what applies to one heavenly visit applies to another, so that the same descriptions fit the experience of Enoch, Moses, Abraham, Elijah, etc.[364]

First, the principle is laid down that glory can be experienced only to the degree one is qualified to share it. The person who would behold God's glory must himself first be "clothed upon with glory," i.e., enveloped in that same glory: ". . . being clothed with robes of righteousness, . . . in glory even as I am, . . . to receive a crown of righteousness, and to be clothed upon, even as I am, to be with me, *that we may be one.*" (D&C 29:12-13; italics added.) Even so with Enoch:

Moses 7:3. [Enoch:] . . . I beheld the heavens open, and I was clothed upon with glory; 4. And I saw the Lord; and he stood before my face, and he talked with me, even as a man talketh one with another, face to face.

Secrets 22:8 (Morfill, p. 28.) And the Lord said to Michael: "Go and take Enoch out from his earthly garments, and anoint him with my sweet ointment and put him into the garments of my glory. . . ." 10. And I [Enoch] looked at myself, and was like one of his glorious ones. And there was no difference. (See also Slavonic Enoch 9, Vaillant, pp. 25f.)

Text B, 22 (in R. H. Charles, *Apocrypha and Pseudepigrapha*, 2:443). After Enoch is "clothed in garments of glory . . . the Lord with his mouth summoned me and said: Have courage, Enoch, fear not, stand before my face to eternity. And . . . Michael brought me before the face of God."

Assumption of Moses, Introduction §3 [". . . it (the Assumption of Moses) shows many affinities with 2 Enoch," Charles, ibid., p. 409]. At his death while still "in the flesh" Moses is met by Enoch-Metatron, who clothes him with light so that he will be able to see the angels; and his body was transformed into "a flame of fire."

BHM 5: xlii. In this Hebrew Enoch Book, R. Ishmael tells how in the seventh temple he "beholds Enoch who has been transformed in the Angel Metatron Sar hā-Panīm [of the Face]," and who tells him how upon becoming an angel he was "clothed with all glories."

The reason for the transformation is clear:

Moses 1:14. . . . I could not look upon God, except his glory should come upon me.

Gizeh 14:21. And no angel could . . . look upon his face, because it is fearful and glorious, and no flesh can look upon him. 14. And I began to tremble and to shake, and fell upon my face.

1:5. . . . and no man can behold all my glory, and afterwards remain in the flesh on the earth.

Evangelium Veritatis, folio XV[r] and folio XV, p. 29. The shock of the sight of God would utterly destroy those unprepared for it.

1:11. But now mine own eyes have beheld God; but not my natural, but my spiritual eyes, for my natural eyes could not have beheld; for I should have withered and died in his presence.

Sophia Jesu Christi 79. No flesh can endure his presence, nor can his appearance be described. But he showed himself in pure and perfect flesh to us on the mountain, and we were sore afraid.

7:3-4. [Enoch:] I was clothed upon with glory; And I saw the Lord.

Gospel of Philip 105:28-34, 106:1ff. You can see only what you are like, therefore on the Mountain of Transfiguration the Apostles had to be made great in order to see the greatness of Christ.

1:11. [Moses:] . . . I beheld his face, for I was transfigured before him.

Evangelium Veritatis, folio XV^v, p. 30. They can bear the knowledge of God to that degree to which they can bear the light.

It is a general principle that applies to all levels of glory; if one is not prepared, the experience of glory can only cause anxiety and alarm:

Moses 1:11. I beheld his face, *for I was transfigured* before him. 25. He [Moses] beheld his glory again, for it was upon him. [Zechariah, Mary, the shepherds in the field, the apostles on the Mount of Transfiguration, etc., all were "sore afraid" in the presence of heavenly glory. Italics added.]

1 Enoch 71:1. And . . . my spirit was translated and it ascended into the heavens: and I saw the holy Sons of God. 10. And with them the Head of Days, His head white and pure as wool, and his raiment indescribable. 11. And *my* spirit was transfigured. [Italics added.]

BHM 5:170. The Metatron [Enoch] . . . said to me: Come in peace, . . . and they guided me to see the Shekinah and presented me before the Throne of Glory to contemplate the Merkabah; and when the Princes of the Merkabah saw me, and the Seraphim of flame, they placed their eyes upon me and I trembled and became ill and fell from my stand and swooned before the Zohar, the sight of their eyes, and the glory of the appearance of their faces.
172. And when the Seraphim turned their faces towards me I feared and trembled and fell from my standing-place and swooned.

Gizeh 14:24. And I was
upon my face . . . and
trembling, and the Lord with
his own mouth called me, and
said: Come here, Enoch, and
listen to my word. 25. . . . one
of the holy ones raised me up
and stood me on my feet . . .
and I held my face down and
covered. [After this interview
when Enoch went down to the
people, *they* could not bear to
look upon *him*. See Moses'
similar experience after
descending Mount Sinai,
Exodus 34:30.]

Accordingly, when the higher glory is withdrawn and
the individual reverts to his own nature, he finds himself
weak and helpless:

Moses 1:9. And the
presence of God withdrew
from Moses, that his glory was
not upon Moses; and Moses
was left unto himself. And as
he was left unto himself, he fell
unto the earth.
10. And it came to pass that
it was for the space of many
hours before Moses did again
receive his natural strength
like unto man.

1 Enoch 39:14. And my face
was changed; for I could no
longer behold.

The Combat of Adam and
Eve 1:301. And the Lord said
to Adam: While you obeyed
me the light was with you and
you could see the most distant
things but now you cannot
even see what is near to you by
the power of the flesh. Then
Adam and Eve fell down
helpless.[365]

Apocalypse of Abraham
30:1 And as he was still
speaking, I found myself
already upon the earth, 2. and
said . . . 3. I am no more now
in the glory in which I was
above, and what my heart
sought to know I did not
understand.

The early Jewish and Christian traditions are full of accounts in which Satan tried to beguile men by counterfeit glory, even appearing as an angel of light. The righteous however are given the discernment of spirits, and are able to endure true glory—their "confidence wax[es] strong" even " in the presence of God." (D&C 121:45.) Accordingly Satan's false glory never deceives the patriarchs:

Moses 1:12. . . . Satan came tempting him, saying: Moses, son of man, worship me.

13. And . . . Moses looked upon Satan and said: Who art thou? For behold, I am a son of God, . . . and where is thy glory, that I should worship thee?

14. For behold, I could not look upon God, except his glory should come upon me, and I were transfigured before him. But I can look upon thee in the natural man. Is it not so, surely?

15. . . . where is thy glory, for it is darkness unto me? And I can judge between thee and God. . . .

16. Get thee hence, Satan; deceive me not; . . .

18. . . . his glory has been upon me, wherefore I can judge between him and thee. Depart hence, Satan.

19. And now, when Moses had said these words, Satan cried with a loud voice, and ranted upon the earth, and commanded, saying: I am the Only Begotten, worship me!

Book of Adam 1:170. After the Angel of Life departed . . . Enoch arose in joy, clothed in glory to preach to the world. But the seven planets conspired against their brethren and announced that the real glory was only a trick crying out: They have stolen our glory! They threw all the elements into confusion.

Falasha Anthology, 100. [Abraham:] I do not know whether thou art a great angel . . . in this glory, because I cannot see thy praise. When angels come to me I feel strong, my soul is fortified . . . but when thou camest my soul was troubled . . . my tongue became heavy and weak.

Apocalypse of Elijah, p. 197. The Son of Destruction shall show himself and say: I am anointed! though he is not. Do not believe him! [Ephraim Syr., 9. He will surely make all the signs which our Lord performs in the world; the dead however, he will not rise up, because he has not power over the spirits.]

20. And . . . Moses began to fear exceedingly; and as he began to fear, he saw the bitterness of hell. Nevertheless, . . . he commanded, saying: Depart from me, Satan, for this one God only will I worship, which is the God of glory.

22. And . . . with weeping, and wailing, and gnashing of teeth, . . . he [Satan] departed hence.

25. And calling upon the name of God, he [Moses] beheld his glory again, for it was upon him.

Gizeh 13:1. But Enoch (manuscript much confused) said to Azael, Depart! [*poreyou*], there is no peace in thee! Great offence [*krima*] hath gone forth from thee . . .

2. And I will no longer detain you or discuss with you because of your trickery and your evil works . . . 3. Then going forth among them [the people] I [Enoch] told them all, and they all feared and a great fear and trembling seized them.

Zechariah 3:2. And the Lord said unto Satan: The Lord rebuke thee, O Satan; . . . 4. Take away the filthy garments from [Joshua] . . . Behold, . . . I will clothe thee with change of raiment. 5. . . . They set a fair mitre upon his head, and clothed him with garments. And the angel of the Lord stood by.

Apocalypse of Abraham 12. (The angels take Abraham to the top of Horeb) 13:7. [The angel:] This one you see is godlessness—it is the [fallen Angel] Azazel [Satan]. 8. Then he said to him: Shame on thee, Azazel! 9. For Abraham's part is in the heaven, but thy part is on earth, 10. which thou hast chosen for thy home . . . 14. Depart from this man . . . 15. for behold his garment [of glory] which once belonged to

thee in heaven is now lain
aside for him, and the
corruption that is his shall pass
over to thee!

1 Enoch 63:7. [The kings of
the earth say]: We have not
believed before him, nor
glorified the name of the Lord
of spirits . . . but our hope
was in the sceptre of our
kingship, and in *our* glory. 8.
And in the day of suffering and
tribulation he saves us not.
[Italics added.]

The faithful cannot escape a cosmic view of things because it is the *creation* that declares the glory of God:

Moses 6:63. . . . all things
are created and made to bear
record of me, . . . all things
bear record of me.

1 Enoch 69:21-24. The
stars . . . winds, lightnings,
. . . and all these believe and
give thanks before the Lord of
Spirits, and glorify Him with
all their power.

7:28. . . . and Enoch bore
record of it . . . saying: . . .
30. . . . were it possible that
man could number the
particles of the earth, . . . it
would not be a beginning to
the number of thy creations.

Secrets 10 (Vaillant). And
without resting I wrote down
the signs of all the creation.

Secrets 10 (Vaillant). And
the Lord called Berebel
[Brabeusel, Thoth] . . . who
was skilled in writing down all
the works of the Lord. And the
Lord said to Berebel: Take a
book from the deposit
[*khranilnitz*], and give a pen to
Enoch, and explain to him and
dictate the books to him. [So
the angel taught Enoch] all the
works [doings, makings] of the
heavens and the earth and the
sea and all the elements and

time-periods and
commandments and
instructions . . . while I wrote
down all the signs [*znamienia,
semiea* = notes]. So he wrote the
360 books of the creation.

Jubilees 2:1. And the Angel
of the Presence spake to Moses
according to the word of the
Lord, saying: Write the
complete history of the
Creation.
4:17. And [Enoch] was the
first among men that are born
upon the earth who learnt
writing and knowledge and
wisdom and who wrote down
the signs of heaven. [The
Greek adds: "and arithmetic
and geometry, and all the
Sophian."]

Creation is presented as a universal ongoing process:

Moses 1:37. . . . The
heavens . . . cannot be
numbered unto man; . . . 38.
And as one earth shall pass
away, and the heavens thereof
even so shall another come;
and there is no end to my
works.

Zohar iii: 61a, b (Brody).[366]
This we have learned: Before
the Holy . . . created this
world, He had created worlds
and destroyed them.

The creation as process is emphasized by the frequent
occurrence of the word *creation* in the *plural*, usually in
proclaiming the greatness and majesty of God—"millions
of earths like this . . . would not be a beginning to the
number of thy creations" (Moses 7:30); "And thou hast
taken Zion to thine own bosom, from all thy creations"
(7:31); "I can stretch forth mine hands and hold all the
creations which I have made; and mine eye can pierce them
also" (7:36); ". . . and all the creations of God mourned"

(7:56); ". . . Zion . . . shall come forth out of all the creations which I have made" (7:64). Such passages clearly imply that creation is an ongoing drama:

Moses 1:38. And as one earth shall pass away, and the heavens thereof even so shall another come; and there is no end to my works.

bin Gorion, 1:286. Seven imperfect worlds were all destroyed because of wickedness.
1:59. There are 18,000 worlds known only to God.
Book of Adam, 1:225. The life-span of each planet is different: Fire and water form circles around the 18,000 worlds.

The same idea is conveyed in the Secrets of Enoch 11 (Charles, *Apocrypha and Pseudepigrapha* 2:436), where the heavenly bodies in their "successive going" are "ever going and returning, [having] rest neither by day nor by night." Thus (Secrets of Enoch 16) "the sun is a great creation, whose circuit lasts twenty-eight years and begins again from the beginning." "Hear Enoch, . . . not to My angels have I told . . . their rise, nor my endless realm, nor have they understood my creating, which I tell thee today." (24:3.) "There is born light from light, there came forth a great age, and showed all creation." (25:3.) "I want to create another world . . . [31:3] . . . and there is no counsellor nor inheritor to my creations." (33:4.) In manuscript R, chapter 10, of the Slavonic Enoch, he sees "the exchanges of all the elements and their progressions, and their manner of changing according to the signs of the Zodiac, and the progress of their changes," and so on.

The idea of creation as an ongoing process involving many participants was, of course, offensive to the doctors with their monistic obsession. "It is a constant concern of the Midrash," writes E. Hahn, "why God needed six days and ten words for the creation when a single gesture would have sufficed."[367] And so they effectively silenced the old teaching of creation as a process.

Equally offensive was the idea of a *plurality of worlds*, countering, as it did, a basic teaching of Aristotle and the evidence of common sense that this world, being heaviest, must necessarily be in the center of everything and mankind the only rational animal, not only on earth, but in all the immensity of the universe. "Millions of earths like this" was quite unthinkable—even comical. "Since God didn't even need this world," as Jonathan Edwards vociferously proclaimed, "why should he want to create even more?" Since "the fullness of good is attained once for all in God . . . ," ran the official argument, "God has no need of a world and is indifferent to it and all that goes on in it."[368] Quite the opposite with Enoch:

Moses 7:30. And were it possible that man could number the particles of the earth, yea, millions of earths like this, it would not be a beginning to the number of thy creations.

Mishnat ha-Zohar 1:127ff.[369] God's creations are *en sof*, "without end."

1:37. . . . The heavens [galaxies], they are many, and they cannot be numbered unto man.
1:33. . . . worlds without number have I created.

Apocryphon of John, p. 27. The heavens, they cannot be numbered to man.

bin Gorion 1:59. The heavens are without number, and every one of the vaults is like an independent world which in turn contains 1,000 other worlds.

Berayta fol. 54a. The foolish Minaeans believe that this is the only world there is! Actually there are worlds without number.

Secrets 13 (Vaillant). And now, my children, I know all things. . . . I have written of the extremities of the heavens and what is in them. I have measured the movements of their hosts. I have completed the counting of the stars, a vast multitude without number. No man can conceive of their revolutions [or orbits]; the angels themselves do not know their number.

2 Enoch 40:2. I have measured and described the stars, the great countless multitude of them. 3. Not even the angels see their number.

With all its pluralism we are never allowed to forget that "from first to last one mind alone dominates the whole boundless complex," since all receive the instructions and their inspiration from a single source:[370]

Moses 1:35. But only an account of this earth, and the inhabitants thereof, give I unto you. For behold, there are many worlds that have passed away by the word of my power. And there are many that now stand, and innumerable are they unto man; but all things are numbered unto me, for they are mine and I know them. 37. . . . The heavens . . . cannot be numbered unto man; but they are numbered unto me, for they are mine.

7:30. . . . millions of earths like this . . . and yet thou art there, and thy bosom is there.

Gizeh 9:5. For thou hast made them all, and hast all authority [exousian], and all things appear before thee and are plainly revealed [akalypta], and thou seest all things.

1 Enoch 84:3. Thou hast made and rulest all things, . . . wisdom departs not from the place of thy throne, nor turns away from thy presence, and Thou knowest and seest and hearest everything.

1 Enoch 39:11. He knows before the world was created what is forever, and what will be from generation unto generation.

7:36. Wherefore, I can stretch forth mine hands and hold all the creations which I have made; and mine eye can pierce them also.

Origen, *P.G.* 11:409. He made all things according to number and measure. For with God nothing is without limit and measure, since by his mind he comprehends all things.

Clement of Alexandria, *P.G.* 9:721f. Psalm 18:2 refers to the plurality of the heavens, where even the demons all recognize that Christ is the Lord. The teaching is from Enoch.

6:61. . . . the Comforter . . . which maketh alive all things; that which knoweth all things, and hath all power . . .

Clement quotes Daniel, quoting Enoch: (*P.G.* 9:700) And I saw all substance. For the Abyss which is boundless, comes under the same *hypostasis* [definition] [as matter], being limited and controlled by the power of God.

One of the most remarkable teachings of the Joseph Smith book of Enoch as found in the Pearl of Great Price book of Moses is the doctrine of a *spiritual creation* of all things that preceded the creation of this earth. Significantly, this doctrine finds its fullest support in the Slavonic Enoch text and is not found in the Ethiopian:

Moses 3:5. . . . For I, the Lord God, created all things . . . spiritually, before they were naturally upon the . . . earth. . .

Secrets 17 (Vaillant). And Enoch answered the people saying: Hear my children! Before anything was [*prezhdye dazhe vsya nye byila*], and before

3:7. . . . and man became a living soul. . . . nevertheless, all things were before created; but spritually were they created.

6:51. I am God; I made the world, and men before they were in the flesh.

6:44. . . . the earth . . . the foundation thereof . . . he laid it, an host of men hath he brought in upon the face thereof.

6:45-46. . . . we . . . cannot deny, . . . for a book of remembrance we have written among us.

the whole creation took place, the Lord established the Age of Creation [n. 2, Adoil], and after that he made all the Creation, both visible and invisible; and after all that he created man in his own image. He gave him eyes to see, ears to hear with, and a mind to counsel; and then he prepared the set times and places. 13. I swear unto you my children . . . that before man was in the womb of his mother we were prepared, each individual, and a place for each spirit . . . and that each should sojourn [here] in his proper time, that man thereby might be tested in the balance. Yea my children . . . there has been prepared in advance a place for every soul. And I have put in writing the work of every man, and no living person can hide himself or dissimulate his works.

Ms. R, ch. 11. I created man with a nature both visible and invisible; and reason recognized his image as another and lesser creation within the greater, and inversely the greater contained the lesser. [Referring to spirit and body as two separate creations.]

bin Gorion, 1:281. The world was created in two stages, the first being a spiritual creation.

2 Enoch 24:4. Before all
things were visible, I [God]
used to go about in the
invisible things. . . . 5. And I
conceived the thought of
placing foundations and of
creating a visible creation.

Secrets 10 (Vaillant). Then
the angel Braboil said: Sit
down and write all the spirits
of men, all those who have not
been born yet, and the places
which have been prepared for
them. All these things were
prepared since before the
foundation of the world.

Zohar iii: 61 s-b Brody: "And
everything which is found in
this world has been before,
and has passed before him and
has been arranged [organized]
before Him . . . all the
creations of the world which
have existed in each
generation, before they came
into this world, have existed
before Him in their *true* form
[*d'yaqnah*], even all the souls of
the children of man have been
before they came down to the
world, have all been formed
before Him in heaven in the
very likeness that they have in
this world.

The council in heaven described in the fourth chapter of
Moses is reflected again in the Enoch section, confirmed by
other Enoch texts:

Moses 6:51. . . . I am God;
I made the world, and men
before they were in the flesh.

Secrets 11 (Vaillant). Enoch
went to the Lord who taught
him all about the Creation and

52. . . . If thou wilt turn unto me, . . . in [his] name . . . whatsoever ye shall ask, it shall be given you. 57. . . . the name of his Only Begotten is the Son of Man. . . . 62. . . . This is the plan of salvation unto all men, through the blood of mine Only Begotten, who shall come in the meridian of time.

his works . . . He saw matter unorganized before the Creation . . . the Council in Heaven . . . He saw Satan Arouchaz aspire and get cast out to become the foundation of lower things, beyond which there is great darkness and nothing.

1 Enoch 48:2. And at that hour the Son of Man was named in the presence of the Lord of spirits. . . . 3. Yea, before the sun and the signs were created, . . . his name was named before the Lord of spirits. 4. He shall be a staff to the righteous whereon to stay themselves and not fall. . . . 5. All who dwell on earth shall fall down and worship before him.

BHM 5:174. [The angels:] God our Lord of the Universe! It is not good what the First Ones say before thee. Wilt thou never create Adam again? [God answered:] I have made and I remove, and I am long-suffering and I deliver! And forthwith they saw me [Enoch], and they said before his face: What is the merit of this one, that he should come up to the highest heights?

A little-known part of the creation story is the great Creation Hymn sung in the great assembly. We hear it reverberating in Enoch's declaration, "All things are created and made to bear record of me." (Moses 6:63.) "At dawn," says the Slavonic Enoch, "the elements sing the Creation Hymn, and all the birds sing and he who gives the light ar-

rives and gives light to his creation," for the morning hymn
is the Creation Hymn. (Job 38:7; *IQS Manual of Discipline*,
pl. 10.) Enoch joins in with "Holy, holy, holy! is the Lord of
spirits: he filleth the earth with spirits." (1 Enoch 39:12.) A
vision was opened up to Enoch by God (Secrets 31:1): "I
made the heavens open to him, that he could see the
heavens sing the song of victory and the gloomless night,"
or as the Gizeh text (1:2) puts it, "A vision of the Holy One
in heaven. He showed me and I heard the holy acclama-
tions of him, and as I heard I also understood everything by
seeing it." That the acclamation is repeated in the Joseph
Smith Enoch is clearly shown in a fragment from the Dead
Sea Scrolls:

Moses 7:31. . . . from all thy creations, from all eternity . . . and naught but peace, justice, and truth is the habitation of thy throne; and mercy shall go before thy face and have no end.	*11 Q Ps^a Creat.* Grace and truth surround his presence; truth and justice are the foundation of his throne. . . . By the knowledge of his mind he brought the dawn, and all the angels who saw it happen sang aloud. For he showed them what they had not known.
	Apocalypse of Abraham 17:14. O Light, which shone before the morning light appeared to thy creatures . . . 15. In thy heavenly abode no other light is necessary.

   In the ongoing creation the establishment of new
worlds is accompanied or represented by a stretching out
of *curtains*. These would seem to keep each world in its
proper relationship to the others. A commonplace of
apocalyptic literature is that God himself is necessarily
screened from sight by a veil, as by the cloud on the Mount
of Transfiguration.

Moses 7:30. . . . millions of earths like this . . . would not be a beginning to the number of thy creations; and thy curtains are stretched out still.

Clement of Alexandria, *P.G.* 9:677. That place itself is one of fire [eternal burnings]. Therefore it is said that it has a veil, lest things be consumed by the sight of [Him]. Only the Archangel can enter into his presence, as a type of which the High Priests once a year entered the Holy of Holies.

T.U. 8:368. The topos of Jeu, where Jeu, "the Father of the Treasure of Light" rules as "King of the Treasure of Light," is separated from other beings by a veil [*katapetasma*].

Gospel of Philip 132:23. The veil at first concealed how God controlled the Creation, but when the veil is rent [we will know]. 133:14. If some are of the tribe of the Priesthood, these will be able to go within the veil with the High Priests.

1 Jeu 39. At this topos the Watchers move the veils aside and you enter into the presence of the Father, who gives you His name and His seal.

The purpose of numerous curtains or veils is to apportion to each world the light it is ready to receive. When Moses asked about the other worlds, the Lord informed him that he was not to know about them at the present and Moses agreed to be satisfied with learning "concerning this earth, and the inhabitants thereof, and also the heavens, and then thy servant will be content."

(Moses 1:36.) Numerous ancient documents attest to the curtains' existence:

> "And . . . all the powers of the universe [*Pleroma*] . . . sang a great hymn of praise, . . . and he received the [creation] hymn, and made a veil for their worlds, surrounding them like . . . a wall." (2. Gnostic Work, 47a., in *T.U.* 8:260.)

> "And that mystery knows . . . why the stars . . . and the disks of the light-givers have arisen, and why the firmament [has come into existence] with all its veils." (Pistis Sophia 214.)

> "The world is a system of concentric shells, veils, or vestments, each a *Hekal* or palace or room of the temple. Man is organized on the same principles." (Old Hebrew Book of Enoch was the Hekhaloth, a term explained in the Zohar, Bereshith 20a.)

> "There is a place from which all aeons and all worlds take their origin and prototype: a place of shadowless light and indescribable joy; . . . and there is a veil between the worlds." (Apocryphon of John 60:116, 118.)

> "The 24 invisible [bodies of heaven] are 10,000 times brighter than the Sun, . . . whose light must pass through many veils [to reach us]" so that we do not see it as it really is. (Pistis Sophia 186.)

"[If] the Guardian of the Inhabited earth [did not spread out its wings to absorb the fire-like rays of the sun] the human race could not survive, nor any other form of life." (3 Apocalypse of Baruch 6:3, 5-6.)

"Fire and water form a circle around the 18,000 worlds [making them a type of unity] . . . Above the veil are the heavens." (For "heavens" read "fire and water," the enveloping cloud; N. Sed. *REJ* 124:75, 39.)

As a place of probation (2 Nephi 2:21), this world must be isolated, both as a testing-ground and as quarantine to avoid infecting others:

Moses 7:36. . . . among all the workmanship of mine hands there has not been so great wickedness as among thy brethren.

Sophia Jesu Christi, 118-19. He has created the veil [curtain, *katapetasma*] between what is imperishable and those who later came into being, so that which is set apart [marked off, numbered] to come into existence might follow after all the other ages and the [primal] chaos, that this flesh might be tested [in struggle] for error. But these formed a veil of spirit.

Sophia Jesu Christi 120. [Light reaches] all the inhabitants of the world of chaos . . . that he might place the veils which were there in their proper order [*hormazein*].

T.U. 8:402. [Jeu:] The
Firmament is equipped with
veils and gates that are
guarded, far removed from the
world in which men dwell.

Hypostasis of the Archons
142:9. There exists a curtain
between the upper and the
lower aeons and shadow
beneath the curtain from
which shadow came matter at
the creation.

1:35. But only an account of   4 Ezra 4:21. The dwellers
this earth . . . give I unto   upon the earth can understand
you.   only what is upon the earth,
                                 and they who are in the
                                 heavens that which is above
                                 the heavenly height.

Book of Adam 1:185. There
are curtains and veils, an
impregnable barrier of living
fire, between the creatures of
a celestial order and those of
the second estate.

Apocryphon of John 1:58.
Adam's deep sleep was really
the putting of a veil between
him and his former
knowledge. 59. The veil shut
Adam off from his memory, as
if he were drugged. 60. His
mind being separated by a veil
from what is really going on in
the universe.

When Moses and Enoch ventured to ask what lay
beyond their veil they were properly reprimanded: to want
to know everything in a single lesson is a human weakness
which is not to be pampered—it is all too easy to ask the

"why" of everything as small children do, but God knows that we are not ready for it:

Moses 1:30. . . . Tell me, I pray thee, why these things are so, and by what thou madest them? 31. . . . And the Lord God said unto Moses: For *mine own purpose* have I made these things. [Italics added.] Here is wisdom, and it remaineth in me.

Secrets 11 (Vaillant). And now, Enoch all that I have explained to thee, and all that thou hast seen on earth, and all that I organized and made . . . there was no counsellor nor assistant; it was I alone . . . who was my own adviser,

32. And by the word of my power, have I created them. . . .

and it was by my word that it was carried out, and my eye beheld it all.

33. And worlds without number have I created; and I also created them for mine own purpose; and by the Son I created them, which is mine Only Begotten.

Secrets 24:3 (Vaillant). Hear, Enoch, for not to My angels have I told my secret, . . . nor have they understood my creating, which I tell thee today. 4. For . . . I alone used to go about the invisible things, . . . 5. and I conceived the thought of placing foundations and of creating a visible creation.

Secrets 11 (Vaillant). He asked for no counsel, his work executed everything, just as his mind conceived everything [Vaillant, n. 14 refers to the Greek version, *pas logos autou ergon.*]

1 Enoch 14:22. Ten thousand times ten thousand [stood] before Him, yet He needed no counsellor.

2 Enoch 25:3. And I [God] was in the midst of the great

light, and as there is born light
from light, there came forth a
great age, and showed all
creation which I had thought
to create. And I saw that it was
good. 4. And I placed for
myself a throne, and took my
seat on it.

Secrets 11 (Vaillant). And
now, Enoch, all that I have
explained to thee, and all that
thou hast seen on earth, and
all that thou hast written in thy
books, it is by my wisdom that
I organized and made all these
things . . . there was no
adviser [counsellor] nor
executive [continuer], it was I
alone . . . who was my only
counsellor, and it was by my
word that it was carried out
[lit., "the thing was my
word"], and my eyes beheld
all. [See F. Lachover & I.
Tishby, *The Wisdom of the Zohar*
(Jerusalem: Byalik Foundation,
1971), 1:127ff, on how God
alone conceives his "works
without end."]

The Zion of Enoch

Enoch was not, of course, the only preacher of righteousness in his dispensation, and like the others met
puzzlement, fear, resentment, and then a measure of
success. People began not only to fear him but to believe
him, "for he walked with God." Some of the accounts
speak of "all the people" or "everybody" going after Enoch,
just as we read that "all the land of Judea" followed John
the Baptist into the wilderness to be baptized. (Mark 1:5.) It
soon becomes apparent in both cases that this is a manner
of speaking; only a select number followed those leaders all
the way.

Moses 6:23. And they were preachers of righteousness, . . . and called upon all men, everywhere, to repent; and faith was taught unto the children of men.

6:26. . . . [As] Enoch journeyed . . . among the people . . . the Spirit of God . . . abode upon him.

6:38. And they came forth to hear him, . . . saying . . . we [will] go yonder to behold the seer. . . .
39. And . . . when they heard him, . . . fear came on all them that heard him; for he walked with God.

BHM 4:129. And [all the people] gathered together to Enoch . . . to hear this thing; and Enoch taught the children of men the way of God. . . . And the spirit of God was upon Enoch, and he taught all his people the wisdom of God and his ways. 130. . . . And all the people were astonished and awed by his wisdom and knowledge, and bowed down to the earth before him.
131. . . . And all the people gathered together unto Enoch . . . and he taught them again to keep the ways of the Lord and gave them all his peace [etc., etc.].

Secrets 16 (Vaillant). When Enoch spoke to his children and the princes, then all the other people in the neighborhood heard that the Lord had called Enoch, and they all assembled to the number of 2,000 men, and came to Azouchan [or Achuzan] where Enoch and his sons and the elders of the people were, and saluted him: Thou blessed of the Lord . . . bless now thy people and glorify us before the Lord, because the Lord has chosen to establish thee [as] one who takes away our sins.[371]

6:54. Hence came the saying abroad among the people, that the Son of God hath atoned for original guilt.

Ms. R: For the Lord has chosen thee before all other men on earth . . . to establish thee [as] one who takes away the sins of men, and as a helper [savior] to the people of the house.

6:36. . . . and from thenceforth came the saying abroad in the land: A seer hath the Lord raised up unto his people.

BHM 4:129. . . . and the saying went forth to every region of the children of Adam: Who is the man who desires to know the ways of the Lord and good works? Let him come to Enoch![372]

The picture of two thousand men coming to recognize and acclaim Enoch at the place where he "and his sons and the leaders of the people were" suggests the modest nucleus of an organization. Their gathering together is the first step in a long process of withdrawing from a wicked world.[373] Enoch himself had already withdrawn, then returned. He joins Adam, Abraham, Job, the Twelve Patriarchs, and Moses, all of whose apochryphal "Testaments" tell how the hero is first carried to heaven in a vision, then returns and describes the vision to his family and followers, then takes a final leave. The sequence of these heroic deaths later developed into a literary genre in which monkish scribes dwell with morbid fascination and dismay on the terrors of death. Enoch's departure is undeniably the most spectacular, setting the standard for fiery chariots and sky-borne hosts later. At the same time, it is the most sober and "scientific," with the exception of Joseph Smith's version, to which we shall refer shortly.

The Jewish sources tell of Enoch's departure with his people from the world's point of view—those who remained behind: "And at that time the children of men sat down before Enoch and he spoke to them. And they raised their eyes and saw something like a great horse coming down from heaven, and the horse moving in the air [wind] to the ground, And they told Enoch what they had seen. And Enoch said to them, 'That horse has come down to the earth to take me; the time and the day approach when I must go from you and no longer appear among you.' And at that time that horse came down and stood before Enoch, and all the people who were with Enoch saw it. And then Enoch went forth, and there came a voice to him saying, 'Who is the man who rejoices in the knowledge of the ways of the Lord God? Let him come this day to Enoch before he is taken from us.' And all the people gathered together and came to Enoch on that day. . . .And after that he mounted up and rode on his way, and all the people went forth and followed him to the number of 800,000 men. And they went with him for a day's journey. And behold, on the second day he said to them, 'Return back from following me lest ye die.' But none of them turned back but went with him. And on the sixth day the number of people had increased, and they stuck with him. And they said to him, 'We will go with thee to the place where thou goest; as the Lord liveth, only death will separate us from thee!' And it came to pass that they took courage and went with him, and he no longer addressed [remonstrated with] them. And they went after him and never turned back from him. And those kings who did turn back ordered a count to be made of all the remnant of men who went out after Enoch. And it was on the seventh day, and Enoch went up in a tempest [whirlwind] of the heavens with horses of fire and chariots of fire. And on the eighth day all the kings who had been with Enoch sent to take the number of the men who had stayed behind with Enoch [when the kings left him] at the place from which he had mounted up into the sky. And all the kings went to that place and found all the ground covered with snow in that place, and on top of the snow huge blocks [stones] of snow. And they said to each other, 'Come, let us break into the snow here to see whether the people who were left with Enoch died under the lumps of snow.' And they hunted for Enoch and found him not because he had gone up into the sky." (*BHM* 4:131.)

One thing that makes this story so noteworthy is the association with other ascensions. The parallels with Elijah are obvious down to the party of searchers Elisha sent. (See 2 Kings 2:11-18.) Adam, Moses, and other worthy men were mysteriously caught up or away at various points in their missions. (Moses 6:64, 1:1, 7:27.) The prophet Baruch, in an account first published in 1866, assembled his people, counseled them to remember Zion since "it must be renewed in glory . . . when the Mighty One will renew His creation," and named seven elders to guard the people who remain until "the new world comes which does not turn to corruption those who depart to its blessedness. . . . For in the heights of that world shall they dwell. And they shall be made like unto the angels, . . . [with] excellency . . . surpassing that in the angels." (2 Baruch 31:1-51.)

The lamentation of his people, "Truly we shall be left in darkness, and there shall be no light to the people who are left" (46:2), is a standard element in the departure of other prophets and apostles. (See the Assumption of Moses, chapter 11.) When the prophet Ezra assembles his people, they mourn: "[Why] hast [thou] forsaken us and sittest in this place? For of all the prophets thou alone art left to us . . . as a lamp in a dark place." Ezra consoles them, mourns for the passing of Zion, sees an apocalyptic vision of great destructions to come, then is "caught away and taken up into the place of such as were like him, after having written all these things. And he is called the scribe of the knowledge of the Most High [a title applied to Enoch, too] for ever and ever." (4 Ezra 12:40–14:50.)

A prophet is thus someone experienced in the process of withdrawal. The Joseph Smith version of Enoch, found in the book of Moses, chronicles Enoch's withdrawal in three stages: (1) After Enoch's return, he gathered his followers and led them out of a dangerous world to a place of safety in the mountains. The Lord fought for them, mountains fled, rivers altered their courses, and all nations feared them. (See Moses 7:13-17.) (2) Safe, the people prospered, finally building a city that lasted 365 years. (See Moses 7:17-20.) (3) At last the entire divine government was of necessity moved clear out of the world—either the blessed Zion or the cursed world would have to leave, and so "Zion, in process of time, was taken up into heaven." (Moses 7:21.) But what happened in the *earthly* city of Zion, between the lines of those three brief verses?

The interest of the Latter-day Saints in the city of Enoch is not simply a literary or even a scientific one. It is historic and prophetic. The city of Enoch is very much our concern. As we read of Enoch's community, a chorus of persistent questions hums in the background: Just how literally is all this to be taken? How are we to imagine the almost unimaginable events of that far-off time?

We cannot dodge such questions, since we are committed to forming as quickly as possible the closest possible partnership with that society.

The first step in dealing with Enoch's reality is to ask just what, according to the written record, Enoch's city is supposed to have been. Ancient records do not, contrary to a once popular belief, simply spring into existence out of wild Oriental imaginations but, as ever-expanding research makes ever plainer, must always be assumed to have some kind of a historical kernel of reality. So we ask, under what circumstances did Enoch's city come into existence. How did it operate? What really became of it? What does the record say?

All the eschatological references in the scriptures to the Zion of Enoch are found in the Prophets and the Psalms of the Old Testament—the New Testament simply quotes them.[374] In the book of Moses, the word *Zion* appears only in chapter 7, where, however, it occurs no fewer than sixteen times, making this chapter the most significant single treatise on the subject. Scholars have long noted that the Prophets emphasize the moral aspect of Zion, while the Psalms, with their royal imagery and archaic ritual background, favor the political. Yet both are speaking of a very

real earthly community, nailed down by references in both
to *"bringing again"* Zion—recognizing that Zion actually
has been on the earth in the past and can be enjoyed by the
Saints again as soon as they are willing to "return to the
original relationship with Yahweh," a condition "in which
alone Israel's filial relationship to God can be renewed and
which God . . . will reestablish in the future."[375] The familiar picture of the Lord "taking possession again of the seat
in Jerusalem" as he collects "his scattered people from all
quarters of their heritage, at a time of gathering" is ordi-
narily couched in the classic terms of the book of Enoch.[376]

The best news—indeed the only wholly good news that
can come to the inhabitants of this wicked earth—is the
bringing again of Zion to bless the earth with the only order
of society acceptable to God and unreservedly beneficial to
man. Zion is any society in which the celestial law is opera-
tive, "and though we cannot claim these promises which
were made to the ancients, for they are not our property,"
the Prophet Joseph reminded his people, ". . . yet if we
are . . . called with the same calling . . . and embrace the
same covenant . . . we can . . . obtain the same promises . . . because we, ourselves, have faith . . . even as
they did." (*Teachings of the Prophet Joseph Smith*, p. 66.) Zion
is a glorious ideal, albeit a rare reality, in the world's history; it is "the Holy Order that God has established for his
people in all ages of the world when he has had a kingdom
upon the earth. We may call it," said Brigham Young, "the
Order of Enoch, the Order of Joseph, the Order of Peter, or
Abraham, or Moses, and then go back to Noah . . .", who,
of course, takes us to Enoch. (*Journal of Discourses* 17:113.)

Indeed, it has been said that a happy condition perhaps
similar to Zion prevailed in Eden itself when Adam faithfully followed God's instruction: "The Holy One of Zion
. . . established the foundations of Adam-Ondi-Ahman."
(D&C 78:15.)

"The Garden of Eden is the Holy of Holies, and the

dwelling of the Lord . . . and Mount Zion [is] the center [or] navel of the earth." (Jubilees 8:19.)

Though the people of Moses' day were not qualified to receive it, nevertheless "God gave him the pattern of Zion and its measure." (2 Baruch 59:4.) The early Christian church is said by R. H. Charles to have modeled itself after Enoch's community, designating its leader as Enoch. The sections about Zion and the New Jerusalem in the Enoch literature are, according to Charles, "the most complete and most consistent of all the sections"[377] and were a great favorite of all those separatist groups, both Jewish and Christian, who took to the desert, fancying themselves to be the one and only true representatives on earth of the church and kingdom of Enoch.[378] As persecuted minorities, they all looked forward with longing to a time when they would come to their own with the glorious return of both the Lord and the city of Enoch. Passages in the Psalms of Solomon establishing a definite association between early Christians in the East and Dead Sea communties like Qumran seem to describe the migration of those eastern communities from Palestine more in terms of Enoch's migration than Moses': "Jerusalem, . . . behold thy children being gathered from the East and West, the North [and South,] . . . and from the distant islands. . . . Lofty mountains he has humbled and made plain before them. (Psalms of Solomon 11:2-4.)

"They that love the assemblies of the Saints fled away from them: and they flew like sparrows from their nests. . . . And the everlasting fountains were restrained, both the abysses and they from the lofty mountains; because none among them did righteousness. . . . At his rebuke the gentiles shall flee from before His face . . . That He may gather together all the children of God. . . . And He shall purify Jerusalem in holiness, as it was of old time. . . . And their King is the Lord's Messiah. (Psalms of Solomon 17:16, 19, 25, 26, 30.)

In the Psalms, the royal coronation has a central place, with the king representing the Lord and the people his Zion. (See Mosiah 2-5 for a well-known year-rite in which the king, though a weak mortal, figures as God's representative.) Enoch's transcendent virtue qualifies him as a vital link in "the order" of the Lord himself. Compare these verses from Doctrine and Covenants 76:56-58 with the apocryphal Slavonic Enoch:

"They are they who are priests and kings, who have received of his fulness, and of his glory; And are priests . . . after the order of Melchizedek, which was after the order of Enoch, which was after the order of the Only Begotten Son. Wherefore, as it is written, they are gods, even the sons of God."

"And when all the people in the region about heard that the Lord had chosen Enoch, they took counsel together and said: Let us go and acclaim [tsyelyim] Enoch. . . . And they hailed Enoch, saying, Blessed art thou of the Lord the king of the eternities! Now bless thy people and glorify them before the face of the Lord, inasmuch as the Lord has established thee as one taking away our sins." (Secrets [Vaillant, pp. 60f.].)

The Hebrew *Life of Enoch* has the kings of the earth hailing Enoch as their supreme head,[379] while the book of Jasher simply repeats the same story, concluding: "And they assembled in all, one hundred and thirty kings and princes, and they made Enoch king over them and they were all under his power and command."[380] All this is according to a principle that was quite unknown only a few decades ago. As stated by Egyptologist J. Zandee, "Not only in Israel, but in all the ancient Near East, every king is a Messiah. . . . There is no difference in principle between the eschatological Messiah and the ruling King as the bearer of salvation. . . . The King is a god, . . . the King is the son of God. . . . The King is as the image of God on earth. . . . The King brings justice to earth. . . . [The King is] the Good Shepherd, . . . [The King is the man of Wisdom]. . . . The King is the [High] Priest [endowed with power]. . . . The King is a cosmic deity."[381] In short, the king is an Enoch, to whom God has promised his own throne.

| Moses 7:59. . . . Forasmuch as thou art God, and I know thee, . . . thou hast made me, and given unto me a right to thy throne, and not of myself, but through thine own grace. | BHM 5:174. The Metatron [Enoch] said: . . . God made for me a throne modeled after the Throne of Glory, I being clothed upon with glory [a wrapping of radiance] and Light [*Zohar*] . . . and beauty and mercy like that of the throne of thy glory. . . . And he caused me to sit upon it, and a herald proclaimed in all the firmament of firmaments, saying, Enoch is proclaimed as a divine King! [175. He puts a crown on his head.] |

| 7:68. And all the days of Zion, in the days of Enoch, were three hundred and sixty-five years. | |

This is the pattern of the year-king of which Enoch is a prime representative.[382]

Above all, Zion is the community of the Saints, the Elect, "the pure in heart" (D&C 97:26), who are "of one heart and one mind" so that there are "no poor among them." (Moses 7:18.) This is the Zion envisioned by the prophets; the book of Moses, the Doctrine and Covenants, and apocryphal works all expressly call it the Zion of Enoch:

| Moses 7:62. . . . to gather out mine elect . . . unto . . . an Holy City, . . . looking forth for the time of my coming; for there shall be my tabernacle, and it shall be | Gizeh 1:3. [This is] about the Elect . . . receive my parable about them; and my Great Holy One will come out of his dwelling-place, 4. and the God of the Age [*aeon*] shall |

called Zion, a New Jerusalem.
64. . . . Zion, which shall
come forth out of all the
creations which I have made.

66. . . . he [Enoch] saw
great tribulations among the
wicked; and he also saw the
sea, that it was troubled, and
men's hearts failing them.

67. . . . and he saw the day
of the righteous, the hour of
their redemption; and received
a fullness of joy.

walk upon the earth, even
upon Mount Zion . . . and he
will appear in the power of his
might from the heaven of
heavens.

5. And all shall be afraid
. . . great trembling and fear
shall seize them, . . . 6. and
the mountains shall be shaken
down . . . and dissolve . . .
7. and the earth shall be
rent . . .

8. But with the righteous
shall peace be made, and upon
the Elect oneness of heart
[*synteresis*] and peace . . . and
He will bless them all, and a
light will appear and bring
peace unto them.

1 Enoch 45:4. Then will I
cause Mine Elect One to dwell
among them . . . 5. and I will
transform the earth and make
it a blessing; and I will cause
Mine elect ones to dwell on it
. . . to dwell before me.
51:15. And the earth shall
rejoice, and the righteous shall
dwell upon it, and the elect
shall walk thereon.

Secrets 17 (Vaillant). All the
righteous who shall escape the
great judgment will be united
in the Great Age, . . . and they
shall be eternal, and they shall
no longer know weariness or
suffering or affliction, nor be
in any danger of violence, nor
fears of the night nor any
darkness, but they shall have

a great light forever . . . a
great paradise, a place of safety
for them to dwell in forever
. . . and their faces shall shine
like the Sun!

The Mandean writings equate Zion to heavenly "firmaments, habitations, worlds, and Jordans," giving the most
vivid and appealing descriptions of such holy places,
which, they say, are to be enjoyed only by the "spirits of
good people . . . the wise and the prudent of the families
of Abel, Seth, and Enoch." There the Saints live without
discord or dissension; they are angelic beings, wise and
gentle, without malice or deceit, constantly visiting each
other. There is perfect agreement among the worlds, each
having its particular glory and rejoicing in the glory of the
others as all share their treasures of knowledge with each
other. They are vast distances removed from each other,
but through their common Lord and God they all share a
common glorious awareness of each other. All are incor-
ruptible and hence without death; they do not grow old or
wear out; their nature is unfading. Their number is fixed
because it is infinite—beyond counting. Each of these
worlds is a Zion, having no law courts, no hunger or thirst,
no cold or heat, no hatred or fear, no war, no slavery, no
harmful creatures or plants. Magnificent buildings stand
beside tranquil seas; flowing springs give life-giving water.
Everything vibrates with joy. The wants of the people are
few. They move through the air by an effortless power of
flight; they are at home in the firmaments and the worlds
and among all the dominions and powers. Their beauty is
within them and shines out, as if they were of pure crystal.
Force also flows through them from the King as they open
themselves to it by persevering in prayer and song. They
study and meditate constantly; they exhale the fragrance of
divine happiness. Each is more remarkable than the other,
each more illustrious.[383]
    It was natural for the church in every age to identify it-

self with the Order of Enoch if only because that order is the only one acceptable to God at any time: "The Lord spake unto Enoch [Joseph Smith, Jun.] saying: Hearken . . . [ye] who are ordained unto the high priesthood . . . who have assembled yourselves together. . . . the time has come . . . ; it must needs be that there be an organization of my people . . . in the land of Zion—[or in other words, the city of Enoch (Joseph)], for a permanent and everlasting establishment and order unto my church, . . . to the salvation of man. . . . If ye are not equal in earthly things ye cannot be equal in obtaining heavenly things." (D&C 78:1, 3, 6.)

For "Zion cannot be built up unless it is by the principles of the law of the celestial kingdom; otherwise I cannot receive her unto myself." (D&C 105:5.) "If my people observe not this law, . . . it shall not be a land of Zion unto you." (D&C 119:6.)

A telling mark of authenticity for the Joseph Smith version is that Enoch's Zion is defined as a society where "there was no poor among them." (Moses 7:18.) The Greek Enoch, which for the first time showed how the ancient sectaries related themselves to the city of Enoch, "shows a great partiality for the lowly and humble. Here we are confronted with the ethics of the poor man; . . . these needy and humble people have to seek solace in the fact that unto them the knowledge of these mysteries will be revealed."384

The presence of such a society is a standing rebuke to the rest of the world. As Brigham Young puts it, "We are following the customs of Enoch and the holy fathers, and for this we are looked upon as not being fit for society. We are not adapted to the Society of the wicked, and do not wish to mingle with them." (JD 10:306.) Enoch was hopeful that his Zion, "a city of refuge, a place of safety for the saints of the Most High God" (D&C 45:66), was here to stay; the Lord indicated to him that this was not to be: "Enoch . . . said unto the Lord: Surely Zion shall dwell in safety forever. But the Lord said unto Enoch: Zion have I blessed, but the residue of the people have I cursed." The separation would have to continue until finally "Zion, *in the process of time,* was taken up into heaven." (Moses 7:20-21; italics added.) We see the division of the people at every stage of the history: when "their enemies came to battle against them," Enoch "led the people of God," while "all nations feared greatly" (Moses 7:13); the most dangerous of them "stood afar off" and even fled to the new land that had risen from the sea. (Moses 7:14-15.) The result was two worlds, Zion, inhabited by people "of one heart and one mind" (Moses 7:18), the other wracked by continual "wars and bloodshed." (Moses 7:16.)

The completeness of the division is strikingly expressed by one of the most ancient of literary devices, rhetorical antithesis:

Moses 7:20. . . . Zion have I blessed,	but the residue of the people have I cursed.
5:15. . . . believed in the Son, and repented of their sins	. . . believed not and repented not.
7:16. . . . but the Lord came and dwelt with his people, and they dwelt in righteousness	And from that time forth there were wars and bloodshed among them.
7:18. . . . they were of one heart and one mind.	7:33. . . . they are without affection, and they hate their own blood.
7:18. And the Lord called his people Zion, because they . . . dwelt in righteousness.	7:36. . . . among all the workmanship of mine hands there has not been so great wickedness as among thy brethren.

When the sectaries of the Dead Sea labeled their society the *Yachad* (lit. unity, oneness) it was a reminder that *unity* is the first law of Enoch's society by which the Saints are expected to live in every dispensation.

Moses 7:18. And the Lord called his people ZION, because they were of one heart and one mind, . . . and there was no poor among them.	Zohar, Noah 76b. R. Jose. From [the Tower story] we learn that as long as the people of the world lived in harmony, being *of one mind and one will,* although they rebelled against the Holy One, the supernal judgment could not touch them; but as soon as they were divided, "the Lord scattered them abroad."
	2 Baruch 30:2. Then all who have fallen asleep in hope of Him shall rise again. . . . And they shall come forth . . . *in one assemblage of one thought.* (Italics added.)

Even after the removal of Enoch's city, the work of redemption continued among "the residue of the people. . . . And *after* that Zion was taken up into heaven, Enoch beheld, and lo, all the nations of the earth were before him; And there came *generation upon generation;* and Enoch was high and lifted up, even in the bosom of the Father, . . . and behold, the power of Satan was upon all the face of the earth." (Moses 7:22-24.) According to this perspective, Noah's sailing was only the last step in a process of evacuation that had lasted for generations. Even after the people had chosen sides—Enoch and the Lord, or Satan— the missionary work still went on.

Moses 7:27. And Enoch beheld angels descending out of heaven, bearing testimony . . . and the Holy Ghost fell on many, and they were caught up by the powers of heaven into Zion.	Apocalypse of Adam (Copt.) 69-70. Downpourings of rain will destroy all flesh, "but mighty angels will come down from heaven and lead away those men to a place where the Spirit of life is to be found."

7:28. And . . . the God of heaven looked upon the residue of the people, and he wept.

Gizeh 8. (And there was a great wickedness in the earth, Satan [Azael and Semiazas] teaching men all manner of ungodliness. 9. Then the great angels . . . went and reported to God, saying, What shall we do?) 10:1. So the Highest sent Istrael [Ms. G⁵ Uriel] to the Son of Lamech [Noah]. 2. Tell him in My name to hide himself [Ms G⁵ 3. Teach the righteous what to do . . . to preserve his soul and escape.] because all the earth is going to be destroyed . . . 3. And teach him how he may escape. . . . 4. (God sent Raphael . . . 9. Gabriel, 11. Michael, to minister in this emergency.) 15. [When God sends down the angels to] destroy all the bastard spirits . . . 17. . . . . all the righteous shall flee and go on living [safely] for a thousand generations.

1 Enoch 105:1. In those days the Lord bade them [angels] . . . testify to the children of earth . . . show [it] unto them; for ye are their guides.

Beatty, 100:4. And angels shall come down, descending into secret places in that day. . . . 5. And over all the righteous and holy he will set a guard of the holy angels and they shall be preserved as the apple of his eye until tribulations and wickedness shall pass by. . . .

2 Enoch 23:80. [God to Enoch:] I will send my archangel Michael, and he will take the boy [Methuselah] to a place of safety.

7:60. . . . in the last days, in the days of wickedness and vengeance, . . . 62. . . . truth will I cause to sweep the earth as with a flood, to gather out mine elect . . . unto a place which I shall prepare, an Holy City, that my people may . . . be looking . . . for the time of my coming; . . . and it shall be called Zion, a New Jerusalem.

Apocalypse of Abraham 29:15f. (Great tribulations will come) . . . 17. [But] of thy people righteous men will be spared . . . hastening in the glory of my name to a place which I have prepared for them ahead of time [Jerusalem].

Until the separation is completed the powers of destruction are held in check. As the book of Moses describes: "Great tribulations shall be among the children of men, but my people will I preserve; . . . [I will] gather out mine elect . . . unto a place which I shall prepare." (Moses 7:61-62.)

Apocryphal documents present that same idea: "And the earth shall be rent, and everything which is upon the earth shall be destroyed. . . . But there shall be great peace for the righteous, and upon the elect shall be security [*synteresis*] and peace, . . . and I will bless them all." (Gizeh 1:7-8.)

"In the days of Enoch . . . God gave them [the wicked] respite all the time that the righteous men Jared, Methuselah, and Enoch were alive; but when they departed from the world, God let punishment descend." (Zohar, Bereshith 56b; cf. Genesis 7:23.)

"Why art thou [Enoch] discomforted with such a vision? Until this day has lasted the day of His mercy; and He hath been merciful and long-suffering towards those who dwell on the earth." (1 Enoch 60:4-6.)

When the angels beg God to get on with the work and wipe out the unworthy human race, he replies, "I have made and I remove, and I am long-suffering and I rescue!" (*BHM* 5:172.)

"And after that [Enoch] showed me the angels of punishment who are prepared to come and let loose all the powers of the waters . . . to bring judgment and destruction on all who dwell on the earth. And the Lord of Spirits gave commandments to the angels who were going forth, that they should *not* cause the waters to rise, but should hold them in check." (1 Enoch 66:1.)

The angels, then, for many years were a kind of shuttle service, preaching repentance and offering escape to all who were willing to listen. Their diligence clears God of the charge of being capricious and cruel in sending the Flood, a favorite argument of skeptics and atheists in every age. According to Jellinek, the primary object of the old Hebrew book of Enoch was to expose that argument's emptiness: "The work of the angels testified that God was just. . . . Enoch testified that he became an angel in heaven, instructed by the angels Shemashasi and Asael, in order to bear personal witness to man that God in sending the Flood was not cruel."[385] This point is clearly brought home in the Joseph Smith version, in which Enoch and the Lord discuss the whole problem frankly and thoroughly, to Enoch's complete satisfaction. (See Moses 7:28-67.)

According to apocryphal writings, Abraham, Ezra, and Baruch, among others, questioned the wisdom and charity of sending total destruction on the human race. "Dost thou think," says the Lord to Baruch, "that in these things the Most High rejoices, or that His name is glorified? . . . Go therefore . . . and instruct the people so far as thou art able, that they may learn so as not to die at the last time, but may learn in order that they may live at the last times."[386] To Ezra God gives a gentle reprimand, "Thou comest far short of being able to love my creation more than I!"[387] And, as we have seen, Enoch in the Joseph Smith account gives the strongest testimony of all—that he actually saw God weep! (Moses 7:28.)

All who were willing to repent were duly removed to a place of safety; it was only those who doggedly refused to listen over a period of years, the wicked "residue of the people," who had to be left behind to perish. Those who took refuge in the ark were by no means all who were saved; many had gone before. This is another interesting phase of the Noah-Enoch relationship.

Moses 7:25. . . . [Enoch] saw angels descending out of heaven. . . . 26. And he beheld Satan; and he had a great chain in his hand, and it veiled the whole face of the earth with darkness. . . . 27. And Enoch beheld angels descending out of heaven, . . . and the Holy Ghost fell on many, and they were caught up by the powers of heaven into Zion.

Beatty 102:2. And while all the earth was shaking . . . and in confusion, 3. the angels were busy carrying out what had been assigned [*syntachthen*] to them.

Apocryphon of John, pp. 73:7. Noah was not alone [in being saved] but men of the generation of the true and faithful [the "unshaken ones"] came to a special place, 11. and there they were enveloped in a cloud of light. 13. And Noah was aware of his divine calling along with those with him when the light enlightened them. For darkness had been poured out over every place upon the entire earth. He took counsel with his angels, 74:1. and the angels were sent down to the children of men.

Apocalypse of Adam, pp. 69-70. After that shall come great angels in high clouds, and take away those people to the place where the spirit of life

is . . . and they will come from
heaven to earth and all the
multitude of flesh will perish
in the water.

Though communities aspiring to the glory of Zion have
been on earth a number of times, it is the final return of
Zion in the last days toward which all the prophets have
looked. And while the church in every dispensation had
certain aspects that resembled the Zion of Enoch, the
closest parallel will be the Zion of the End-time.

Moses 7:62. I shall prepare
. . . an Holy City, that my
people may . . . be looking
forth for the time of my
coming; for there shall be my
tabernacle, and it shall be
called Zion, a New Jerusalem.
64. And there shall be mine
abode, and it shall be Zion,
which shall come forth out of
all the creations which I have
made; and for the space of a
thousand years the earth shall
rest.

Jubilees 1:27. And He [God]
said to the angel of the
presence [Sar hā-Panīm or
Enoch]: Write for Moses from
the beginning of creation till
my sanctuary has been built
among them for all eternity.
And the Lord will appear to
the eyes of all, and all shall
know that I am the God of
Israel . . . and King on Mount
Zion for all eternity. And Zion
and Jerusalem shall be holy
. . . until the sanctuary of the
Lord shall be made in
Jerusalem on Mount Zion, and
all the luminaries be renewed
for healing and for blessing for
all the elect of Israel, and that
thus it may be from that day
unto all the days of the earth.

That the city "shall be called Zion, a new *Jerusalem*"
seems an obvious anachronism in a book written
supposedly before the Flood; yet the idea is strikingly
confirmed in the Testament of Levi, a very early Jewish
writing totally ignored until the present century,[388] in
which is a prophecy expressly attributed to Enoch: "For the
house [*oikos*] which the Lord shall choose for himself *shall be*

called Jerusalem, as is contained in the book of Enoch the Righteous." (Testament of Levi 10:5.)

R. H. Charles quotes parallel passages on this theme from the book of Enoch and the book of Jubilees to show that the latter is in the authentic Enoch tradition, since, as he states, "the resemblance in word and thought . . . can hardly be accidental."[389] He underlines key words to establish the relationship:

1 Enoch 5:9. *They shall complete the number of the days of their life* And their lives shall be increased *in peace,* And the years of their *joy* shall be multiplied.	Jubilees 23:27, 29. And the days shall begin to grow many and increase amongst these children of men. . . . 29. And all their days they shall complete and live in peace and joy.

A recent article in *Scientific American* indicates that some of the conventional ideas of early Judaism and Christianity must be drastically altered in view of new documentary discoveries; M. E. Stone notes that "chief among these [discoveries] were the Book of Enoch and the Book of Jubilees, both translated from the Ethiopic in the 19th century." Then he places the following passages from Enoch and Jude in parallel to show that "it is evident that the Book of Enoch served as a source for the Letter of Jude . . . and for other early Christian writings."[390]

Gizeh 1:9: And behold! He cometh with the myriads of His holy ones, to exercise judgment upon all, and to destroy all the ungodly; And to convict all flesh of all the works of their ungodliness which they have ungodly committed, and of all the hard things ungodly sinners have spoken against them.	Jude 1:14-15: It was of these also that Enoch in the seventh generation from Adam prophesied, saying, "Behold, the Lord came with his holy myriads, to execute judgment on all, and to convince all the ungodly of all their deeds of ungodliness which they have committed in such an ungodly way, and of all the harsh things which ungodly sinners have spoken against him.

Now are these parallels, given as proof positive of the authentic affinity of ancient writings, any more compelling than these between the same ancient sources and the book of Moses given to us through the Prophet Joseph Smith?

Moses 7:62. And righteousness will I send down out of heaven; . . . and righteousness and truth will I cause to sweep the earth as with a flood, to gather out mine elect from the four quarters of the earth, unto a place which . . . shall be called Zion, a New Jerusalem. . . . 64. And there shall be mine abode, and it shall be Zion, which shall come forth out of all the creations which I have made; and for the space of a thousand years the earth shall rest.

7:66. But before that day he saw great tribulations among the wicked; . . . 67. . . . and he saw the day of the righteous, the hour of their redemption, and received a fulness of joy. . . .

1 Enoch 39:5. Here mine eyes saw their dwellings with His righteous angels, And their resting-places with the holy. . . . And righteousness flowed before them as water and mercy like dew upon the earth: Thus it is amongst them for ever and ever. And in that place mine eyes saw the Elect One of the righteousness and of faith, And I saw his dwelling-place . . .

Apocalypse of Abraham 29:14. But before the Age of Righteousness and abundance begins, the lawless Gentiles must suffer my judgments, through the people of thy tribe, whom I have set apart for myself. 15. In those days I will bring over all the creatures on earth ten plagues. . . . 17. But of thy tribe will righteous men be preserved . . . who will hasten in the name of my glory to a place prepared ahead of time [Jerusalem] . . . 18. [where] they shall live in security . . . in the age of the righteous.

Of the many striking figures of speech which definitely link the peculiar language of the Joseph Smith Enoch with that of the ancient sources, none is more interesting than that dealing with the preservation of the Ark, a passage which obviously puzzles the Ethiopian scribes, but which stands out clearly in the Joseph Smith text:

Moses 7:43. Wherefore Enoch saw that Noah built an ark; and that the Lord smiled upon it, and held it in his own hand.

1 Enoch 67:2. And now the angels are making a wooden [building? R. H. Charles notes: "This account differs from 89:1, where it is said that Noah himself makes the ark"], and when they have completed that task I will place My hand upon it and preserve it.

The Latter-day Saints have been taught to view their own dispensation as the ushering in of the final restoration of Zion. The Church itself, never again to be taken from the earth, must ever more closely approximate the Zion of Enoch as those "which have been scattered shall return to . . . build up the waste places of Zion . . . to be established, no more to be thrown down." (D&C 103:11, 13.) It is the same work under the same auspices: "I am the same which have taken the Zion of Enoch into mine own bosom; . . . even as many as have believed in my name." (D&C 38:4.) The Latter-day Saints "are they who have come . . . to the general assembly and church of *Enoch*, and of the Firstborn." (D&C 76:67; italics added.) "The Lord spake unto [Enoch] Joseph Smith, Jr., saying: . . . it must needs be that there be an organization of my people, . . . in the land of Zion—Or in other words, the city of Enoch [Joseph], for a permanent and everlasting establishment and order unto my church." (D&C 78:1-4.)

Zion is the common designation of the Church established in the world: "the land of Zion" being "in other words, the city of Enoch." (D&C 78:3-4.) Even though the work is still in its preliminary stages, one is justified in saying, "this is the new chapel," when only the foundations are in. Thus the Church can be called Zion even though its work has barely begun: "My people must be tried in all things, that they may be prepared to receive the glory . . . of Zion" (D&C 136:31), and if they are faithful "they shall have power after many days to accomplish all things pertaining to Zion" (D&C 105:37). The Saints are told not to despair: "Concern not yourselves about Zion, for I will deal mercifully with her" (D&C 111:6), and "Zion shall be redeemed in mine own due time" (D&C 136:18), "although she is chastened for a little season" (D&C 100:13). Brigham Young constantly reminded the Saints of the preparatory nature of the work in which they were engaged:

"We have commenced to organize, I will say partially, in the Holy Order that God has established for his people in all ages of the world when he has had a kingdom upon the earth. We may call it the Order of Enoch, the Order of Joseph, the Order of Peter, or Abraham, or Moses, and then go back to Noah, and then step to our own position here, and say that we will organize as far as we have the privilege, . . . under the laws of the land. Many branches of industry have been organized here to help to sustain each other, to labor for the good of all, and to establish cooperation in the midst of the Church in this place." (JD 17:113-14.)

In the years following the entrance into the Salt Lake Valley he placed the greatest emphasis on the theme of preparation and the uses of adversity:

"I never attributed the driving of the Saints from Jackson county to anything but that it was necessary to chasten them and prepare them to build up Zion." (JD 13:148.)

"We are not yet prepared to go and establish the Centre Stake of Zion. The Lord tried this in the first place. . . . He gave revelation after revelation; but the people could not abide them." (JD 11:324.)

"Are we fit for Zion? . . . Could we stay in Independence? No, we could not. . . . Can the Saints see? No, or a few of them can." (*JD* 15:3.)

"Then do not be too anxious for the Lord to hasten his work. Let our anxiety be centered upon this one thing, the sanctification of our own hearts, the purifying of our own affections, the preparing of ourselves for the approach of events that are hastening upon us. This should be our concern, this should be our study, this should be our daily prayer, and not be in a hurry to see the overthrow of the wicked." (*JD* 9:3.)

"Suppose Joseph had not been obliged to flee from Pennsylvania back to York State, would he have known as much as he afterwards knew? Suppose he could have stayed in old Ontario County in peace, without being persecuted, could he have learned as much as he did by being persecuted? . . .

"Joseph could not have been perfected, though he had lived a thousand years, if he had received no persecution. . . . You may calculate when this people are called to go through scenes of affliction and suffering, are driven from their homes, and cast down, and scattered, and smitten, and peeled, the Almighty is rolling on His work with greater rapidity." (*JD* 2:7-8.)

It was even so with ancient Israel: "They had to travel to and fro to every point of the compass, and were wasted away, because God was determined to save their spirits." (*JD* 4:53.)

"While we were in Winter Quarters, the Lord gave to me a revelation. . . . I talked it to my brethren; . . . but with the exception of one or two of the Twelve, it would not touch a man. . . . I would have given [millions] if the people had been prepared to then receive the kingdom of God according to the pattern given to Enoch. But I could not touch them." (*JD* 18:244.)

The excuse for the Saints' reluctance was clearly their total preoccupation with their own separation from the world, which was violent and forcible but a necessary prelude to Zion—"gather ye together, O ye people of my church, upon the land of Zion. . . . Let them . . . who are among the Gentiles flee unto Zion. And let them who be of Judah flee unto Jerusalem." (D&C 133:4, 12-13.) They were looking for a place of safety, "the land of Zion, . . . for a defense, and for a refuge from the storm, and from wrath when it shall be poured out without mixture upon the whole earth." (D&C 115:6.) Building the city had to come later.

The spectacular departure of Enoch's Zion will be matched by its no less astonishing return. There are things here beyond the scope of men's everyday experience: "The redemption of Zion must needs come by power." (D&C 103:15.) Once established in her place, Zion serves as a sort of bridgehead, preparing the way for the return of Enoch's Zion, when the two shall fuse.

Moses 7:63. Then shalt thou and all thy city meet them there, and we will receive them into our bosom, and they shall see us; and we will fall upon their necks, and they shall fall upon our necks, and we will kiss each other.

1 Enoch 39:1. And it shall come to pass in those days that the elect and holy children will descend from the high heavens, and their seed will become one with the children of men.

4 Ezra 13:36. When Zion appears it is completely *parata et aedificata*—a city wholly finished and perfect—coming like a mountain cut out without hands, whose builder and ruler is God.

D&C 45:11. Wherefore . . . let me show unto you even my wisdom of him whom ye say is the God of Enoch, and his brethren, 12. Who were separated from the earth, . . . a city reserved until a day of righteousness shall come.

Berl. Manich. Copt. Ms. p. 12. Kap. 1:1. When my Apostle [Enoch] shall raise himself up he shall be lifted up along with his church, and they shall be lifted up [elevated] from the earth. 5. It shall take the form of my assembly [*ekklesia*] and be free in the height.

The "Enoch" of the Dead Sea Scrolls

Just in time for the latest episode in this examination into the book of Enoch comes the long-awaited translation of the Dead Sea Scroll book of Enoch. (J. T. Milik and M. Black, eds., *The Books of Enoch, Aramaic Fragments of Qumran Cave 4*, Oxford: Clarenden Press, 1976.) Father J. T. Milik, one of the first scholars on the scene when the scrolls were discovered, was assigned thirty-two fragments of the books of Enoch from Qumran Cave IV; and all scholars working on Enoch have eagerly waited during the last quarter century to see what new information would be added, what theories might be toppled, what hypotheses confirmed by these documents in Aramaic, the earliest of all known Enoch texts.

These documents, dating from the third to the first centuries B.C., corroborate the other Enoch literature that we have. There *was* a real book of Enoch, which was once written in five parts. This seriously challenges those critics who have claimed for years that ancient sectaries threw everything into Enoch that they wanted to pass off as scripture.

It's an added delight for Latter-day Saints to read that Professor Milik finds the Greek texts to be much superior to the Ethiopian texts—the Joseph Smith account in the Pearl of Great Price is closer to the Greek than to the Ethiopian. Latter-day Saints will also note with interest Professor Milik's deduction that one text, the Gizeh text, was undoubtedly prepared to be buried with the deceased—a parallel with the usage intended for the Abraham text.

Furthermore, Professor Milik works with the fascinating hypothesis that Enoch had prepared an account of the creation and the law of God that naturally predates Moses' account in Genesis and sees Genesis 6:1-4, long a puzzling passage to the biblical scholar, as a quotation from that earlier Enoch source. This is *exactly* what happens in the Joseph Smith source: Moses quotes Enoch on events shortly after the creation.

As we have already seen, the Enoch story runs into the oldest literature of the human race; and Professor Milik finds links with the mythological heroes of Sumer and Babylonia, with the astronomy of Egypt and Phoenicia, and the ideas about the earth of Mesopotamia. Even though Professor Milik does not seem to recognize the full importance of the "Enoch figure," he provides some evidence that undercuts yet another scholarly supposition: that Enoch was invented out of the hopes and yearnings of Messianic Jews in the second century B.C.; in fact, however, these very people were shunning the Enoch material at that very time. Milik reviews some important texts that show the writers of the Aramaic text gradually losing their interest in Enoch material during the first century, then the Essenes turning away from it, the writers at Masada actually expunging the name of Enoch and putting Noah in its stead, while the Christians, on the other hand, treasured it highly and embellished it with so many astrological flourishes that they unintentionally undermined Enoch's credibility for future generations.

In all of these ways, the Qumran IV Enoch fragments reinforce rather than reinterpret what we as Latter-day Saints already knew about Enoch. But these newly translated pieces add one genuinely new bit of information to our store—something that is probably the most objective test yet of Joseph Smith's prophetic powers.

What always impressed me as the oddest detail of the Joseph Smith account of Enoch was the appearance out of the blue of the name of the only nonbiblical individual named in the whole book—Mahijah. (Moses 6:40.) Mahijah is the one who asks Enoch searching questions, and in answer is told about the place Mahujah, where Enoch began this particular phase of his mission. (Moses 7:2.) It was therefore with a distinct shock of recognition that, after having looked through all but the last of the Aramaic Enoch fragments without finding anything particularly new, and coming to those very last little fragments, I found the name Mahujah leaping out of the pages again and again. (Pp. 300, 302, 305, 311, 314.) Could this be our Mahujah or Mahijah? As a matter of fact it could be either, not only because the semi-vowels *w* and *y* are written very much alike in the Aramaic script and are sometimes confused by scribes, but also because the name as written in 4QEn, MHWY, is the same as the MHWY-EL who appears in Genesis 4:18 as the grandfather of Enoch, transliterated in the King James Bible as *Mehuja-el,* which name also appears in the Greek Septuagint as *Mai-el* and in the Latin Vulgate as *Mavia-el,* showing that Mahujah and Mahijah were the same name, since *Mai* (the Greek had no internal "h") could come only from Mahi-.

So what? A coincidence—a giant or a Watcher called Mahujah or Mahijah. But far more than a coincidence when taken in its context. The only thing the Mahijah in the Book of Moses is remarkable for is his putting of bold direct questions to Enoch, thus giving the patriarch an opening for calling upon the people to repent, referring them to the book of remembrance, and telling them of the plan of salvation. And this is exactly the role, and the only role, that the Aramaic Mahujah plays in the story. The name is found in none of the other Enoch texts and neither is the story: it is peculiar to the version Joseph Smith gave us and the oldest known Enoch manuscripts. The following translation is from Milik and Black, lest the writer be charged with forcing the text.

Moses 6:39. . . . when they heard him . . . fear came on all them that heard him.	4QEnGiants[b]1.20. [Thereupon] all the giants [and the nephilim] took fright
6:40. And there came a man unto him, whose name was Mahijah, and said to him: Tell us plainly who thou art and from whence thou comest?	and they summoned MHWY and he came to them: And the giants asked him and sent him to Enoch [. . .] saying to him: Go then [. . .] and under pain of death you must [. . .] and

listen to his voice; and tell him that he is to explain to you and to interpret the dreams.

6Q8 1. [. . .] Ohya and he said to MHWY: "[. . .] and (I?) do not tremble. Who showed you all (that), tell [us(?)] [. . .]" And MHWY said: "[. . .] Baraq'el, my father, was with me."

6:41. And he said to them: I came out from . . . the land of my fathers, a land of righteousness unto this day

4QEnGiants^c. [Ohyah, following MHWY's report]: . . . my accusers [. . .] they dwell in [heaven]s, for they live in holy abodes, . . . they are more powerful than I.

6:42. And . . . as I journeyed . . . by the sea east, I beheld a vision: and lo, the heavens I saw. . . .
7:2-3. . . . As I was journeying . . . I . . . went up on the mount; . . . I beheld the heavens open.

4QEnGiants^b. [MHWY . . . rose up into the air] like the whirlwinds, and he flew . . . and crossed Solitude, the great desert [. . .] And he caught sight of Enoch, and he called to him and said to him: "An oracle [. . .]"

6:45. Enoch: . . . we . . . cannot deny. . . . 46. For a *book* of remembrance we have written among us, according to the pattern given by the *finger* of *God* . . . in our own language.

4QEnGiants^a Frag. ii 7. [. . .] to you, MH[wy][. . .] the two tablets [. . .] and the second has not been read up till now. 8. The *boo[k* of [. . .] The copy of the second tablet of the Epistle [. . .] written] by Enoch, the distinguished scribe's *own hand* [. . .] and the *Holy One*, to Shemihazah and all [his] com[panions].

6:47. And as Enoch spake forth the words of God, the people trembled, and could not stand in his presence.

4QEnGiants^a Frg. 4. [. . .] Ohyah said to Ha[hyah, his brother . . .] . . . they prostrated themselves and

began to weep before
[Enoch(?) . . .].

6:48. And he said to them:
. . . We are made partakers of
misery and woe.
6:49. . . . carnal, sensual,
and devilish, and are shut out
from the presence of God.

4EnGiants*a* Frg. 8. The
longest fragment: The
depravity and misery of the
people described. Their
petition is rejected: God has
cast them out. All is "for the
worst."

6:52. . . . If thou wilt turn
unto me . . . and repent . . .
asking all things in his name,
. . . it shall be given you.

(Closing line) And now,
loosen your bonds (of sin)
which tie [you] up [. . .] and
begin to pray.

7:13. And . . . he [Enoch]
led the people of God, and
their enemies came to battle
against them; and he spake the
word of the Lord, and the
earth trembled, . . .

4QEnGiants*c*. (Ohyah the
enemy of Enoch): ". . . by the
strength of my power, [I had
attacked] all flesh and I have
made war with them . . . they
live in holy abodes, and . . .
they are more powerful than
I."

and the roar of the lions was
heard out of the wilderness;

and all nations feared greatly.

[Thereupon . . .] the
roaring of the wild beasts came
and the multitude of the wild
animals began to cry out
[. . .]. And Ohyah spoke
. . . My dream has
overwhelmed(?) [me] [. . .
and the s]leep of my eyes [has
fled].

7:37. . . . these shall suffer.
. . . 38. . . . these . . . shall
perish in the floods; and
behold, I will shut them up; a
prison have I prepared for
them.

4QEnGiants*a* Frg. 7i. Then
Ohyah [said] to Hahya[h, his
brother . . .]. Then he (sc.
God?) punished . . . the sons
of the Watchers, the giants,
and all [their] beloved ones will
not be spared [. . .] he has

imprisoned us and you he has
subdued (lit. tegaf, seized,
confined).

Bearing in mind that the Aramaic fragments are few
and very small and arranged in whatever order the editors
think best, it is still possible to see that the themes of the
Joseph Smith account emerge clearly amidst all the very obvious changes and vicissitudes that have occurred to the
ancient texts.

KEY TO ABBREVIATIONS

The pseudepigraphic works found in this paper—Apocalypse of
Abraham, Apocalypse of Adam, Apocalypse of Baruch, Apocalypse
of Elijah, 2 Baruch, 1 Enoch, 2 Enoch (Secrets of Enoch), 3 Enoch,
Jubilees, 4 Ezra, Psalms of Solomon, Testament of Adam, and
Testament of Moses—may all be conveniently found in James
Charlesworth, *The Old Testament Pseudepigrapha*, 2 vols. (Garden
City, N.Y.: Doubleday, 1983–85). The citations frequently represent
the author's own translations. Similarly, materials from the Nag
Hammadi literature—Apocryphon of James, Apocryphon of John,
Gospel of Philip, Hypostasis of the Archons—may be found in James
M. Robinson, *The Nag Hammadi Library in English* (San Francisco:
Harper & Row, 1977). Other works will be cited according to the edi-
tion from which they were taken. The following works are cited in
the body of the text:

Apocalypse of Abraham
In Paul Riessler, *Altjudisches Schrifttum ausserhalb der Bibel*, 2nd
ed. (Heidelberg: F. H. Kerle, 1966).

Apocalypse of Adam
In Douglas M. Parrott, ed., *Nag Hammadi Studies*, vol. 11
(Leiden: E. J. Brill, 1979).

Apocalypse of Elijah
In Herbert P. Houghton, "The Coptic Apocalypse," *Aegyptus* 39
(1959): 195ff.

Apocryphon of John
In *Die Gnostichen Schriften des Koptischen Papyrus 8502*, ed. Walter
C. Till, vol. 60 of *Texte und Untersuchungen zur Geschichte der
Altchristlichen Literatur* (Berlin: Akademie Verlag, 1955). Also in

James Robinson, *Nag Hammadi Library in English* (Leiden: E. J. Brill, 1977).

Beatty
Chester Beatty Collection in Campbell Bonner, *The Last Chapters of Enoch in Greek* (London: Christophers, 1937). See also Sir Frederic G. Kenyon, *The Chester Beatty Biblical Papyri* (London: Emery Walker, 1933-41).

Berayta
Nicholas Sed, "Une Cosmologie juive du haut moyen age: La Berayta di Maᶜaseh Bereshit," *Revue des Etudes Juives* 123 (1964): 259-305.

Berl. Manich. Copt.
Berlin Manichäean Coptic Manuscript, *Manichaische Handschriften der Staatlichen Museen Berlin* (Stuttgart: W. Kahlhammer, 1940).

BHM
Bet ha-Midrash, 6 vols. (Jerusalem: Wahrmann Books, 1967).

Bin Gorion
M. J. Bin Gorion, *Die Sagen der Juden* (Frankfurt: Kütter & Loening, 1913).

Black
Matthew Black, *Apocalypsis Henochi Graece* (Leiden: E. J. Brill, 1970).

Bonner
Campbell Bonner, *The Last Chapters of Enoch in Greek* (London: Christophers, 1937).

Book of Adam
Livre d'Adam, in *Dictionnaire des Apocryphes*, 2 vols. (Paris: Migne, 1856). See note 32.

Cedrenus
Georgius Cedrenus, *Compendium Historiarum* 1:17 in *Corpus Scriptorum Historiae Byzantinae* 4, ed. I. Bekker, 1838.

Combat of Adam and Eve
Livre du Combat d'Adam et Eve, in *Dictionnaire des Apocryphes*, 2 vols. (Paris: Migne, 1856).

Dictionnaire
Dictionnaire des Apocryphes, 2 vols. (Paris: Migne, 1856). See note 32.

Ethiop. Bk. Mysts.
Silvain Grébaut, *Livre des Mystères du ciel et de la Terre,* in *Patrologia Orientalis.*

Ev. Verit.
Micel Malinine, ed., *Evangelium Veritatis* (Zurich: Rascher Verlag, 1956).

Falasha (Anthology)
W. Leslau, ed., *Falasha Anthology* (New York: Yale University Press, 1951).

Gizeh
Gizeh Fragment in appendix 1 of R. H. Charles, *The Book of Enoch* (London: Oxford University Press, 1913).

Iesous Besileus
Iesous Besileus ou Basileusas, ed. R. Eisler (Heidelberg: C. Winter Verlag, 1930).

Jewish Encyclopedia
W. Popper, ed., *The Jewish Encyclopedia,* 12 vols. (New York: Funk and Wagnall, 1904).

N. Sed. REJ
Nicholas Sed, "Une Cosmologie juive du haut moyen age: La Berayta di Ma'aseh Breshit," *Revue des Études Juives* 123 (1964).

Mid. Rab.
Harry Freeman, *Midrash Rabbah* (London: Soncino, 1961).

Ms. R.
In Andre Vaillant, *Le Livre des Secrets d'Henoch* (University of Paris: Institut d'Etudes Slaves, 1952).

P.G.
J. P. Migne, *Patrologiae Graecae,* 161 vols. (Paris: J. P. Migne, 1857).

P.L.
Patrologiae Latinae, 221 vols. (Paris: J.-P. Migne, 1879).

P.O.
Patrologia Orientalis.

Secrets of Enoch (Morfill)
W. R. Morfill, *The Book of the Secrets of Enoch* (Oxford: Clarendon Press, 1896).

Secrets (Vaillant)
Andre Vaillant, *Le Livre des Secrets d'Henoch* (University of Paris: Institut d'Etudes Slaves, 1952).

Sophia Jesu Christi
> In volume 60 of *Texte und Untersuchungen zur Geschichte der altchristlichen Literatur* (Berlin: Akademie Verlag, 1955).

Testament of Abraham
> In W. Leslau, ed., *Falasha Anthology* (New York: Yale University Press, 1951).

T.U.
> *Texte und Untersuchungen zur Geschichte der altchristlichen Literatur* (Berlin: Akademie Verlag, 1955).

Zohar
> *The Zohar*, trans. Harry Sperling and Maurice Simon (New York: Rebecca Bennet, 1958).

11 QPSa Creat.
> "Hymn to the Creator," in J. A. Sanders, *Discoveries in the Judeaen Desert of Jordan*, vol. 4 (Oxford: Clarendon Press, 1965), pp. 89-92.

NOTES

1. The book of Moses, heading to chapter 1.

2. Joseph Smith, *History of The Church of Jesus Christ of Latter-day Saints*, B. H. Roberts, ed. (Salt Lake City: Deseret News, 1902) 1:133.

3. *Pearl of Great Price: Being a Choice Selection from the Revelations, Translations, and Narrations of Joseph Smith* (Liverpool: F. D. Richards, 1851), p. 1.

4. Smith, *History* 1:139.

5. Ibid., 1:135-36.

6. Ibid., 1:131-33.

7. R. H. Charles, *The Book of Enoch* (London: Oxford University Press, 1913), p. ix, n. 1. Compare his *Apocrypha and Pseudepigrapha of the Old Testament*, 2 vols. (Oxford: Clarendon Press, 1912) 2:163, where he maintains that "some of its authors . . . belong to the true succession of the prophets, . . . exhibiting on occasions the inspiration of the O.T. prophets."

8. Charles, *Book of Enoch*, pp. xcv-ciii, indicates that many "passages of the New Testament . . . either in phraseology or idea directly depend on or are illustrative of passages in 1 Enoch." "In the New Testament," according to a current *Encyclopaedia Britannica*, 24 vols. (Chicago: Encyclopaedia Britannica, 1973) 8:604, "Enoch himself is mentioned in Luke iii:37; Heb. xi:5; and Jude 14, while there is reference to him in Jude 4-15, Matt. 19:28, 26:24, Luke 16:9, John 5:22, 1 Thess. 5:3, 1 Pet. 3:19ff., and Revelation.

9. Charles, *Book of Enoch*, p. xcv.

10. Ibid., pp. xii-xiii.

11. Ibid., pp. lxx-lxxix for the Jewish sources, pp. lxxxi-xci for the Christian.

12. Carl Schmidt, ed., *Pistis Sophia*, trans. by Violet MacDermot (Leiden: E. J. Brill, 1978), p. 247.

13. Ibid., p. 349.

14. Eugenio Zolli, "Henoch," in *Enciclopedia Cattolica*, 12 vols. (Città del Vaticano: Ente per l'Enciclopedia Cattolica per il Libro Cattolico, 1951), 6:1405.

15. Charles, *Book of Enoch*, p. x; it was second only in influence to the canonical Daniel, Klaus Koch, *Ratlos vor der Apokalyptik* (Gütersloh: Gerd Mohn, 1970), pp. 19-20.

16. Adolf Jellinek, *Bet ha-Midrash*, 6 vols. (Jerusalem: Wahrmann Books, 1967) 2:xxx. Hereafter cited as *BHM*.

17. Ibid. For a list of Enoch citations in Cabalistic writers, see Isaac Myer, *Qabbalah* (Philadelphia: Isaac Myer, 1888), p. 167.

18. "So far only two Aramaic fragments have been published. . . . In view of this important discovery it might seem premature to publish a Greek text before the publication of these fragments. . . . Unfortunately this has not proved to be possible; and the prolonged delay . . . of the Aramaic Enoch and latterly the confused situation with regard to the custody of the Aramaic mss., make any further postponement of this provisional Greek edition inadvisable." (Matthew Black, *Apocalypsis Henochi Graece* [Leiden: E. J. Brill, 1970], p. 7.)

19. Adolf Jellinek, "Hebräische Quellen für das Buch Henoch," *Zeitschrift der deutschen morgenländischen Gesellschaft* 7 (1853): 249.

20. Charles, *Book of Enoch*, p. ix.

21. C. C. Torrey, *The Apocryphal Literature* (New Haven: Yale University Press, 1945), p. 27.

22. St. Augustine, *City of God* 15:23.

23. Hans-Friedrich Weiss, *Untersuchungen zur Kosmologie des hellenistischen und palästinischen Judentums* (Berlin: Akadamie-Verlag, 1966), p. 119.

24. H. Leclerq, "Henoch," in F. Cabrol and H. Leclerq, *Dictionnaire d'Archéologie Chretiénne et de Liturgie*, 15 vols. (Paris, Librairie Letouzey et Ane, 1925) 6:2245-46.

25. Charles, *Book of Enoch*, p. ciii.

26. This attitude is illustrated in the author's "Christian Envy of the Temple," in *Jewish Quarterly Review* 50 (1959): 99ff.

27. In his work *Peri Archon*, 1:iii:3 (J.-P. Migne, *Patrologiae Graecae*, Paris: J.-P. Migne, 1857, hereafter cited as P.G.) 11:147-48 and 4:35

(P.G. 11:409), Origen appeals to "The Book of Enoch" to support his theories of the creation, but when Celsus quotes Enoch he objects: "Even less should things be taken seriously which Celsus seems to have picked up and misunderstood from the Book of Enoch." (*Contra Celsum* 5:54; *P.G.* 11:1265.) He says things are "very much mixed up" and "in the churches not taken very seriously as Scripture (divine)," since they contain "matter not preached (uttered) nor heard in the churches of God," which nobody would be foolish enough to take literally. (*Contra Celsum, P.G.,* 11:1268-69.)

28. A. J. Maas, "Henoch," in *The Catholic Encyclopedia,* 15 vols. (New York: Robert Appleton Company, 1910) 7:218.

29. J. Plastaras, "Henoch," in *New Catholic Encyclopedia,* 17 vols. (New York: McGraw-Hill Book Company, 1967) 6:1019.

30. Michael E. Stone, "Judaism at the Time of Christ," *Scientific American* 228 (January 1973): 80-82.

31. The Syncellus fragment, from his *Chronographia* 1:47, found in *Corpus Scriptorum Historiae Byzantinae* 41, ed. Wilhelm Dindorf (Bonn: Weberi, 1829), is also reproduced in appendix 1 of Charles, *Book of Enoch,* p. 305. Reference to this was made by Georgius Cedrenus, circa A.D. 1100 in his *Compendium Historiarum* 1:17 in *Corpus Scriptorum Historiae Byzantinae* 4, ed. I. Bekker, 1838. See also P.G. 121:41, 44-45, 476.

32. G. B., "Livre d'Henoch," in J.-P. Migne, *Dictionnaire des Apocryphes,* 2 vols. (Paris: Migne, 1856), 1:396, in *Troisième et Dernière Encyclopédie Théologique,* Tomes 23 and 24. Hereafter cited as *Dictionnaire.*

33. G. B., "Livre d'Henoch" in Migne, *Dictionnaire* 1:397. It is quoted by Peter Alphonsus, and is simply a Latinized rendering of the well-known Moslem merchant's creed: *Al-kāsib ḥabīb ullāh!*

34. Nathaniel Schmidt, "Traces of the Early Acquaintance in Europe with the Book of Enoch," *Journal of the American Oriental Society* 42 (1922): 45.

35. Ibid., p. 47.

36. Ibid., p. 47.

37. Ibid., p. 46.

38. John McClintock, "Enoch, Book of," in *Cyclopaedia of Biblical, Theological, and Ecclesiastical Literature,* 12 vols. (New York: Harper & Brothers Publishers, 1870) 3:225.

39. See author's discussion in *Since Cumorah: The Book of Mormon in the Modern World* (Salt Lake City: Deseret Book, 1970), pp. 32-35.

40. James Strachan, "Enoch," in *Dictionary of the Apostolic Church,* ed. James Hastings, 2 vols. (New York: Charles Scribner's Sons, 1916), 1:334.

41. Schmidt, *Book of Enoch*, p. 50, placing Postel's meeting with the priest around 1536.

42. Ibid.

43. "Livre d'Henoch," in Migne, *Dictionnaire* 1:399.

44. Schmidt, *Book of Enoch*, p. 51.

45. Michael Stuart, "Christology of the Book of Enoch," *The American Biblical Repository*, 2nd Series, 3 (January 1840): 88.

46. Schmidt, *Book of Enoch*, p. 51.

47. Ibid., pp. 51-52.

48. Ibid., p. 52.

49. "Livre d'Henoch," in Migne, *Dictionnaire* 1:400. However, in 1736, Johann Albert Fabricius in his *Codex Pseudepigraphus Veteris Testamenti*, 2 vols. (Hamburg: T. C. Felginer, 1722), 1:22, gathered and reproduced all available passages from the church fathers concerning Enoch ("Livre d'Henoch," in Migne, *Dictionnaire* 1:399).

50. McClintock, "Enoch, Book of," 3:225.

51. Stuart, "Christology," 3:89.

52. Schmidt, *Book of Enoch*, p. 52.

53. Stuart, "Christology," 3:89. Among Bruce's treasures was the Codex Brucianus 96, a long Coptic Christian work which is strongly influenced throughout by the Enoch tradition.

54. Ibid., 3:89.

55. J. E. H. Thomson, "Apocalyptic Literature," in James Orr, ed., *The International Standard Bible Encyclopedia* 5 vols. (Grand Rapids: William B. Eerdmans, 1939), 1:164.

56. McClintock, "Book of Enoch," 3:225.

57. Thomson, "Apocalyptic Literature," 1:164.

58. "Livre d'Henoch," in Migne, *Dictionnaire* 1:400.

59. "Livre d'Henoch," in Migne, *Dictionnaire* 1:394, 403. De Sacy's work appeared in the *Magasin encyclopédique*, ann. 6, 1:382, and included chapters 1-3, 11-16, 22, and 32, all from the Paris manuscript.

60. Richard Laurence, "A Charge Delivered at the Triennial Visitation of the Province of Munster, in the Year 1826," editorial in *The British Critic, Quarterly Theological Review, and Ecclesiastical Record*, Series 4, 2 (1826): 162, 131-33, 160-62, pursuing Laurence with relentless fury.

61. Ibid., p. 163.

62. Ibid., pp. 165-66.

63. Stuart, "Christology," 3:90.

64. "Livre d'Henoch," in Migne, *Dictionnaire* 1:400-401.

65. S. De Sacy, in *Journal des Savants* (October 1822), pp. 545-51, 587-95.

66. Andreas Gottlieb Hoffmann, *Das buch Henoch in vollständiger uebersetzung mit fortlaufendem commentar, ausführlicher einleitung und erläuternden excursen*, 2 vols. (962 pages), (Jena: Croeker, 1833-38). R. H. Charles ignores this item in his list of translations, *Apocrypha and Pseudepigrapha* 2:186.

67. "Livre d'Henoch," in Migne, *Dictionnaire* 1:393-394. A. F. Gfroerer was director of the Stuttgart Library.

68. "Livre d'Henoch," in Migne, *Dictionnaire* 1:394.

69. This translation of the Book of Enoch is contained in "Livre d'Henoch," Migne, *Dictionnaire* 1:425-514.

70. *Fraser's Magazine* 48 (November, 1833) contains a review of the second edition of Laurence's Enoch. Recently there has been available in bookstores *The Book of Enoch the Prophet*, "Literally Translated from the Ethiopic" by Richard Laurence, LL.D. A reprint from an edition edited, with variations, and published by John Thomson, Glasgow, 1882"; 1966 edition, Seattle, Washington. The text differs from the recent reprint, *The Book of Enoch the Prophet* (London: Kegan Paul, Trench and Co., 1883).

71. They were Edward Murray, *Enoch Restitutus*, or "an Attempt to separate from the books of Enoch, the book quoted by Saint Jude"; D. M. Butt, *The Genuiness of the Book of Enoch Investigated;* John Overton, *An Inquiry into the Truth and Use of Enoch* . . . (1822). The neglect of these writings is noted in "Livre d'Henoch," Migne, *Dictionnaire*, 1:398.

72. Stuart, "Christology," 3:90.

73. Thomson, "Apocalyptic Literature," 1:164.

74. Stuart, "Christology," 3:89.

75. Schmidt, *Book of Enoch*, p. 47.

76. Algernon Herbert, *Nimrod* (London: Printed for R. Priestey, 1828) 1:36.

77. George H. Schodde, *The Book of Enoch Translated from the Ethiopic with Introduction and Notes* (Andover: Warren F. Draper, 1882).

78. Michael Stuart, "Future Punishment, as Exhibited in the Book of Enoch," *The American Biblical Repository*, 2nd series, 4 (July 1840): 10.

79. Ibid., 4:11.

80. Stuart, "Christology," 3:130.

81. Ibid., 3:129.

82. Glaire & Walsh, eds., "Enoch," in *Encyclopédie Catholique*, 18 vols. (Paris: Parent Desbarres, 1846), 11: 214-15.

83. J. B. Frey, "Apocryphes de l'Ancien Testament," in L. Pirot, ed., *Dictionnaire de la Bible, Supplement* (Paris: Librarie Letouzey et Ane, 1928) 1:369.

84. K. Koch, *Ratlos*, pp. 7-9.

85. C. P. Van Andel, *De Structuur van de Henoch-Traditie en het Nieuwe Testament* (Utrecht: H. Kemink & Son, 1955), p. 1.

86. Michael E. Stone, "Judaism at the Time of Christ," *Scientific American* 228 (January 1973): 80-82.

87. Geo Widengren, *The Gnostic Attitude*, trans. and ed. Birger A. Pearson, (Santa Barbara: Institute of Religious Studies, 1973), pp. 41-45.

88. E. M. Sowerby, *Catalogue of the Library of Thomas Jefferson*, 5 vols. (Washington: Library of Congress, 1959) 5:vii.

89. Ibid., 1:1.

90. Stuart, "Christology," 3:91; italics added.

91. Ibid., 3:92-93.

92. Ibid., 3:102.

93. Ibid., 3:103.

94. Parley P. Pratt, "The Apocryphal Book of Enoch," *Millennial Star* 1 (July 1840): 61.

95. Ibid., pp. 62-63.

96. Campbell Bonner, *The Last Chapters of Enoch in Greek* (London: Christophers, 1937), p. 3.

97. A. L. Davies, "Enoch, Book of," in Hastings, ed., *Dictionary of the Apostolic Church* 1:334. See also note 40.

98. O. Plöger, "Henochbücher," *Die Religion in Geschichte und Gegenwart* (Tübingen: J. C. B. Mohr, 1959), p. 222.

99. Charles, *Book of Enoch*, p. xxiv; one important manuscript dates "possibly as early as the 15th century," p. xxiii, and another from the 18th century, p. xxii.

100. Plöger, "Henochbücher," p. 222.

101. Ibid., p. 223-24.

102. Bonner, *Last Chapters*, p. 22.

103. Ibid., p. 24.

104. Van Andel, *Structuur*, p. 7.

105. Charles, *Book of Enoch*, pp. xxiv-xxv.

106. Ibid., p. xxvi.

107. Samuel Terrien, "Enoch, Books of," in *Encyclopedia Americana*, 30 vols. (1970), 10:395.

108. Plöger, "Henochbücher," p. 224.

109. Terrien, "Enoch, Books of," 10:395.

110. Weiss, *Untersuchungen zur Kosmologie*, p. 126. See also O. Eissfeldt, *Einleitung in das Alte Testament* (Tübingen: Mohr, 1964), p. 843.

111. Emmanuele da San Marco, "Henoch, Libro di," in *Enciclopedia Cattolica*, 12 vols. (Città del Vaticano: Ente per l'Enciclopedia Cattolicae per il Libro Cattolico, 1951), 6:1407.

112. David Winston, "The Iranian Component in the Bible Apocrypha, and Qumran," *History of Religions* 5 (Winter 1966): 197.

113. Terrien, "Enoch, Books of," 10:395.

114. Andre Vaillant, *Le Livre des Secrets d'Henoch* (University of Paris: Institut d'Etudes Slaves, 1952), p. iii.

115. Ibid., p. iv.

116. Ibid., p. i.

117. Ibid., p. i.

118. Ibid., p. v.

119. Ibid., p. viii.

120. Ibid., p. xi.

121. Ibid., p. xxii.

122. Ibid., p. xxiii.

123. Charles, *Book of Enoch*, p. xcvff.

124. Vaillant, *Secrets d'Henoch*, p. viii.

125. Terrien, "Enoch, Books of," 10:394.

126. Charles, *Book of Enoch*, p. xvii.

127. Bonner, *Last Chapters*, p. 3.

128. Ibid., p. 4.

129. Ibid., pp. 12-13.

130. Sir Frederic G. Kenyon, *The Chester Beatty Biblical Papyri* (London: Emery Walker, 1933-41) 8:12.

131. Bonner, *Last Chapters*, p. 17.

132. Kenyon, *Beatty Biblical Papyri* 8:5-7.

133. Van Andel, *Structuur*, p. 3.

134. Ibid., p. 4.

135. Schmidt, *Book of Enoch*, p. 44.

136. Ibid., pp. 44-45.

137. Charles, *Book of Enoch*, pp. lxx-lxxix.

138. Marc Philonenko, "Une Citation Manichéenne du Livre d'Hénoch," *Revue d'Histoire et de Philosophie Religieuses* 52 (1972): 337-40.

139. Black, *Apocalypsis Henochi*.

140. Ibid.

141. *BHM* 2:xxx.

142. McClintock, "Enoch, Book of," 3:228.

143. Jellinek, "Hebräische Quellen," p. 249.

144. *BHM* 2:xxx-xxxii.

145. *BHM* 3:vii, 83-102.

146. *BHM* 4:xi-xii, 129-132.

147. *BHM* 5:xli; Frg. XXIV, pp. 170-90.

148. Pierre Batiffol, "Apocalypses Apocryphes," in F. Vigouroux,

ed., *Dictionnaire de la Bible*, 5 vols. (Paris: Letouzey and Ane, 1895-1912), 1:757.

149. Frey, "Apocryphes," 1:357.

150. Schmidt, *Book of Enoch*, p. 47.

151. Ibid., p. 45.

152. Jellinek, "Hebräische Quellen," p. 249.

153. J. T. Milik, "Prière du Nabonide et autres écrits d'un cycle de Daniel," *Revue Biblique* 63 (July 1956): 407-415.

154. Frank M. Cross, "The Manuscripts of the Dead Sea Caves," *Biblical Archaeologist* 17 (February 1954): 3.

155. Black, *Apocalypsis Henochi*, pp. 6-7.

156. D. Barthelemy and J. T. Milik, eds., *Discoveries in the Judean Desert, 1: Qumran Cave 1* (Oxford: Clarendon, 1955), p. 3.

157. Terrien, "Enoch, Books of," 10:394.

158. Nahman Avigad, *A Genesis Apocryphon* (Jerusalem: Hebrew University, 1956), p. 19.

159. Terrien, "Enoch, Books of," 10:394.

160. *Livre d'Enoch* 1:425-26.

161. Frey, "Apocryphes," 1:357.

162. Carl Christian Clemen, "Die Zusammensetzung des Buches Henoch, der Apokalypse der Baruch und des Vierten Buches Esra," in *Theologische Studien und Kritiken* 71 (1898): 211-46, cit. Charles, *Book of Enoch*, p. xliii.

163. Charles, *Book of Enoch*, pp. xlvii-xlviii.

164. Ibid., pp. xxx-xlvi.

165. Michael Stuart, "Christology," 3:132. Later, in 1891, T. K. Cheyne pointed out "Essene and Zoroastrian elements" in the Enoch literature; cit. Charles, *Book of Enoch*, p. xlii.

166. Charles, *Book of Enoch*, p. xxxv, emphasis added.

167. Davies, "Enoch, Book of," 1:334.

168. M. Rist, "Enoch, Book of," in *Interpreter's Dictionary of the Bible* (New York: Abingdon Press, 1962) 2:103.

169. Thomson, "Apocalyptic Literature," 1:166.

170. Van Andel, *Structuur*, p. 1.

171. Ibid., pp. 5-7.

172. Summarized by Van Andel, *Structuur*, p. 9.

173. Ibid., p. 11.

174. Ibid., p. 43.

175. Ibid., p. 47.

176. Ibid., p. 51.

177. Ibid., p. 68.

178. Ibid., pp. 69-70.

179. Ibid., p. 114.

180. Ibid., p. 48.

181. Raphael Jehudah Zwi Werblowsky, "Enoch, Books of," in *Encyclopedia of Jewish Religion* (New York: Holt, Rinehart, Winston, 1965), p. 129.

182. Stuart, "Christology," 3:105. He finds "by far the most interesting and important part of the book" is that which develops its christology, p. 99.

183. Ibid., 3:105.

184. Ibid., 3:105.

185. Ibid., 3:113.

186. Ibid., 3:128.

187. Stuart, "Future Punishment," 4:10.

188. Ibid., 4:10.

189. Ibid., 4:10.

190. Ibid., 4:11; Stuart, "Christology," 3:133.

191. Stuart, "Christology," 3:123.

192. Stuart, "Future Punishment," 4:5.

193. G. Volkmar, "Beiträge zur Erklärung des Buches Henoch nach dem äthiopischen Text," *Zeitschrift der deutschen morgenländischen Gesellschaft* 14 (1860): 87.

194. Schmidt, *Book of Enoch*, p. 45.

195. Vaillant, *Secrets d'Henoch*, p. xiii. J. B. Frey, another Catholic, avers that "the finest and most important part" of the Enoch literature is possibly a Christian interpolation. (Pirot, *Dictionnaire de la Bible, Supplement*), pp. 358-59.

196. Charles, *Book of Enoch*, p. xxxiii.

197. See John Marco Allegro, *The Dead Sea Scrolls* (New York: Penguin Books, 1956), pp. 134-80.

198. G. W. Anderson, "Enoch, Books of," *Encyclopaedia Britannica*, 24 vols. (1973), 8:604-5.

199. Van Andel, *Structuur*, p. 113.

200. Matthew Black, "Eschatology of the Similitudes of Enoch," *Journal of Theological Studies*, New Series, 3 (1952): 4, quoting T. W. Manson.

201. Batiffol, "Apocalypses," 1:757. Enoch reflects the Judaism of Palestine during the transition to Christianity and to Rabbinism according to Zolli, another Catholic writer. ("Henoch," 6:1405-6.)

202. Quoted by G. Santillana, *Hamlet's Mill* (Boston: Gambit, 1969), p. 10.

203. Hugh Nibley, "The Genesis of the Written Word," *New Era* 3 (September 1973): 38-50.

204. *The Zohar*, trans. Harry Sperling and Maurice Simon (New York: Rebecca Bennet, 1958), Bereshith, 37b.

205. *BHM* 3:xxxii.

206. Eusebius, *Praeparatio Evangelica* 7:viii and 11:vi, in P.G. 21:520, 856f.

207. Epiphanius, *Adversus Haereses* 1:ii, 26, 8, in P.G. 41:34lf.

208. Vaillant, *Secrets of Enoch*, p. x.

209. H. Gunkel, "Der Schreiberengel Nabu im Alten Testament und im Judentum," *Archiv für Religionswissenschaft* 1 (1898): 299.

210. "Testament of Abraham," in W. Leslau, ed., *Falasha Anthology* (New York: Yale University Press, 1951), p. 100.

211. Georgius Cedrenus, *Historiarum Compendium* 1:17 of vol. 4 in series. See note 31.

212. N. H. Tur Sinai, "Shitir Shame, die Himmselschrift," *Archiv Orientalni* 17 (1949): 433.

213. A. Leo Oppenheim, "Mesopotamian Mythology II," *Orientalia* 19 (1950): 155-56.

214. M. J. Bin Gorion, *Die Sagen der Juden* (Frankfurt: Kuttier & Loening, 1913) 1:100.

215. Ian Henderson, *Myth in the New Testament* (Chicago: Regnery Company, 1952), p. 16, congratulates contemporary theology in having risen through demythologizing above the quasi-physical ideas of Paul. According to Origen, the church rejects any involvement with a physical universe whatsoever, nothing in its teachings being *kata physin;* the trouble with the Greek myths is that they are tainted with the physical. (P.G. 6:1260.) Arnobius says such questions as "What is man? What is the origin of the soul? Whence comes evil? How large is the earth?" etc., are completely irrelevant: "Leave these things to God and care for your soul!" (Arnobius, *Adversus Nationes,* 2:61, *Corpus Scriptorum Ecclesiasticarum Latinorum* 4:97.) According to an official Roman Catholic handbook, whoever says or believes that the physical heavens have any relationship whatever to God and the divine orders of Cherubim and Seraphim is anathema (H. J. K. Denzinger, *Enchiridion Symbolorum* [Rome: Herder, 1957], no. 2:206). Whoever studies the Creation, the Chariot or asks what is above, below or beyond or what will be in the eternities, "it were better for him had he not come into the world!" (Mishnah, Hag. 2:1).

216. Nibley, "Genesis," pp. 42-43.

217. Clemens Alexandrinus, *Stromata* 1:23; 153; in Theodorus Hopfner, *Fontes Historiae Religiones Aegyptiacae* (Bonn: A. Marc and E. Weber, 1922), p. 370.

218. H. Gunkel, *Zum religionsgeschichtlichen Verständnis des Neuen Testaments* (Göttingen: Vandenhoeck & Ruprecht, 1910), p. 29.

219. 1 Enoch 106:19; Bonner, *Last Chapters*, p. 3. Chapter 106 is not included in the translations of Laurence, being a fragment of the book of Noah. Since the Ethiopic Enoch was the first known, its

chapters and verse numbers are standard for all Enoch texts; thus 1 Enoch 106 designates the same section, no matter in what language it is found.

220. Mayer Lambert, "Que portaient les tables de pierre?" *Revue des Études Juives* 82 (1926): 45-48.

221. Geo Widengren, *The Ascension of the Apostle and the Heavenly Book* (Uppsala: Lundquistska Bokhandeln, 1950), p. 7.

222. Ibid., p. 28.

223. Edwyn Robert Bevan, *Sibyls and Seers* (Cambridge: Harvard University Press, 1929), p. 116. Initiates to Greek mysteries must record their inspired versions on tablets and deposit them in the temple archives. (Pausanias 9:39.14.)

224. August Freiherrn von Gall, *Basileia tou Theou* (Heidelberg: Carl Winters Universitatsbuchhandlung, 1926), pp. 313-14.

225. 1QM (Scroll of the War of the Sons of Light Against the Sons of Darkness) 12:3, in Yigael Yadin, *Scroll of the War of the Sons of Light* (Oxford: Oxford University Press, 1962), pp. 314-15.

226. Mosiah 5:5-15, where the acceptance of the covenant goes with the general engraving and sealing of names.

227. Widengren, *Ascension*, pp. 11-12.

228. Ibid. pp. 7, 10-11.

229. Samuel Mercer, *The Pyramid Texts*, 4 vols. (New York: Longmans, Green and Co., 1952), 1:76-77 (No. 2550.267).

230. Timothy Archbishop of Alexandria, "Discourse on the Abbaton," in E. A. W. Budge, *Coptic Martyrdoms in the Dialect of Upper Egypt* (London: British Museum, 1914), pp. 482-83.

231. Yadin, *Scroll of the War*, pp. 314-15.

232. Bin Gorion, *Sagen* 1:263-66.

233. *The Zohar*, Breshith 37b.

234. Bin Gorion, *Sagen* 1:263.

235. Barhadbshabba, *On the Founding of the Schools*, in *Patrologia Orientalis* (Paris: Firmin-Dicht, 1908; hereafter cited as P.O.) 4:352.

236. Nibley, "A New Look at the Pearl of Great Price," *Improvement Era* 72 (November 1969): 120.

237. Bin Gorion, *Sagen* 2:143.

238. D. A. Khvol'son, *Die Ssabier und der Ssabismus*, 2 vols. (St. Petersburg: Buchdruckei der Kaiserlichen Akademie der Wissenschaften, 1856), 2:502-3.

239. *Apocalypse of Adam*, in Douglas M. Parrott, ed., *Nag Hammadi Studies*, vol. 11 (Leiden: E. J. Brill, 1979), folio 85, lines 24-25, 31 (p. 195); also see folio 79, line 27 (p. 183).

240. Schmidt, *Pistis Sophia*, pp. 246-47.

241. Bin Gorion, *Sagen* 1:261-62.

242. *BHM* 3:14:xxxii.

243. Bin Gorion, *Sagen* 1:269.

244. Van Andel, *Structuur* p. 19.

245. Meyer, *Qabbalah*, pp. 98f. The claim is repeated in the *Zohar*, Bereshith 37b.

246. Bin Gorion, *Sagen* 1:257.

247. Van Andel, *Structuur*, pp. 41ff; Moses 8:2.

248. Leslau, "Testament of Abraham," p. 100; italics added.

249. Ascension of Isaiah 9:21-22.

250. Ibid., 9:22.

251. Origen, *In Genesim*, in *P.G.* 12:73, 81, 84.

252. Charles Leonard Woolley, *Abraham* (London: Faber, 1936), p. 182.

253. 4 Ezra 14:22.

254. Charles, *Apocrypha and Pseudepigrapha* 2:470.

255. 2 Baruch 6:8-10.

256. In these passages the document is called a "testament." (Carl Schmidt, *Gespräche Jesu mit seine Jüngern nach der Auferstehung, ein katholisch-apostolisches Sendschreiben des 2 Jahrhunderts*, vol. 43 [3rd series, vol. 13] of *Texte und Untersuchungen zur Geschichte der Altchristlichen Literatur* [Leipzig: Hinrichs, 1919], pp. 164-65.)

257. Cross, "The Manuscript of the Dead Sea Caves," p. 3.

258. Davies, "Enoch, Book of," 1:334.

259. Michel Malinine, ed., *Evangelium Veritatis* (Zürich: Rascher Verlag, 1956), folio 12r, p. 23.

260. 4 Ezra 14:20.

261. Malinine, *Evangelium Veritatis*, folio 12r, p. 23.

262. M. J. Lagrange, *Le Messianisme chez les Juifs* (Paris: J. Gabalda, 1909), p. 46.

263. Geo Widengren, "Synkretistiche Religionen," *Religionsgeschichte des Orients in der Zeit der Weltreligionen*, ed. B. Spuler (Leiden: E. J. Brill, 1961), pp. 77-78ff.

264. 2 Enoch.

265. Apocryphon of James, folio I:1, lines 28-32, I:2, lines 7-18, in James Robinson, *Nag Hammadi Library in English* (Leiden: E. J. Brill, 1977), p. 30. This text, discovered in 1945, is one of the most enlightening commentaries on the subject of secrecy and transmission, "Since you have asked me to send you a secret discourse delivered by the Lord to Peter and me . . . I am writing it in Hebrew letters and sending it to you alone. . . . Make every effort to avoid/prevent the document's reaching a lot of people, the Savior not wishing to tell these things to all of us of the Twelve. . . . Ten months ago I sent you another discussion/talk which the Savior had with me in se-

cret. . . . The Twelve used to have sessions in which they would recall things the Savior had said to them individually, alone or in public, and then write them down in books."

266. 2 Enoch 54:1; italics added.

267. Apocryphon of John, in *Die Gnostichen Schriften des Koptischen Papyrus Berolinensis 8402*, ed. Walter C. Till, vol. 60 of *Texte und
Untersuchungen zur Geschichte der Altchristlichen Literatur* (Berlin:
Akademie Verlag, 1955). Page numbers refer to the Coptic manuscript. Codex 1, p. 75, lines 15-20; p. 76, line 1. Page 76, lines 10-15,
contains a curse on whoever gives up this (writing) as a present or in
return for food or drink or clothing or anything of that nature.

268. 2 Enoch 48:6; italics added.

269. Malinine, *Evangelium Veritatis*, folio 12r, p. 23. It is no secret
that when Jesus explains it to Mary, a cloud envelops them, forming
seven veils of flame, so that even the angels could see or hear nothing of what was going on. (Sebastian Euringer, "Die Binde der
Rechtfertigung," *Orientalia* 9 [1940]:245.)

270. Apocryphon of John, codex 1, p. 76.

271. 4 Ezra 14:45-46.

272. 4 Ezra 14:6.

273. 4 Ezra 14:46.

274. Bin Gorion, *Sagen* 2:270.

275. Bin Gorion *Sagen* 1:263.

276. *Thaʿlabī Qiṣaṣ al-Anbiyā* (Cairo: Muṣṭafa al-Ḥalabī al-Bābī
wa-Awladuhu, 1354 A.H.), p. 242. A very good source.

277. John Marcos Allegro, *The Treasure of the Copper Scroll* (Garden City: Doubleday, 1960), pp. 120ff.

278. Syncellus 1:53-55.

279. Silvain Grebaut, *Livre des Mystères du Ciel et de la Terre* 2:24,
in *P.O.* 6:412.

280. Oppenheim, "Mesopotamian Mythology," 19:155.

281. A. Moret, *Histoire de l'Orient* (Paris: Les Presses Univer-
sitaires de France, 1929), pt. 1, pp. 85-86, 96-97, 141-44.

282. Syncellus 1:51. See note 31 above and note the additional
references to Eusebius in Syncellus 1:50-51.

283. Van Andel, *Structuur*, p. 74.

284. Gerhard Fecht, "Der erste Teil des sogenannten
Evangelium Veritatis," *Orientalia* 32 (1963):327-31.

285. Malinine, *Evangelium Veritatis*. f. 12r:23; 11:22, 1, 38f.

286. Grevaut, *Livre des Mystères* 4:4, in *P.O.* 6:430-31.

287. Carl Schmidt, *Gnostische Schriften in koptischer Sprache aus
dem Codex Brucanius*, vol. 8 of *Texte und Untersuchungen zur Geschichte
der Altchristlichen Literatur* (Leipzig: J. C. Hinrich, 1892), p. 342.
(Hereafter cited as T.U. 8.)

288. Widengren, *The Ascension of the Apostles*, pp. 74-76.

289. Athenasius, *De Decretis Nicaena Synodi*, 5, in *P.G.* 25:424, discussing 1 John 2:7.

290. Schmidt, *Book of Enoch*, pp. 46-47.

291. Jubilees 4:19.

292. Leo Koep, *Das himmlische Buch in Antike und Christentum* (Bonn: P. Hanstein, 1952), pp. 46ff.

293. Davies, "Enoch, Book of," 1:334.

294. 4 Ezra 14:22.

295. 1 Enoch 39:2.

296. Kenyon, *Beatty Biblical Papyri* 8:8.

297. Charles, *Book of Enoch*, p. ix.

298. "The Kephalaia," in H. J. Polotsky, ed., *Manichäische Homilien* (Stuttgart: W. Kohlhammer, 1934) 1:25.

299. This motif is discussed in Hugh Nibley, *The Message of the Joseph Smith Papyri* (Salt Lake City: Deseret Book, 1975), pp. 214-17.

300. Ibid., pp. 94-103. It is significant that at this point in the Joseph Smith version the hero is declared to be a victor over the waters, since to the casual reader that seems quite irrelevant.

301. For the sources, Paul Riessler, *Altjüdisches Schrifttum ausserhalb der Bibel*, 2nd ed. (Heidelberg: F. H. Kerle, 1966), p. 1267. It has been traced to Ebionite and Essene circles closely related to the communities of the Dead Sea Scrolls. Unfortunately, we are here reduced to using Riessler's German translation of the Old Slavonic text.

302. Koch, *Ratlos*, pp. 16, 19ff.

303. The sources are discussed and some of them are collected and translated in J.-P. Migne, *Troisième et Dernière Encyclopédie Théologique*, vol 23 (Paris: J.-P. Migne, 1856), pp. 297ff. It is to this work that our page numbers refer in the following parallel columns.

304. Text in E. A. W. Budge, *Coptic Martyrdoms*, pp. 225-49, translation pp. 474-96. A full account of the findings of the book by Timothy, giving strong indication of its authenticity, is included in the text, folios 1b, 41-5b.

305. Here is powerful confirmation of the Book of Mormon version. Other "forty-day accounts," especially the Coptic *Évangile des Douze Apotres*, first published in 1913 (in *P.O.* 2:132-37), and believed by no less an authority than Origen to be older than the Gospel of Luke, tell a story very close to 3 Nephi: The Lord asks the Twelve one by one if there is any last request; and when some of them are too embarrassed to ask him more, he tells them not to hold back, since he knows their minds already—exactly as in 3 Nephi 28:4-7. Most significant is that the final questions they ask him always have to do with the problem of death and the possibility of coming to terms with it or even avoiding it—the problem of the Three Nephites.

306. Migne, *P.G.* 23:338, citing St. Ephraim and St. Jerome.

307. The subject has been thoroughly studied by Leo Jung, "Fallen Angels in Jewish, Christian, and Mohammedan Literature," *Jewish Quarterly Review*, new series 16 (1925-26): 45-88, 171-205, 287-336, and by Bo Reicke, *The Disobedient Spirits and Christian Baptism* (Copenhagen: E. Mucksgaard, 1946).

308. Thus there are many stories of two fallen angels, going by various names—*BHM* 4:ix-x:127-28 (Shamkhasi and Asael); 5 (no. 2): xxxix (Harut and Marut); Bin Gorion, *Sagen* 1:319-21; (Aza and Azael)—whose behavior matches that of the Watchers.

309. Joseph A. Fitzmeyer, *Genesis Apocryphon* (Rome: Biblical Institute Press, 1971), pp. 51-55 (col. 2, lines 1-26).

310. Georgius Cedrenus, *Historiarum Compendium* 1:18, and P.G. 121:44.

311. Moshe Emanueli, "The Sons of God Took Wives Whomever They Chose," *Beth Mikra* 60 (October-December 1974): 150-52.

312. Noted by Van Andel, *Structuur*, p. 15.

313. Gizeh Fragment 15:3-4, in Charles, *The Book of Enoch*, p. 292.

314. Hippolytus, *De Christo et Antichristo*, in P.G. 10:733, 737, 925-29, 933.

315. Black, *Apocalypsis Henochi*, p. 39. 1 Enoch 99:10-12.

316. 2 Enoch 18:7. Ms. R. in Vaillant, *Secrets d'Henoch*, p. 92. The Watchers "came down and broke their promise, . . . defiling themselves with the wives (*zhenami*) of men, and so debased themselves." (Ibid., p. 18.)

317. Psalms of Solomon 8:9-11.

318. Black, *Apocalypsis Henochi*, pp. 23-24.

319. Gizeh Fragment 15:2-4. The passage puzzles Charles, *Book of Enoch*, appendix 1, p. 294, as it obviously did the Greek scribes.

320. Clement of Alexandria, *Stromata*, in Migne, P.G. 9:24.

321. Gizeh Fragment 8:1ff, in Charles, *Book of Enoch*, p. 280, giving Mss. G^g and G^3.

322. "Life of Enoch," in *BHM* 4:130; *The Zohar*, Bereshith 56a.

323. *The Zohar*, Bereshith 56a.

324. Ibid., Bereshith 56b.

325. 1 Enoch 97:8-10.

326. "Livre d'Adam," in Migne, *Dictionnaire* 1:56.

327. E. G. Graeling, "The Significance and Origin of Genesis 6:1-4," *Journal of Near Eastern Studies* 6 (1947):197.

328. Text in Philonenko, "Une citation manichéenne," 52:338.

329. Text in G. Ricciotti, "Apocalypsis Pauli syriace," *Orientalia* 2 (1933): 22-24.

330. Vaillant, *Secrets d'Henoch*, pp. 70f.

331. Ibid., pp. 10f.

332. Commented on by Koch, *Ratlos*, pp. 25-27.

333. For the changing point of view, three books by Nigel Calder are instructive, namely, *The Restless Earth: A Report on the New Geology* (New York: Viking, 1972); *Violent Universe: An Eye-Witness Account of the Commotion in Astronomy* (New York: Viking, 1969); and *The Weather Machine* (New York: Viking, 1975).

334. The righteous dwell in the mountains and the wicked in the deep. Harry Freedman, *Midrash Rabbah* (London: Soncino, 1961) 1:257; "Livre du Combat d'Adam," in Migne, *Dictionnaire* 1:296; Hipploytus, fragment in *P.G.* 10:709; B. Beer, *Leben Abrahams* (Leipzig: O. Leiner, 1859), quoting Rabbi Eleaser.

335. Sylvain Grébaut, *Les Miracles de Jesus*, in P.O. 17:826-29.

336. Text in Nicolas Sed, "Une Cosmologie Juive du haut moyen age: La Berayta di Ma'aseh Bereshit," *Revue des Études Juives* 123 (1964): 259-305, explaining how the Watchers weep for the evil world here below.

337. Grébaut, *Livre des Mystères*, in P.O. 6:431.

338. "Livre du Combat d'Adam et Eve," in Migne, *Dictionnaire* 1:362.

339. For references, Nibley, "Treasures in the Heavens," in *Dialogue: A Journal of Mormon Thought* 8 (Autumn 1973): 77-78, 81-84; or *Old Testament and Related Studies*, The Collected Works of Hugh Nibley, vol. 1 (Salt Lake City: Deseret Book, 1986), pp. 174-75, 181-85; or *Nibley on the Timely and the Timeless* (Provo, Ut.: Religious Studies Center, Brigham Young University, 1978),pp. 49-84.

340. F. Tempestini, "Livre d'Adam," in Migne, *Dictionnaire* 1:118.

341. Weiss, *Untersuchungen zur Kosmologie*, p. 121.

342. Schmidt, T.U. 8:345.

343. Eusebius, *Praeparatio Evangelica* 9:17, in P.G. 21:708.

344. Syncellus 1:60 and Cedrenus 1:21, lines 11-13. See note 31 above and *P.G.* 121:41-42.

345. Clement of Alexandria, *Eclogae Ex Scripturis Propheticis*, P.G. 53:4.

346. E. Hahn, "Hadîth cosmogonique et Aggadah," *Revue des Études Juives*, new series, 1 (1937):55.

347. McClintock, "Enoch, Book of," 3:227.

348. Stuart, "Christology," 3:129.

349. Ibid.

350. Hugo Rahner, *Spirit and Nature: Papers from the Eranos Yearbooks*, ed. Joseph Campbell (Princeton: Princeton University Press, 1982), Bollingen Series 30:1, 1:145f.

351. Henderson, *Myth in the New Testament*, p. 16.

352. "Livre d'Henoch," Migne, *Dictionnaire* 1:397.

353. Grébaut, Livre des Mystères, in P.O. 6:433.

354. Many examples are given in Sheila Ostrander and Lynn Schroeder, *Psychic Discoveries Behind the Iron Curtain* (New York: Bantam Books, 1970), in which the most skeptical scientists in the world find themselves perplexed.

355. Lyall Watson, *Supernature* (New York: Anchor Press, 1973), pp. 263, 274-76; Carmen Blacker, in Claus J. Bleeker, *Initiation, Studies in the History of Religion* (Leiden: E. J. Brill, 1965), pp. 96ff. Studies have shown tht people who live in high mountains are more susceptible to psychic phenomena.

356. Clement of Rome, *Recognitiones* 1:106, in Migne, P.G. 1:1207-10.

357. Hans Dieter Betz, "Das Verständnis der Apokalyptik in der Theologie der Pannenberg-Gruppe," *Zeitschrift für Theologie und Kirche* 65 (1968): 265.

358. Schmidt, T.U. 8:345.

359. Weiss, pp. 83-84, citing Jerome, in P.L. 22:546.

360. F. Tempestini, "Livre d'Adam" in Migne, *Dictionnaire* 1:166.

361. Charles, *Book of Enoch*, p. 147.

362. Ibid., p. 149f; and Van Andel, *Structuur*, p. 40.

363. Van Andel, *Structuur*, p. 41.

364. The cases of Moses and Enoch are particularly interchangeable, either by ancient scribes or modern interpreters, as noted by Montague Rhodes James, *Apocrypha Anecdota* (Cambridge : Cambridge University Press, 1893), pp. 166-71.

365. Myer, *Qabbalah*, p. 388.

366. Ibid.

367. Hahn, "Hadîth cosmogonique et Aggadah," p. 62.

368. Arthur O. Lovejoy, *The Great Chain of Being* (New York: Harper Torchbooks, 1960), pp. 43-44.

369. F. Lachover, *Mishnat ha-Zohar* (Jerusalem: Byalik Foundation, 1971), 1:127ff.

370. Nibley, "Treasures in the Heavens," pp. 83-85.

371. Vaillant, *Secrets d'Henoch*, pp. 60f. The word for establish, appoint (*postaviti*) means also "ordain" (as a priest), dedicate, appoint as a substitute; reflexively, to take a duty upon oneself, implying that Enoch is not the Savior but one "after the order of him." (Moses 6:67.)

372. An intriguing problem is raised by the occurrence in the Joseph Smith account of Enoch of the names Mahijah (Moses 6:40) and Mahujah (Milik, *Books of Enoch*, p. 311) in connection with the ritual questions "Tell us plainly who thou art and from whence thou comest?" For by an odd coincidence the first publication of proper

names from the Tell Mardikh archives, discovered in 1974 and proven to be by far the oldest library in the world, begins the list with the two names Mi-ka-yah and Mi-ka-il, both asking the question "Who is . . . ?" [G. Pettinato, "The Royal Archives of Tell Mardikh-Ebla," *The Biblical Archaeologist* 39 [May 1976]: 50.)

373. Martin Buber, "Abraham the Seer," *Judaism* 5 (1956): 295 gives some indication of why withdrawal is so important.

374. By far the greatest number of passages are found in the Psalms and Isaiah; there are twenty-five references in Jeremiah, including Lamentations. The word occurs only seven times in the New Testament, six of them referring to the Messiah, the King or Ruler of Zion. Of the forty-four occurrences of the name in the Book of Mormon, thirty-four are by Nephi, almost all of them being from Isaiah; the four in Mosiah are all from Isaiah; the five citations in 3 Nephi all deal with the fulfillment of the prophecy.

375. This difference of orientation between the Psalms and the Prophets is discussed by Ulrich W. Mauser, *Christ in the Wilderness* (London: SCM Press, 1963), pp. 36ff.

376. Ibid., pp. 50f.

377. Charles, *Book of Enoch*, p. 1.

378. Van Andel, *Structuur*, pp. 23-26, 31-39.

379. *BHM* 4:130f.

380. Book of Jasher 3:5-10. Passages such as this which closely follow both the Hebrew and the Slavonic Enoch show that the book of Jasher used very ancient sources and was far more than a medieval romance.

381. J. Zandee, "Le Messie: conceptions de la royauté dans le Religion du Proche-orient," *Revue de l'Histoire des Religions* 180 (1971): 4ff.

382. F. Tempestini, *Livre d'Adam*, in Migne, *Dictionnaire* 1:21, 27f., 232.

383. Van Andel, *Structuur*, p. 115.

384. *BHM* 5:24:xlii.

385. Ibid.

386. 2 Baruch 67:3; 76:4.

387. 4 Ezra 8:47.

388. Charles, *Apocrypha and Pseudepigrapha* 2:283. Condemned by the Reformation, it's authenticity "was summarily rejected," until "the twentieth century sees this book at last come into its own."

389. Charles, *Book of Enoch*, pp. 2-3.

390. Stone, "Judaism at the Time of Christ." p. 80.

Index